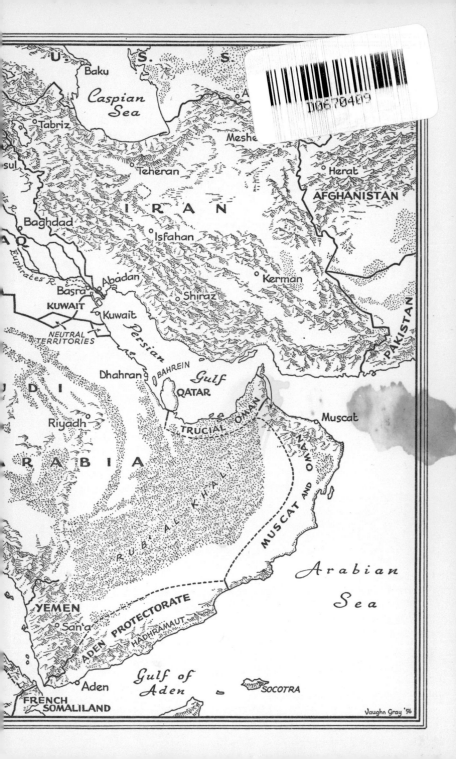

HERITAGE
OF THE
DESERT

The Arabs and the Middle East

By

HARRY B. ELLIS

THE RONALD PRESS COMPANY • NEW YORK

Library of Congress Catalog Card Number: 56–11292

PRINTED IN THE UNITED STATES OF AMERICA

To
ANN

Preface

The Arabs themselves, the lands in which they live, and the continuity of Arab life, stretching back like a richly freighted caravan into the mists of antiquity, possess a color and vitality which I hope have emerged in this book. I have tried to explain the Arabs as I grew to know them during nearly three years spent as Middle East correspondent of *The Christian Science Monitor*. I have also tried to tell why the Middle East is so deeply important to the rest of the world.

In so doing I have concentrated on the Arabs because they are the dominant people of the Middle East. The Israelis also are included, because of the profound effect their presence is having on the unsettled Arab world.

Turkey, Iran, and Afghanistan, important in other ways, are excluded from the book except as they impinge on the story of the Arabs, which lies at the core of an understanding of the Middle East. Likewise, the Arabs of North Africa are excluded, because they are at a different stage of development and possess a largely separate orientation from the Arabs of the Middle East.

My debt to my wife during the preparation and writing of this book cannot be adequately expressed. Often she bore alone, while I was traveling, the difficulties of living as a Western woman in the Arab world. With gratitude and love, this book is dedicated to her.

I must also gratefully acknowledge my debt to those scholars, historians, and Middle East specialists on whose labors I have drawn. A selected bibliography of their work appears at the end of this book. In particular I would like to acknowledge my debt to Dr. Philip K. Hitti for details of Arab history, and to George Lenczowski for his work on the modern politics of the Middle East.

Transliteration of Arabic words into English is varied. In this book I have sought to use styles endorsed by recognized Arabic scholars, while at the same time preserving familiarity for the reader. Thus no absolute uniformity of transliteration is claimed. All pictures in the book are my own, taken during my travels in the Middle East.

HARRY B. ELLIS

Sherborn, Massachusetts
August, 1956

Contents

vii

HERITAGE
OF THE
DESERT

CHAPTER 1

Middle East in Perspective

Far down in southeastern Saudi Arabia the country's only railroad makes a stop at the date palm oasis of Hofuf. It was afternoon prayer time when the train reached Hofuf, one day when I rode the line, and Arabs broke from the train and ran out into the desert on all sides, some to pray, others to relieve themselves in the sands. Lacking water, the more devout of the men washed themselves symbolically in sand and knelt to their prayers, while the business of the station—the loading and unloading of baggage, the shouts of the station crew—went on around them.

A number of great-wheeled carts, drawn by white donkeys painted orange with henna dye, stood on the platform to receive the bundles and chests of those passengers getting off. By one cart stood a tall Arab woman, completely veiled in black from head to toe, with not even her eyes visible to me on the train.

She was taller than any of the men around her and stood like a black statue, immobile among the swirl of white-robed men, surpassing them in dignity and bearing. Yet she was, of course, since this was Arabia, merely the humble and obedient wife of some one of them; for, at an apparent command, she reached out a long slim arm from beneath the folds of her robes and climbed over the wheel of one of the carts to sit in its back, the gold-embroidered tassel which embellished the front of her robe swinging as she moved. I caught a glimpse of bright blue material beneath, and then the black settled in again like a cloud, and once again the woman was a shrouded impersonal figure, seated nobly on a sack of grain.

Suddenly, with no show of impatience in her demeanor, the performance was reversed, and she clambered over the side of the cart to stand once more in the hubbub, until she was directed to take her place in a second cart. The train lurched, the praying Arabs scrambled chattering to their seats, and a moment later the cart bearing the woman was out of sight, on its way, perhaps, to some humble home of mud, deep within the date palm groves of the Hofuf oasis.

The woman and the scene in which she played her part were symbols both of the antiquity and the continuity of Middle Eastern life. Two thousand years ago, in this oasis, women in similar robes traveled in the same kind of carts drawn by the ancestors of this white donkey. The lives of the people of Hofuf have changed little in those 2,000 years. As it was in the past, so today, Hofuf is a town of mud buildings, the larger of them whitewashed, set within its groves of date palms near the shores of the Persian Gulf. The tiny shops of Hofuf still serve the Bedouin nomads who come in off the desert to barter their camels and sheep for the cloth, dates, and coffee they will take back with them to their wanderings across the sands.

So hot and arid is the Arabian desert, and so vast, that almost no influence in history has been able to penetrate

Arabia to disturb the lives of the people who live there. To visit Hofuf today in the middle of a sandstorm is to look upon a scene of utter dreariness and yet one of agelessness, as though the sand and wind had burst and blown against these walls since time began, and as though women in black, walking close to the walls, had shrouded themselves against the weather and against men's eyes since life began in the desert, thousands of years before.

The people who live in Arabia, including those of Hofuf, are Semites, specifically Arabs, forming one branch of the great Semitic family which had its origin in the Arabian peninsula. Through the ages, beginning about 3500 B.C., the Semites of Arabia sent up waves of migration to populate the lands north of Arabia which today are called the Middle East. Each wave of migration was given a different name in history, Babylonian, Amorite, Phoenician, and Hebrew among them.

To this last-named tribal group, the Hebrews, who settled in Palestine about the thirteenth century B.C., it fell to elevate the desert concept of religion to monotheism, or the worship of one God. The Hebrews gave Judaism to the world, and, almost 1,300 years later, Christianity. A third great monotheistic religion was born in Arabia in the seventh century A.D., when the Arabs, another branch of the Semites, founded Islam, the religion of Moslems.

Impelled by the zeal of their new faith, the Arabs swept up from Arabia to establish an empire stretching from the Atlantic Ocean on the west to the borders of China on the east, and embracing almost everything in between. The Arab Empire, which lasted until A.D. 1258, was the standard-bearer of learning during the Middle Ages. Many manuscripts of the ancient Greeks were transmitted to Europe through their translation into Arabic during the period of the Arab Empire. In astronomy, mathematics, medicine, and other fields the Arabs were pioneers.

When their empire finally fell before the Mongol invasion from Central Asia, the Arabs had so thoroughly Arabicized the Middle East that it has remained the Arab world in name to this day. Arabic is its major language, and Islam is its chief religion. The Ottoman Turks, who built their empire on the remains of the Arab domain, adopted the religion of the Arabs, as had the Mongols before them.

Under the Ottomans, who ruled the Middle East from A.D. 1516 through World War I, the Arabs remained dormant until the end of the nineteenth century. At that time the Western powers, anxious to establish lines of communication to their own empires in Asia, began to penetrate the Ottoman lands. Forerunners of the Western invasion were schools founded in the Middle East by the British and French and by Protestant missionaries from the United States. These schools implanted in Arab thought social and political ideas prevalent in the West, with stress on the liberty of individuals and nations.

Arab nationalism was roused, and secret societies centered in Damascus and Beirut began to circulate the concept of pan-Arabism, which meant the ideal of an independent Arab kingdom embracing all the Arabic-speaking peoples and free of Ottoman rule. By the outbreak of World War I the ferment of Arab nationalism had spread to the point that the Arabs, in return for a promise for an independent kingdom after the war, threw in their lot with the British and revolted against their Ottoman masters. This Arab Revolt, led by an Arab prince named Feisal and advised by T. E. Lawrence and other Englishmen, tied down Turkish troops and contributed to Allied victory over the Ottoman-German axis in the Middle East.

Britain and France, however, conceived of the Middle East as their own sphere of influence, and to this end they secretly planned the division of the postwar Arab world into British and French zones. This arrangement was confirmed by formal mandates assigned to Britain and France by the League of Nations. France obtained a mandate over what had been the former Turkish provinces of Syria and Lebanon, while Britain received mandates over Palestine, Transjordan, and Iraq.

The independent Arab kingdom was not to be, and the Arabs, believing that they had been betrayed by Britain, turned their roused nationalism against the mandate powers. A further inconsistency existed from the point of view of the Arabs. Under the terms of their mandate over Palestine, the British were obliged to facilitate the establishment of a national home for the Jews in the Holy Land.

To the Arabs this was anathema, since they regarded Palestine as an Arab land. To many Jews, however, the return of their nation to Palestine was a divinely ordained mission. Palestine had known only occasional Hebrew sovereignty since 586 B.C., when the walls of Jerusalem had been breached by Chaldean (Babylonian) troops and the Jews had gone into exile. In all the intervening years the dreams of a great portion of world Jewry had centered on Palestine, the "promised land," the land of their fathers in which Hebrew culture and genius, made known to the world through the Old Testament, had reached its zenith. It was toward Palestine that Zionism, a political movement founded by Theodor Herzl in 1897, increasingly had yearned in its quest for a homeland.

Beautifully, prophetically, and possibly tragically in view of recent history, the unknown author of the 137th Psalm, during the exile in Babylon, set down the feeling of home-less Jews for Palestine.

By the rivers of Babylon, there we sat down, yea, we wept, when we remembered Zion.

. . .

How shall we sing the Lord's song in a strange land?
If I forget thee, O Jerusalem, let my right hand forget her cunning.
If I do not remember thee, let my tongue cleave to the roof of my mouth; if I prefer not Jerusalem above my chief joy.

. . .

As a result of this situation the British mandate over Palestine was a three-cornered tug of war, with the Jews, steadily strengthened by immigration, struggling to establish a homeland, with the Arabs resisting the Jewish incursion, and with the British striving to govern the land and mediate between the two. Upshot of the mandate period was the departure of the British from Palestine in 1948, the Arab-Israeli war of the same year in which the Arabs were defeated, and the establishment of the Zionist state of Israel.

Elsewhere throughout the mandated Middle East the fires of Arab nationalism, expressed in terrorism and revolt, forced the gradual relinquishment of the mandates. Syria and Lebanon became independent republics in 1945. Earlier, in 1930, Britain had granted independence to the Kingdom of Iraq. Independence for the Hashemite Kingdom of Jordan followed in 1946. The Arab world, after World War II, was free of foreign rule, though it had lost Palestine to the Jews.

Internally, the Arab scene at this time was marked by the impact of Westernization in many ways. Almost every Arab land saw a developing struggle between the conservative, feudal, traditional leaders of the past and young Western-educated Arabs striving to establish responsible parliamentary government in their lands. In Syria and Egypt, particularly, this struggle was marked by army *coups d'etat.*

A cleavage developed between the top and bottom layers of society as the upper classes deserted the old Islamic culture and patterned their living habits after those of Westerners, including the purchase of automobiles, refrigerators, and Western clothes. Hoping to mount at least the first rung of the ladder now being climbed by their leaders, peasants deserted their fields and flocked to the cities.

A new class of white-collar Arabs came into being, disdaining work with their hands, but with little outlet for their clerical skills save in swollen government bureaucracies. As the old patterns of society crumbled, frustration took the form of political extremism, including that of the xenophobic Moslem Brotherhood, dedicated to the excision of the Western influences causing such change in the Arab world.

The same Arabs who sought out the prestige products of the West were suspicious of the United States for her role in the creation of Israel and hostile to Britain and France because of the experience of the mandates. The end of the mandates had left the Arabs politically divided, weak, and unsure of themselves. Inter-Arab rivalries had been set in train, dominated by the growing clash between Egypt and Iraq for leadership of the Arab world.

Lebanon, bequeathed a confessional system of government by the French, experienced deteriorating relations between Moslem and Christian Lebanese. Jordan, artificially carved out of the desert by the British in 1921, was too poor to support itself and increasingly became the pawn of stronger Arab powers. Overpopulated Egypt, with less than five per cent of her land arable, faced the problem of providing for a population which doubled every 50 years.

Saudi Arabia's people grew restive as their royal family became profligate on income from oil. Syria was torn by indecisive squabbles among its civilian politicians, broken by frequent army seizures of the government. Only Iraq, with a vast agricultural potential to be developed through income from oil, was a land of promise among the Arabs; and even here the presence of feudalism threatened a future struggle in the land. Relations between Israel and the Arabs continued to deteriorate, with the two sides unable to agree on terms which would change their present armistice to real peace.

Into this situation, in 1955, stepped the Soviet Union, seeking to gain a direct voice and influence in the Middle East, source of more than half of the world's oil and the gateway to Africa and south Asia. To gain their ends the Soviets sided with the Arabs. By arming the Arabs heavily, and in particular Egypt, the Soviets may hope to launch a new Arab-Israeli war. In such a war the Arabs would probably be defeated, some Arab governments would fall, and in their wake popular-front-type governments might rise, in which Arab Communists would play important roles.

Failing to achieve war, the Soviets are offering to invest so heavily in development projects which the Arabs need that Arab trade and economic dependence would be shifted from West to East. The Arabs see through such a trend and many of them deplore it. But the Soviet Union is willing to buy Arab agricultural output, especially Egyptian cotton, which increasingly is squeezed out of world markets by surpluses grown in the United States.

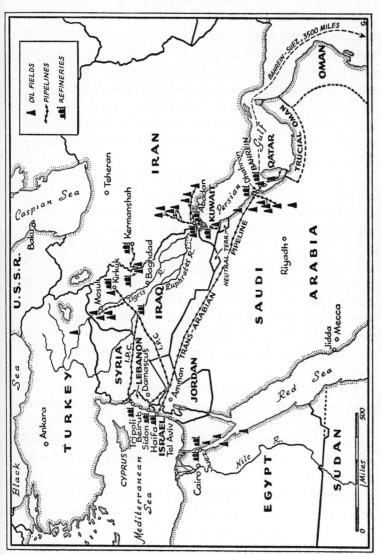

Middle East Oil Fields, Pipelines and Refineries.

Because the West's reservoir of friendship is so low in the Middle East, the United States, Britain, and France are in a difficult position to combat the Soviet campaign. Yet a non-Communist Middle East is vital to the West. In a press conference March 31, 1956, President Eisenhower declared that the Middle East "is of great—as a matter of fact, it is of extraordinary—importance to all the free world." The President noted that western Europe was turning from coal to oil for its energy and that this oil came from the Middle East.

Brought out at the press conference was the fact that three-fourths of the world's proved oil resources are to be found in the Middle East. Europe's daily consumption of oil, it was said, is expected to rise from about 6,000,000 barrels a day in 1955 to 16,750,000 a day in 1965. Oil from the Arab world and Iran today supplies western Europe with more than three-quarters of its total petroleum requirements. Without this oil from the Middle East, the deficiency would have to be made up from the Western Hemisphere, thereby depleting, at a time of steadily increasing demand, the reserves of Canada, the United States, and South America.

Oil is the fuel of peace. Even more is it the lifeblood of war. The stupendous production of war matériel in the United States, decisive in World War II, was made possible only by the unprecedented consumption of oil. Oil was the fuel which carried that production to the war fronts.

No strategist dares depend on Middle East oil in the event of a third world war. Should war come, the oil of Arabia and Iran likely would be denied to both sides by the interdiction of air and sea power. Allied forces would have to be fueled by Western Hemisphere oil. Thus the continued flow of Middle East oil in peace time is vital to the preservation of American reserves.

To Britain the continued flow of Middle East oil is, if anything, more important than it is to the United States. If Britain were to lose her sources of Middle East oil, the British industrial machine, fueled by this oil, would grind to a halt.

In 1955 the Middle East produced approximately 162,-000,000 metric tons of crude oil, or more than 20 per cent of the world total of 785,000,000 metric tons. In the world picture, the United States was by far the leading producer with an estimated 357,000,000 tons, followed by Venezuela with 111,000,000 tons. The Soviet Union trailed third among individual countries, with a production of 70,000,000 tons, according to official Soviet figures. (This marked an increase of more than 20 per cent over 1954 production, attributed by the Soviets to rapid development of the Volga-Ural region.)

Within the Middle East total of 162,000,000 tons, the Kuwait Oil Company (half American-owned) led with 55,-000,000 tons, followed by the Arabian American Oil Company (wholly American-owned) with just under 47,000,000 tons, the Iraq Petroleum Company (23.75 per cent American-owned) with nearly 34,000,000 tons, and the National Iranian Oil Company (whose oil is produced by an international consortium of which five American companies own eight per cent each), 16,000,000 tons. Other Middle East producing areas included the island of Bahrein, whose company is American-owned, and the peninsula of Qatar on the Arabian mainland, whose output is British-controlled.

Even this volume of production scarcely hints at the total nature of Middle East reserves, since annual production throughout the world is carefully controlled to meet complex market needs. In Saudi Arabia alone, for example, the

Arabian American Oil Company (Aramco) has discovered a single field whose reserves are believed to exceed the total proved reserves of the entire United States.

Oil is not the only factor of importance in the Middle East. It has become a truism to say that this area is the crossroads of the world, lying athwart three continents. The statement may mean little to the average American, however, until he understands that a ship cannot reach the Far East from Europe—unless it goes all the way around Africa—without passing in sight of Israel, Egypt, and Saudi Arabia, to name only three Middle East countries affected.

The same is true of road travel. A European wishing to travel overland from his homeland to Africa would, willynilly, pass through the heart of the Arab world. No less is this true of travel by air. Today the major air routes leading from Europe to Asia and to Africa cross the Middle East, touching down at the international airports of Beirut or Cairo.

An area so located has escaped few of history's wars. Rulers from Darius the Persian to Alexander the Greek, from Genghis Khan and Tamerlane the Tartar to Napoleon, and even down to Kaiser Wilhelm II, sent their legions through the Fertile Crescent in efforts to break over from one continent to another. On the cliffs of the Dog River, 10 miles north of Beirut, capital of Lebanon, so many world conquerors have chiseled their names in stone that the bank of the stream is a living scroll of history. Here, on a single wall of rock, stand inscriptions attributed to Tiglath-pileser III and Sennacherib, among other Assyrian kings, to the Egyptian Ramses II, to Napoleon, and even to General Allenby, as though each conqueror, gazing bemused upon the marks of those who had gone before, had scratched his own record upon the rock.

As in the past, so in any future intercontinental war, the Middle East almost certainly would be a theater, a probability strengthened by the new importance of oil. Thus no strategist, Eastern or Western, dismisses the Middle East from his planning. The United States in particular possesses in the Dhahran air base in eastern Saudi Arabia its closest bomber base to the southern Soviet Union.

For these reasons and others, including the plight of 900,-000 Palestine Arabs made homeless by the Arab-Jewish war, it is important to understand an area which looms as the next testing ground between the Soviets and the West, an area in which the Communists have a great deal to gain and the United States a great deal to lose.

CHAPTER 2

Black Tents of Kedar

As far back as history records, Arabia has been one of the least hospitable lands on earth—a vast peninsula of scorched deserts and waterless limestone steppes, intruded at places in the north and west by black volcanic peaks rising like humpbacked whales above the sands. Across this wind-swept and sunburned wilderness, tent-dwelling Bedouins have wandered throughout the ages, clustered in fiercely isolated tribal groups, living in uneasy and often hostile relationship to one another and to the few green oases where men led more settled lives.

The isolation, and hence racial and cultural purity, of these nomads was complete. Ringed in by some of the most terrible deserts on earth, the heart of Arabia never has been subject permanently to a foreign flag or, indeed, to a lasting invasion of any kind. Behind the barriers of the Hejaz Mountains to the west and the desert itself on every other side, the nomad of Arabia has been left free to develop his pattern of existence, as free in the twentieth century as in every century before. No influence in history has basically disturbed the continuity of Bedouin life. Thus, in almost every essential, the career of the Bedouin today is the same as that lived by the tent-dwelling patriarchs of Old Testament days, who wandered across the face of the Middle East.

Here is the fascination inherent in Bedouin life today, that in the goat-hair tent in which the nomad dwells, the robes he wears, the implements he uses, and the customs of his tribal existence are preserved the essentials of that original Semitic life whose attributes have become familiar to the Western world through the pages of the Old Testament, and whose most basic character traits still are found in the grain of the otherwise heterogeneous Arabs of the present. For the Westerner to visit a Bedouin encampment today, or a desert oasis where the lives of nomads and townsmen mingle, is to step back into the milieu of that Semitic life which gave rise to the three great monotheistic religions of the world, a continuity of history made possible by the stern geography in which the Arabian dwells.

"And he will be a wild man; his hand will be against every man, and every man's hand against him," it is written in Genesis 16:12 of Ishmael, commonly regarded in Bedouin lore as the progenitor of their desert kind. And the writer of Leviticus describes the desert furnace in which the Bedouin lives (Lev. 26:19, 20) as a land whose heaven is as iron and whose earth is as brass, where "your strength shall be spent in vain: for your land shall not yield her increase, neither shall the trees of the land yield their fruits." A more apt description of the Bedouin and of the land in which he dwells could scarcely be found.

The Bedouin, the camel, and the date palm, it has been said, are the three great actors in the drama of the desert, and of this triumvirate the Bedouin is the chief. He is a raiser of camels and sheep and holds every other pursuit, with the exception of hunting and raiding, to be beneath his dignity as a man. Agriculture and the settled life of the oasis he scorns, though occasionally he deals with the townsman in exchanging a few of his animals for clumps of dried dates, a sackful of grain, and the simple clothing he wears.

He is fiercely independent, and proud of the fact that he is the only man who can exist in the desert. Thus he is certain he is the equal of any man and, indeed, the superior of all who follow sedentary ways.

I have seen a ragged barefoot Bedouin, fresh from the sands, advance boldly across Persian rugs in the majlis, or court, of an Arab prince, a majlis crowded with Arab notables in gold-embroidered robes and Westerners in business suits. The prince rose gravely to greet the new arrival and pointed out to him a seat along the wall, among his other guests. There the nomad sat calmly, fixing curious glances on the others in the room, with no hint in his hawklike features that the poverty of his dress lessened his status in any way.

The story is told of King Hussein of the Hejaz that the monarch treated with icy contempt the fawning of city Arabs from Jidda and Mecca, but hastened to the window in response to the rude "Ya, Hussein!" called out by a Bedouin beneath his wall. In his heart the King may have despised the tribesman, but he was well aware that the tenure of any ruler in Arabia depended upon the loyalty of the desert tribes; and he knew also that one dealt with Bedouins on terms of equality.

This pride of the Bedouin is centered in what he terms the "blood" of his tribe, and the nomad traces back his tribal genealogy in sonorous terms. Fierce rivalry exists among the tribes; and until the present Saudi dynasty outlawed tribal raiding (only through the threat of superior force and the distribution of largess to the tribes), the custom of ghazzu, or the stealing of one another's cattle and goods, was a staple of desert life.

Ghazzu was a game, a sport, a condition of survival, and still provides a clue to Bedouin character. In a land as barren as Arabia, where almost nothing but desert grasses grows except in scattered oases, the nomad of the desert, scorning work as he does, knew in the old days almost no way to increase his wealth save by the "dishonest" method of seizing the goods of a strange or enemy tribe. This action served the double purpose of swelling the raider's own flocks and herds, by which he measured his wealth, and, should the victim have belonged to an enemy tribe, of paying off old scores against a foe. Besides, in the last analysis, raiding and all that it implies was embraced within the way of life which most appealed to the Bedouin's fierce and untamed nature.

To the Bedouin, raiding brought out everything noble and sporting in a man. If he was to survive the swift surprise of the desert raids, he must become a rider par excellence, both on camel and horseback, and he must handle a gun and dagger with more skill than did his opponent. The successful raider, the bold and dashing leader of many ghazzus, was honored above all other men by the Bedouin. Boys in their one-piece dishdashas, or "nightshirts," hung about the campfires of their elders, listening with glistening eyes to the tales of past raids, and longing for the day when they, too, might join the ranks of the raiders.

As the Bedouin himself has said, and in truth still feels: "Deny me the right to raid and you deny me the breath of life!" What football and baseball mean to the American, and cricket to the Briton, raiding meant, and even more, to the desert Arab. He would not bend his hand to sow seed, or scarcely to tend his own sheep and goats, and the main part of his day was spent in indolence about the coffee hearth of his sheikh. But let the terrible cry be raised that raiders were on the way, or let his leaders call for a ghazzu of their own, and he would leap to the saddle in a moment.

Raiding, too, was controlled by its rules, as rigidly enforced as any others in the desert. Bloodshed itself was not the prime object of the raid, though men often were killed in the fighting. The object was to deprive the opponent of his goods and add them to one's own, to do this by surprise if possible, and then to melt away into the desert before the shaken defenders could rally to pursue.

If the odds should prove roughly equal, then the fighting of that particular ghazzu might be sharp. If the defenders, however, sizing up the situation with practiced eye, saw that they were greatly outnumbered, they would flee into the desert to live and fight another day. Or, should the attackers learn that they had been anticipated, and that the defenders were grimly deployed and ready, they might beat a retreat across the dunes to their own tents, hopeful that their identities, muffled behind their kaffiyahs, or headcloths, would remain unknown. That very evening the sheikh of the would-be attackers might greet the leader of the tribe almost attacked and entertain him at coffee, both men masking their suspicions behind an elaborate façade of desert courtesy.

One of the most striking features of ghazzu was its brand of chivalry, similar to, but far antedating, the chivalry brought back to Europe by the Crusaders. A woman of the besieged tribe knew with absolute certainty that she and her children were safe, though the battle might rage around them and the temper of the attackers grow fierce in their lust for loot. A raider might enter a woman's tent to grapple with her husband, seize her carpets, coffee pots, and other legitimate spoil, and drive off the family's camels and other livestock. But the tent itself must be left intact for the distraught mistress. Sufficient food must be left for herself and her children. Her camel saddle, and her riding beast itself, must not be touched.

To violate this law of sanctuary would be for the raider to court death, should a sheikh of his own tribe, or even one of his fellow tribesmen, catch him in the act. Stories are legion in the desert of leaders of ghazzus who cut down with the sword one of their own men who so far forgot himself in battle as to seize a bracelet or necklace from a woman of the vanquished side. There was a reason for this; for to abuse any woman in ghazzu would be for the raider to jeopardize the safety of his own family under a system whereby he might end up in defeat the next day.

Thus, in a land where insecurity was bred into the very roots of life, some system of protection had to be devised if life was to be carried on at all. There were a dozen reasons why every tribesman, sooner or later, would need to travel outside his own dirah, or tribal grazing range, whether to sell camels in a distant oasis, to pay his respects to a neighboring sheikh, to attend a wedding held in the territory of another tribe, or to make the Islamic pilgrimage to Mecca.

So the desert Arab, practical always in the conduct of his life, developed the system of rafiq to ensure at least something of normal intercourse in his dangerous world. The result, strange to the Western sense but perfectly logical to the Arab, was a system whereby tribes which normally were mortal enemies would allow each other's members, under sponsorship of rafiqs, to travel in safety and even in honor through the ranges of their most persistent foes.

The word "rafiq," denoting a system which, unlike the currently outmoded ghazzu, still prevails in Arabia, means literally friend or companion. The rafiq is a member of the tribe through whose territory the traveling Bedouin intends to pass, and his chief function is to preserve the stranger from molestation by members of the rafiq's own tribe. Thus in the old days, when ghazzus were frequent, the rafiq stepped outside the circle of firelight when camp had been pitched and darkness had settled over the desert and hurled his strange cry to the heavens.

"Look you, O men of the Mutair, here am I, Abdullah, a man of the Mutair, and I say to you, this traveler is of the Bani Khalid, journeying to Riyadh and the palace of Malik [King] Saud; so let none molest us; and whoso heareth me, let him come to us and dine or drink coffee and welcome; but molest us not!"

Four times the rafiq repeated this cry, once to each corner of the camp, and whatever men of the Mutair may have been waiting in the darkness either came forward to drink the traditional cup or stole away. For to attack a stranger guarded by a tribal rafiq would have brought down upon themselves, as well as upon their tribe, the contempt of the Bedouin world, quite apart from any punishment the King might visit upon them.

The rafiq, who may be any member of a tribe, from the sheikh himself down to the most humble tribesman, has other duties to perform as protector, quite as valid today as in the days of ghazzu. When his client has traversed the rafiq's dirah and is ready to pass to the range of a neighboring tribe, the rafiq must arrange for a member of the new tribe to take over the protector's duties.

Should the rafiq for any reason be unable to accompany the client personally on his journey, he may give to him instead his camel stick, a piece of equipment which every tribesman carries, and on which the rafiq first will have notched the wasm, or identifying mark, of his tribe. Then the rafiq must pass the word throughout the length and breadth of his dirah that such and such a client now bears his marked stick, and that all members of the tribe are to regard the traveling stranger, armed with that notched cane, as under the protection of the rafiq himself.

Equal to the Bedouin's warlike character is his love of poetry. The past glories of each tribe have been handed down in Arabic verse—committed to memory, since almost no Bedouin can write—to which the tribesmen love to listen around their campfires at night, their long black hair streaming in ringlets about their shoulders and the whites of their eyes glistening in the light of the flames.

With all his rugged individuality, however, the Bedouin lives a miserable existence by almost any standards but his own. Confined largely to its own dirah, the tribe wanders across the face of the desert, following the path of the infrequent water wells, seeking those widyan, or valleys, where the scanty rains of winter may have brought forth a meager crop of green. Only the thin walls of his goat-hair tent shield the nomad from the terrific heat of summer and from the rolling sand which the khamsin wind sometimes raises in searing clouds during the hottest months.

Without the camel the Bedouin could not survive these trying days. The camel is his steed, on whose sloping back some tribesmen erect the shrouded dhalla, or cage, within which their veiled womenfolk can ride in seclusion. The Bedouin drinks the camel's milk, weaves its hair into cloth, uses its dung for fuel, and occasionally, when the rules of hospitality demand, eats his camel's flesh. Even camel urine is used, as the only shampoo strong enough to kill the lice with which the Bedouin's uncut hair is afflicted.

The Bedouin's attitude toward women is complex. Allowed by the Koran, the Moslem scripture, to possess as many as four wives at a time, the average nomad has but one for the simple reason that he can afford no more. This one wife he treats with the most confining jealousy, as far as outsiders are concerned. Whenever a strange man appears near her husband's tent, the Arab woman disappears behind a curtain into the family section of the dwelling, there to remain until the stranger goes away.

One morning in central Arabia I visited an elderly herder of camels for King Ibn Saud. The herder was short and spare of stature, with a hard merry twinkle to his eyes, and a strident voice above a fiercely pointed beard. With a mixture of impatience and courtesy he welcomed me to his tent and ushered me to a seat on the carpeted floor, before he himself leaned back against the camel saddle that formed the seat of honor. Suddenly he leaped up and peered over the striped qata, or curtain, separating the women's section of the tent from the part in which we sat. Only this movement, and his barked order for coffee to be prepared, gave me any inkling of the presence of women in the tent, so silent was the other side of the partition all the time I was there. So it was, invariably, on visits to other Bedouin tents.

Several times I came upon Bedouin women with their veils thrown back, but the only time I saw these women with no veils on at all was when riding in an Aramco exploration car toward the Rub al-Khali in southern Arabia. Without warning our car breasted a dune and fled down the slope into the very center of a Bedouin camp. The long low outlines of black tents were spaced about the hollow, while in the center was the dark mound of a water well, dug down through the sand to the rock below, its rim darkened by the hoofs and ropes of many years. All unaware we had come upon this camp and saw women in dresses of bright orange and red, devoid of their black robes, staring at us from their sections of the tents.

Other women of the tribe, like so many walking shadows in their black outer robes, wound their graceful barefoot way to and from the water well, balancing copper kettles and other utensils on their heads.

Children in knee-length white shifts stared at us open-mouthed, but for some reason we saw no men. Perhaps they slept in the family sections of their tents, or, more likely, they were in the majlis of their sheikh. But the sheikh's tent, wherever it might be in this hollow, we did not see. Some of the men, of course, were out with the flocks, but not many; for the true Bedouin scorns the work of herding, and spends his idle day instead in the shadow of his tent or before the coffee hearth of his elders, drawing lines in the sand with his stick and saying "aye aye" and "nay nay" with his fellows. Thirty seconds, I suppose, I saw that camp scene before it disappeared behind a dune, yet I recall it still as a scene of warmth, color, and human charm, in a desert otherwise so barren.

It falls to the lonely herdsman, out in the burning sun all day, to guard the tribal flocks from whatever dangers there may be and then to lead them back at night to the friendly shelter of the camp. Here the camels are couched about each tent, to ruminate and grumble through the darkened hours, while the sheep are bedded down inside the ring of camels, with the youngest lambs tethered to the ropes of the tent.

Over the ages the Bedouin has developed certain narrow, though highly specialized, skills. He is able to read the least sign in the desert around him that may lead him to water in his arid land. From boyhood the skeletons of camels he has passed on the long summer treks, and the blown sand mounds of human graves, have warned him that he must learn his desert well. The hoofprint of a camel in the sand is the kind of book he reads, and he knows at a glance, because his safety may depend upon it, the age, sex, and type of beast that made the mark, the speed with which its owner was riding, and the probable purpose of his journey, whether peaceful or otherwise.

The Bedouin, in short, is a man fierce and unpredictable, lightning in mood; ready to rob out on the desert itself, but shielding his victim with his life should the latter demand the protection of his tent; hospitable within his tent door, suspicious without; vivid of speech, jealous of his women; a man ruled by emotion rather than by reason—above all, a man molded by the pitiless environment in which he lives.

His world, little changed through the ages, is the crucible of the desert, in which the spiritual life of the Semites developed Judaism and hence, by indirection, Christianity, and more recently Islam, the dominant religion of the modern Arab world. The Bedouin himself is that Semite who, because of the isolation of his homeland, most nearly resembles the progenitor of all Arabs. Living "in a desert place, and in the waste howling wilderness," he compresses within himself those traits which are recognized as Semitic in the Arab world today.

CHAPTER 3

Persistence of Semitic Life

Many city Arabs profess to scorn the Bedouin and his way of life. These urban Arabs would feel, and look, profoundly ill at ease in a Bedouin tent, suspicious of the food that would be served them, repulsed by the ignorance and lack of cleanliness around them, feeling a sense of kinship—if at all—only in their common religion and language. The sophisticated lives of these Arabs, often Western-educated and living in Beirut, Damascus, or Baghdad, have moved far from the desert simplicity from which all Arabs have sprung.

Nonetheless, however much these Arabs despise the Bedouin's way of life, most of them acknowledge that some of the most enduring characteristics of their race had their origin in the Semitism of the Arabian Peninsula. In other words, the Bedouin traits still lie at the base of Arab character today. This persistence of Semitic life, and its acknowledgment by modern Arabs, was exemplified in the career of the late Ibn Saud, the desert leader who welded the unruly tribes of Arabia into a kingdom comprising nine-tenths of the peninsula. His character and accomplishments made him the one man through whom, consciously or otherwise, town Arabs could trace back with pride their own link to Semitic desert life.

Theirs was admiration of a man who was a Bedouin to the bone. In fact, the life he led, making him a figure second only to Mohammed the Prophet in the imagination of many Arabs, was largely the projection of Bedouin virtues on a heroic scale. In the history of the Semites Ibn Saud was a man who would have been as much at home 2,000 years ago as he was in the desert milieu of his own times. He combined within himself those qualities which have been dear to the desert Arab since long before the advent of Islam, and which many city Arabs still lurkingly admire.

He was fierce in battle, magnanimous to a fallen foe, severe but always just in execution of the Koranic law of "eye for eye, tooth for tooth," lavish to his guests, hospitable to all, adroit in the spinning of desert tales, possessed of a great gusto for making love (he himself estimated he had had as many as 300 Bedouin wives), meticulous in the practice of Islam as he saw it, ruthless upon those Moslems who fell short of the standard he set. These attributes were made all the more impressive by his physical stature, for he towered a full head above most Arabs. Finally, he had an undoubted genius for leadership, based upon a sound knowledge of the Bedouin people among whom he lived.

The fact that Ibn Saud was a king in the Semitic tradition was illustrated by the manner in which he conducted his morning majlis, to which every Arab was free to come to lay grievances before the King, interpreter of the Koran, supreme law of the land. One morning, for example, a poor woman of the desert came before the King and complained that her husband had been killed because another man had fallen out of a palm tree and landed on his back. Under the desert law of "eye for eye, tooth for tooth," the woman demanded retribution from the King as he sat in audience before the people.

His massive frame hunched forward, the monarch suggested that money might be paid instead. But the woman was adamant. Under Koranic law hers was the right to exact from the culprit "wound for wound, stripe for stripe." Whereupon the great Lion of the Desert decreed that either the woman must accept the money offered or she herself, in fulfillment of her right, must climb the same palm tree and fall upon the man as he had fallen upon her husband. After short reflection the woman chose the money and went away.

This happened in Saudi Arabia less than 50 years ago, and yet it strikingly resembled the case decided by an earlier Semitic king, Solomon, when he decreed that a baby be divided between two women, each of whom claimed it as her own. Both kings were faced by angry disputants, beyond whom were gathered many people watching closely what the king did. In both cases the wisdom of the monarch averted further tragedy and gained the approval of the people. In I Kings 3:28 it is written of Solomon that "all Israel heard of the judgment which the king had judged; and they feared the king: for they saw that the wisdom of God was in him, to do judgment." Similarly, it might be said that the people of Saudi Arabia heard in their tents what their own King had done, and gave their approval to his interpretation of Semitic law.

It was no accident that these cases were alike. Ibn Saud, as a Semite of the desert, was bound by the Islamic law which in its code of conduct had developed from the Mosaic system which Solomon was required to obey. The Mosaic code of conduct was a desert code, wrought out during the wilderness travail of the Hebrews. Conditions of life in Arabia have changed so little since then that the same contingencies still arise in the desert as those which the Mosaic code was designed to meet.

The children of Israel were shepherds, divided into tribal groups, dwelling in goat-hair tents, the black "tents of Kedar," as the Song of Solomon calls them. In abode, dress, occupation, and law the Arabian Bedouins of today are very like their early Semitic cousins. A Bedouin camp, as has been seen, is a collection of individual tents, pitched often in a loose semicircle below the crowns of surrounding dunes, focused on a water well. When a neighboring sheikh enters the camp, or their own leader passes by, the men of the tribe stand in their tent doors—the open side of the tent—and watch his progress across the sands. In Exodus 33:8 it is written that when Moses went out to the tabernacle, pitched outside the camp, "all the people rose up, and stood every man at his tent door, and looked after Moses, until he was gone into the tabernacle."

Moses was leader of the people. Yet when Jethro, his father-in-law, came to visit him, Moses "did obeisance, and kissed him," because Jethro was his father-in-law and older than he. More than one visitor received in audience by the late Ibn Saud found himself in a large room apparently alone with a small elderly man, who conversed cheerfully and then made a sign with his hand, at which the gigantic frame of the King himself rose from a corner and came forward at his father's bidding.

Jethro was a humble priest of Midian, serving a local tribal deity, while Moses was the transcendent religious leader who led his people to the worship of a monotheistic God. The father of Ibn Saud was a modest man, completely overshadowed by the political and military genius of his son. Yet in both cases the younger men—Moses and Ibn Saud—paid strict heed to the Semitic custom of obeisance of the young before the old. Ibn Saud refused even to enter a second story room when he thought his father was in the room below, lest he figuratively walk on the head of his father.

The Bible shows the persistence of Semitic life, for almost every department of "modern" Bedouin life was clearly foreshadowed in the Scriptures of the ancient Hebrews. Let us go back for a moment to ghazzu, and assume that a Mutair section had attacked an Ajman camp one dark morning before dawn and found the defenders too strong. Indeed, an Ajman defender was about to put a Mutair attacker to the sword when, with a lunge, the Mutairi grasped the tent pole of his opponent and invoked the protection of the tent. At that moment the Ajmani became, under desert law, the protector of the man who had attacked his tent, obliged to defend him with his own life if need be.

This strange relationship between friend and foe makes little sense to the Westerner until he learns something of desert life and the antecedents of Semitic law. In Leviticus (19:33, 34) the Hebrews are enjoined not to vex the stranger in their midst for "ye were strangers in the land of Egypt"; and the writer of Deuteronomy (23:15, 16) warned the children of Israel not to deliver "unto his master the servant which is escaped from his master . . . He shall dwell with thee, even among you, in that place which he shall choose in one of thy gates, where it liketh him best."

The reason for this leniency was the same in ancient times as it is today. Under desert conditions no Bedouin (including the Hebrew) knew which day he might be conqueror and which day conquered; indeed, what day he might be a slave, seeking to escape. Without some concept of sanctuary he could have felt no security in his wild and turbulent land.

On one level the Old Testament is a sacred religious history, fundamental to the religions of the Christian and Jew, and to a lesser extent to that of the Moslem as well. On another level, secondary but almost equally enthralling, it is the richly colored story of a Semitic people in their long travail up out of the desert into the land of the sown; and of their contacts and conflicts with other Semitic peoples who had gone up from Arabia into the Fertile Crescent before them. Viewed in this context, against the background of Bedouin life as it is lived in Arabia today, it is a deeply persuasive record of the persistence of Semitic life.

Research, in support of this persistence, indicates that many of the peoples who inhabited the ancient Middle East —Babylonians, Canaanites, Phoenicians, and Hebrews among them—were closely related, deriving from an original Semitic stock and sharing at some time in the past a common homeland. Key to this theory, as outlined by Dr. Philip K. Hitti, is language. Decipherment of early cuneiform writings, coupled with the comparative study of the Assyro-Babylonian, Hebrew, Aramaic, Arabic, and other tongues discloses these languages to be cognates; that is, derivatives of a single mother tongue. In particular, these languages are similar in certain key words, including those denoting numbers, personal pronouns, certain parts of the body, and in terms describing blood kinship. Supporting studies show that the people who spoke these tongues were strikingly similar in some of their social institutions and religious beliefs, and even in certain physical characteristics.

"The inference," according to Dr. Hitti, "is inescapable; the ancestors of these various peoples—Babylonians, Assyrians, Chaldaeans, Amorites, Aramaeans, Phoenicians, Hebrews, Arabians, and Abyssinians—before they became thus differentiated must have lived at some time in the same place as one people."[1]

The locale of that "same place" still is a matter of dispute, though the weight of evidence points to the Arabian Peninsula. Concerning the "one people," there is no question. It was the original Semitic race in whose image the Arabian Bedouin of today is cast.

Down through the ages the one determining factor of Arabian life has been the aridity of the land. Only in scattered oases and in the seacoast fringes of the country has settled existence been possible. A result of this sterility has been nomadic movement within Arabia itself. At certain points in history, however, the wanderings of Semitic tribes —impelled, apparently, by pressure of population upon the land—has grown more restless and has swollen into general migrations up out of the peninsula into the more favored lands to the north.

The first such wave is placed about 3500 B.C., when a Semitic migration moved up Arabia's east coast and gradually struck root in the fertile valleys of the Tigris and Euphrates rivers. There, over a period of time, the Semites abandoned their nomadism and amalgamated with the non-Semitic Sumerians of the valley to become the Assyrians and Babylonians of history. (It was from one of these Sumerian cities, Ur of the Chaldees, that Abraham the patriarch, a nomad who refused to settle down, gathered up his family, tents, and cattle and moved westward toward the land of Canaan.)

[1] Philip K. Hitti, *History of the Arabs* (London: Macmillan & Co., Ltd., 1951), pp. 9, 10.

About the same time, a similar Semitic wave moved up the west coast of Arabia (or possibly northward through East Africa) to settle with the Hamitic peoples of the Nile valley. In the Egyptians who resulted from this mixture, however, the Hamitic strain was dominant, and gradually the Semitic character of the Arabian tribes was modified. Thus modern Egypt, though traditionally the leader of the Arab world, is basically neither Semitic nor Arab, a fact which northern Arabs opposed to Egypt's leadership are wont to point out.

Another 1,000 years passed, until, about 2500 B.C., the Semitic Amorites went up from Arabia into the Fertile Crescent, where a portion of them called Canaanites moved into western Syria and Palestine. Another section of this people settled the coastal plain of Lebanon and became known as Phoenicians. (A noted Phoenician was Hiram, King of Tyre, commissioned by Solomon to furnish "cedar trees out of Lebanon" for the temple of the Lord which Solomon purposed to build.)

It is to the third great pulse of Semitic migration, however, that the chief laurels belong. Sometime between 1500 and 1200 B.C., a group of Semitic tribes called Hebrews (guided by an Arabian nomad named Hobab, who served them "instead of eyes" in the wilderness) moved through the area of Sinai up into southern Syria and Palestine, the land called "promised" by the Hebrews. These Hebrew tribes were no more numerous, and in some cases even less so, than some of the other Semitic groupings which had left their mark upon the ancient world. To the Hebrews alone, however, it fell to dignify that spiritual life of desert and oasis which all the Semites shared into a concept of monotheism destined to base the religions of the Western world.

Other Semitic migrations followed, notably that of the Nabataeans about 500 B.C., a nomadic people who established themselves north of the Gulf of Aqaba and hewed their capital, Petra, from the rose-red sandstone cliffs of the Wadi Musa, or Valley of Moses.

The history of these centuries of migrations was tangled. Indeed, the picture of the ancient Middle East was made kaleidoscopic by movements of peoples, by wars and rumors of wars, by the rise, reign, and fall of empires. It was an era given continuity largely by the trade which, from earliest times, had linked the Eastern world of India and China with the fertile lands of the Middle East across the caravan routes of Arabia.

In all these events the Semitic peoples played their parts, sometimes as conquerors, at other times as conquered, often as the traders who cemented the area together. Throughout the conflicts of history the inherent Semitism of these people, except in the modified case of Egypt, remained strong. Arabia, as the fount of pure Semitism, had given up its people to the lands of the north. The stage had been set for the last great act of Semitic migration—the sweep of the Arabs themselves across the Middle East.

CHAPTER *4*

Pigeons on the Roof

Our search for understanding of the Arabs, the last great Semitic group to move up from Arabia, begins at Beirut, capital of Lebanon, on the eastern shores of the Mediterranean Sea. Though Beirut sometimes is called gateway to the Arab world, it is not exclusively for this reason that the search begins there. Rather is it that Beirut, from the start of 1952 to the summer of 1954, was home for my family and myself. My own appreciation of the Arabs came as much from living among them as from any conscious work I did as a journalist, and to this day when I want to put across a conception of the Arabs there seems no clearer way than to cite a Beirut game which we called "pigeons on the roof."

In Beirut the roofs of the houses are flat, and almost every afternoon some of the humbler men of the city go up to their roofs to play this unlawful but enticing game. Attaching a white cloth to a long slender pole, they begin to wave the pole back and forth through the air, all the while whistling strangely and gazing searchingly up at the sky.

36

Sometimes of a late afternoon in Beirut I saw as many as half a dozen Arabs, each perched on his own roof, waving poles, whistling, and paying scant attention to each other.

Below them the racket of the crowded dusty streets went unconcernedly on: donkeys laden with sacks of dried dates picking their way with quick dainty steps, barefoot children darting among the hoofs of animals and the feet of passers-by, now and then a herd of scrawny goats foraging for a bit of green, and above all and through all the incessant horns of sleek new automobiles forcing their way through the narrow lanes.

High above the heads of the pole wavers on the roofs flew the quarry they sought—pigeons released from the dovecots of the city for their afternoon flight and airing. Wheeling dark against the sun and flashing silver as they turned, each flock of birds dropped lower and lower in the sky, toward some man whose strangely compelling whistle and waving pole drew them down, until, with a flutter and preening of wings, they settled into a dovecot on the roof, perhaps their own, or just as likely one they never had seen before.

The rules of the game were simple. Once a bird was in the air it became, regardless of previous ownership, fair game for that Arab who, with consummate skill, could lure it down to his own pigeon house on his roof. Then it was his to fatten if he wished, to eat that night, or to hawk in the streets with a dozen of its plucked fellows, hanging limply from a stick.

To a Western sense this was stealing, but to the simple Arab of Beirut it was merely an accustomed part of the eccentric pattern of living he carried on in his sprawling metropolitan city. Some said the game was legal. Others, particularly those who eschewed the practice, claimed that on the statute books was an ordinance prohibiting the stealing of another man's birds. But, lawful or not, I never saw a policeman so much as glance up at the odd panorama on the roofs.

This game with pigeons typifies the prevailing atmosphere of Arab life—raucous, competitive, fiercely so, lived with a careless disregard for the finer points of law, but withal with an enormous gusto. It is a mosaic made up of so many conflicting strands of history, religious backgrounds, tribal customs, and governmental systems, overlaid with the dead weight of a poverty which in itself breeds lawlessness and strife, that in complexity and variety it is a fair rival to the patterns of the Persian rugs found in so many Arab homes.

Even in its outward symbols the Arab way of living is foreign to the average Westerner. It is repugnant to him to find a modern apartment house—with rents as high as he would pay back home—surrounded by the litter and decay of a neighborhood of mud and tin shacks, and with the streets noisome with the refuse of years. To the Westerner, this unzoned appearance suggests disorder, and disorder of a kind it certainly is. Yet beneath the clutter of Arab urban life exists a complex series of relationships, rigid and severe, cunningly worked out over decades and even centuries to permit peoples of differing, and often opposing, religious and cultural backgrounds to dwell together in peace.

The pattern is made all the more obscure to the Westerner by the attitude of individual Arabs toward him, so that early in his experience he gains the impression that all Arabs are united in the desire to fleece him, the stranger in their midst. What he does not realize is that Arabs who share avarice toward him may also share antipathies toward each other so deeply rooted in the factional history of the

Middle East that they are subordinated only by the need to cooperate with each other in everyday affairs.

Thus, the Westerner may know enough to settle the fare before he steps into a taxicab, in order to avoid an argument later on. Yet he may not realize that of three drivers—equally tenacious as to fare—one may be a Druze, another a Sunni Moslem, and the third a Christian, factors which have given them widely differing communal experience and outlook. They—and the communities in which they live—marry, divorce, treat their womenfolk, their servants, and their leaders according to the strict notions of their forebears, and they form inflexible opinions concerning the bigotry of those who disagree with them.

At first the Westerner, introduced to this Arab mélange, tends to see only the dark side of the picture. He deals with government officials and runs into such a bureaucratic tangle that he grimly understands those many Arabs—again the tinge of lawlessness—who sidestep the red tape by giving "baksheesh" to someone in the know who can "fix it up."

He orders a chair or a table from a local carpenter, and is promised a date of delivery. The day arrives, but the chair does not. The carpenter is outraged that the customer even asks why. So many obstacles and delays have risen to hinder the carpenter's work! He shrugs, however. The customer shall have his chair; though, the workman adds darkly, since he wants it in such a hurry it may not be faultless work. And it seldom is.

Gradually, however, it begins to seep in upon the Westerner that the Arab has other qualities which brighten the potpourri. Arab hospitality, he learns, is a virtue almost overwhelming. The very merchant who tried to swindle him that afternoon would, were the Westerner to visit him in his home, lavish food and drink upon him without stint, even to the end of his larder.

Every Arab, rich or poor, holds hospitality as a lighted candle in his heart, and no guest goes away without feeling the warmth of his host's welcome. This is a quality universal throughout the Arab world, a tradition handed down to the city Arab from his ancestors in the desert, where the nomad welcomes the stranger to his tent, even as Abraham, sitting in his tent door in the heat of the day, caused a calf to be dressed and gave milk to the three men who came to see him, before he would suffer them to state their business.

The Westerner learns, too, that the neighboring Moslem matron who comes to his home on Christmas, her head shrouded in black, to offer Damascus sweets to his family, may have no motive other than a gracious sense that this is a feast day precious to the Nasrany, the Christian. He learns, sometimes much later, that if he is to be equally courteous, he and his wife must present themselves with a gift at their neighbor's door on Moslem holy days.

Thus, slowly a more rounded picture of the Arab comes into focus for the stranger. If he remains long enough, he may begin to see that the thing which has troubled him most, the stain of lawlessness running through the current of Arab life, is not encouraged by Arabs en masse, as he had thought. It is deplored by many, by Arabs who feel themselves victimized by a system of life which they do not fully comprehend, but to which they, their fathers, and their fathers' fathers have been subject as far back as can be told.

The fact is that all Arabs, however much they are divided today by dynastic squabbles, religious schisms, and even admixtures of blood, do indeed share a heritage reflected in certain common qualities or traits, some of them charming, as hospitality, others less so, as avarice. Whatever the nature of these distinguishing features, the Westerner who stays long in the Arab world learns to recognize in them the qualities which most truly should be called Arab. They are, in fact, the characteristics which mark the Arabs as having once been a single race dwelling, many centuries ago, long before the advent of Jesus, in the heart of the Arabian peninsula.

It is there, to the great bowl of the Arabian desert, that we must go to find the source of the story of the Arabs, a story which at one time flamed across and dominated the known world, and which, down to the present day, has continued as a sometimes wavering but always colorful tale.

CHAPTER 5

Age of Empires —
Arab and Ottoman

About the year A.D. 610 an Arab named Mohammed of the Quraysh tribe of Mecca proclaimed to the people of his city that a new monotheism called Islam had been revealed through him. It was a religion, according to its founder, which followed directly in the line of the earlier Semitic monotheisms of Judaism and Christianity; and, like its monotheistic predecessors, it came as a stern rebuke to the paganism and polytheism in which its immediate world was engulfed.

God is One, Mohammed taught. He is all-powerful, the Creator of the universe. There is a judgment day and a heaven and hell. Both places, it was held, occupied specific locales. Heaven, which was the reward of the faithful, included in magnified form the pleasures of the physical senses. Hell, to which the unfaithful were consigned, was a place of affliction and punishment.

Bit by bit, as his experience and influence grew, Mohammed added to these basic teachings a body of law designed
to regulate the political and religious minutiae of the Islamic
state. At the center of this law were the five pillars, or religious requirements, of Islam: the profession of faith (no
god whatsoever but Allah; Mohammed is the messenger of
Allah); ritual prayer (to be said in the prescribed manner
in the Arabic language, regardless of the nationality of the
suppliant); almsgiving; fasting (notably the month of
Ramadan); and the pilgrimage to Mecca, to be performed
at least once by each Moslem.

Politics and religion were combined in the Islamic concept. Islam itself became the state. The imam, or spiritual
leader, became also the commander of the armies of the
faithful and the temporal ruler in every respect. (This is
a concept which still causes conflict between some politically minded Moslems, including members of the Moslem
Brotherhood, who would have a completely Islamic state,
and those Arab leaders who desire a separation of church
and state. Most recently the conflict has been sharp in
Egypt, where the Moslem Brotherhood has been suppressed
by President Gamal Abdel Nasser.)

Mohammed, as many Semitic prophets before him, was
an unschooled man. Many of his convictions, according to
Moslem tradition, came as he meditated in a small cave
named Hira outside the city of Mecca. He began to teach
apparently in his thirtieth year; and after his death, the
words of his teachings were set down by his disciples and
codified in the Koran, which, in the view of Moslems
throughout the world, is the word of God revealed through
His prophet Mohammed.

The dependence of Moslem scripture upon the Old and
New Testaments is apparent. Adam, Noah, Abraham (re-

garded as the spiritual ancestor of Islam), Ishmael, Lot, Joseph, Moses, Saul, David, Solomon, Elijah, Job, and Jonah appear prominently in the surahs, or chapters, of the Koran and form, according to Moslems, the line of prophets which led down to Mohammed.[1] Among New Testament characters Zacharias, John the Baptist, Jesus, and Mary the mother of Jesus are stressed, the latter two with particular respect.

Though its original and astonishing acceptance came in the early years of its founding, Islam today is by no means a spent force in the world. Even today one out of every eight persons on earth—more than 300,000,000 in all—is a follower of Mohammed. Most of this enormous group of people live in the world's warm belt, along the path of conquest followed by the early Arabian Moslems. Yet there are Moslems dwelling as far north as Finland, who must cable to Mecca or to Cairo to learn when Ramadan, the month of fasting, begins and ends, since the sun and moon lie differently in the northern sky than they do along the equator.

A new mosque and Islamic center of modified Moorish design recently was opened in Washington, D. C. Similarly, mosques exist in the capitals of many other Christian countries of the world. The Republic of Indonesia, sixth most populous country on earth, is Moslem. So is Pakistan, one of the world's newest nations. Currently Islam is having a vogue among some American Negroes in New York, to whom Islam's claim of racial equality appeals.

The heart of Islam, however, remains Arab. It was in Arabia that the movement started; and it is to Arabia, specifically to Mecca, to which every Moslem is enjoined by the Koran to make a pilgrimage at least once in his lifetime. Almost every day of every year, if one could adopt a global

[1] See Philip K. Hitti, *History of the Arabs* (London: Macmillan & Co., Ltd., 1951), p. 125.

view, pilgrims might be seen converging on Mecca by plane, car, boat, train—and some still by camel. More than 300,000,000 persons, suppositionally at least, bow in the direction of Mecca five times each day, in obedience to the second pillar of Islam.

Mecca is the forbidden city of Islam. No non-Moslem is allowed within its precincts. I have driven up the road from Jidda on the Red Sea toward Mecca as far as a military encampment, where scowling soldiers stopped me. To have pushed on through would have meant, at the very least, arrest. Islam is the state religion of Saudi Arabia, and the law is clear. No infidel is to view the sacred city, containing within its great square the Ka'bah and Black Stone, to be circumambulated and finally kissed by each pilgrim as a crowning point in his journey of a lifetime. Even the Saudi government airline, since it carries passengers of other faiths, will not land at Mecca; nor do its planes fly over the city, lest an infidel passenger peer down through the heat-charged air over the Hejaz Mountains at the forbidden site.

Islam claims another lien on our interest, however, quite apart from religion. It was Islam which gave impulse to the last great Semitic migration of history, an irresistible out-pouring of people from the Arabian peninsula; Semites eaten up with the zeal of the new faith, who flung the borders of empire to the Atlantic Ocean in the west and as far as China to the east. This was the Arab Empire, es-tablished by the followers of Mohammed.

Until the time of the Arabian prophet, the history of the Middle East had been written largely by Semitic peoples, but not by Arabs as such. (The Arabs are a branch of the Semitic family, given the name Arab to differentiate them from earlier Semitic groupings, such as the Amorites, Ca-naanites, Hebrews, and others.) In rhythmic waves, beginning with the Babylonians about 3500 B.C. and ending with the Nabataeans about 500 B.C., the Semites had gone up from Arabia to found their kingdoms and nations.

One thousand years after the Nabataeans came the next Semitic wave, launched by the religion of Islam. These Semites were Arabs, the followers of Mohammed. So deeply did they burn the mark of their religion, character, and language upon the Middle East that its impress never has been removed. From that day to this the greater portion of the area has been called by a single name—the Arab world.

One historian has put it aptly that the Bedouin was the raw material of Islam. Mohammed preached first to the Bedouins of Arabia, and his teaching was directed toward a Semitic character which down through the ages had warmed to a clear-cut call outlining specific duties to be performed in return for a paradise to be gained. The zeal of the new religion soon was to carry it beyond the confines of Arabia proper, a land already conquered by the faith. In this outward thrust it was the Bedouin who wielded the sword of the zealot, fired by the promise that to succumb in battle for Mohammed was to gain a paradise beyond compare, and fired, equally, no doubt, by a lust for the riches of the fertile lands to the north.

This combination of zeal and ferocity produced one of the most explosive forces in history. Within 100 years after the death of the Prophet Mohammed (A.D. 632), the armies of Islam had overrun not only the lands of the Fertile Crescent but had embraced North Africa to the Atlantic as well, had advanced through Spain, and had even obtained a foothold in southern France. To the east, the Islamic hordes had conquered parts of India and Central Asia, and were at the gates of China.

Of this period of expansion, unprecedented in the history

of the world, D. G. Hogarth wrote that the Arabs "assimilated to their creed, speech, and even physical type, more aliens than any stock before or since, not excepting the Hellenic, the Roman, the Anglo-Saxon, or the Russian."[2] To their empire the Arabs brought a religion, Islam; a language, Arabic; and their own blood. The Islamization of their realm was pervasive; its Arabization, less so, though most of that area which we call the Middle East has remained Arabic from the time of conquest to the present.

One thing, however, the desert Arabs could not bring, and that was a culture. Their gift in this respect was to assimilate, not to originate; and their legacy to the world came down through assimilation. They settled among the conquered peoples, intermarried, absorbed elements of other cultures—Persian, Indian, Syrian, Egyptian—and the result was a civilization which at its zenith shone as a light of the mediaeval world. Arabic became the language of learning. In mathematics, astronomy, geography, medicine, alchemy, architecture, and in the arts of oration and romantic poetry (always opposed by puritannical Islam) Moslems of many backgrounds became the savants of the world.

Islam reigned supreme, and Arabic as a language conquered also. But the leaders of the empire no longer were Arabs so much as they were mixtures of Persian, Syrian, Egyptian, and other strains. The Arab of the desert had been absorbed and vanquished racially when he settled down, though his religion and language had first conquered the peoples among whom he came. The Arab remained pure only in the great bowl of Arabia, inaccessible as always to outside influence.

The culmination of Islamic glory came in the golden age

[2] D. G. Hogarth, *The Penetration of Arabia* (London: Alston Rivers, Ltd., 1905), p. 7.

of Baghdad, during the caliphate of Harun al-Rashid (A.D. 786–809), caliph of "The Thousand and One Nights." Fact seems hardly outstripped by legend in recording the wonders of Baghdad. A wedding is described in the Arabic literature of the time at which 1,000 pearls of great size were thrown from a golden tray upon the young couple as they sat on a golden mat studded with precious gems. When the caliph went out on parade, 100 lions marched before him. In the Hall of the Tree of the caliph's palace, an artificial tree of gold and silver bore in its branches birds of the same metals, complete with mechanical chirping.

Poets, singers, musicians, dancers crowded to the court of the caliph. Along Baghdad's wharves lay hundreds of ships pouring into the city ivory, gold, and black slaves from eastern Africa; white slaves and furs from Scandinavia and Russia; spices, minerals, and dyes from India; musk, silk, and porcelain from China. The adventures of Sinbad the Sailor, a man of Baghdad, are scarcely more marvelous than the travels of the Moslem merchants of the day, men who voyaged as far north as Finland and Sweden, as far east as China, and to Africa in the south.[3]

Of all the glory that was Baghdad little remains today in the mud-walled city of that name on the banks of the Tigris River in Iraq. Indeed, little of the glory that was Islam's elsewhere has survived, save in such structures as the Umayyad Mosque in Damascus and the famed Alhambra of Granada, Spain.

To pass down the Street Called Straight in Damascus; to shed one's shoes before entering the Umayyad Mosque; to walk through the mosque across acres of magnificent rugs given by Moslems the world over; to listen to the soft intoning of suppliants; to do all this, is to glimpse the splendor

[3] See Hitti, *History of the Arabs,* pp. 301-05.

that must have been at one time in Damascus, Baghdad, and elsewhere.

Two great dynasties rose during the period of this Arab Empire. The first was the Umayyad, which established its capital in Damascus. This city, indeed, was the first metropolis to be wrested from the Byzantine Empire by the Arabs swarming up from Arabia. In September, A.D. 635, following a long siege, Damascus surrendered to the army of the Arabs led by Khalid ibn al-Walid. Earlier, almost all of Palestine had fallen to the Islamic hordes, fighting their way north. Jerusalem itself held out until 638, and the Palestinian city of Caesarea until 640.

Following the capture of Damascus and its Syrian hinterland, the Arabs pushed north and eastward into northern Mesopotamia, Armenia, and Georgia. Other Islamic forces moved south through Palestine toward Egypt, following what Dr. Philip K. Hitti has called "the same beaten track along the coast trod by Abraham, Cambyses, Alexander, Antiochus, the Holy Family, Napoleon, and Djemal Pasha. It was the international highway of the ancient world connecting its most important centres of civilization."[4] The final fall to the Arabs of Alexandria in 646 (the Arabs temporarily had seized Alexandria in 642, only to lose it back to the Byzantines) symbolized the conquest of all Egypt.

West of Egypt the Islamic armies poured through North Africa, conquering all in their way. Operating out of the port of Alexandria, a new Arab navy pillaged successively Cyprus, Rhodes, and Sicily. By 713 Spain had become a province of the Arab caliph in Damascus. Only in southern France were the Arabs finally stopped in their push into Europe, by Charles Martel in a battle between Tours and Poitiers in 732.

[4] *Ibid.*, p. 161.

Eastward the Arabs had conquered Iraq and Persia after the conquest of Syria. Iraq, especially, fell easily, since the Semitic peoples of that country felt closer kinship to the Semitic Arabs than to their Persian overlords. By 643 the conquest of most of Persia had brought the Arabs to the gates of India.

In Damascus, meanwhile, a long internecine struggle for the caliphal succession after the death of Mohammed brought to the fore Mu'awiyah, founder of the Umayyad dynasty. In 661 Mu'awiyah was proclaimed caliph (temporal and spiritual ruler) of Islam, and Damascus rather than the Arabian peninsula itself became the capital of the Arab Empire. Involved in the struggle for succession was the slaying, engineered by Mu'awiyah, of al-Hasan and al-Hussein, grandsons of the Prophet Mohammed. These slayings caused the breaking away from Damascus of those Moslems, concentrated in Iraq, who believed that the caliphate should descend by blood relationship from the Prophet. These latter Moslems were called Shiites, as opposed to the Sunni dynasty, or Umayyads, of Damascus. The breach between Shiites and Sunnis has never been healed and forms today the central schism of Islam.

In naming his son Yazid as his successor, Mu'awiyah established the principle of hereditary succession which was followed, not only by the Umayyads, but by the Abbasids who followed them, and even by modern Moslem potentates, as witness the Sauds of Saudi Arabia. During the Umayyad dynasty, which embraced 14 caliphs and lasted from A.D. 661 to 750, the Arab Empire pushed to its greatest expansion, from the Atlantic Ocean on the west (including Spain and North Africa), across the Indus River in India, to the borders of China itself. Umayyad conquests in the east included what today is Afghanistan, Chinese Turkestan, the border provinces of India (which became part of the Moslem state of Pakistan in 1947), and such famous Central Asian cities as Bokhara and Samarkand.

Even during the long period of Umayyad glory, strife among various houses within the dynasty, accompanied by corruption and maladministration in office, weakened the Umayyad throne and laid the groundwork for its collapse before the onslaught of a new and determined enemy in the east. This enemy was a coalition of Islamic forces led by the Abbasids, who were headed in turn by Abu al-Abbas, a great-great-grandson of al-Abbas, uncle of the Prophet Mohammed. In 749, at al-Kufah in Iraq, Abu al-Abbas was enthroned as the first Abbasid caliph. Within a year the Umayyads had been humbled to the dust by the Abbasids, who strove to eradicate every vestige of their Damascus predecessors, even to the exhuming of Umayyad graves and the destruction of the corpses.

Baghdad, in Iraq, became the Abbasid capital, and this shift eastward from Damascus symbolized the gradual change of the Islamic empire from an Arab to a Persian base. Persians and other eastern races dominated the governments of the Abbasids, in contrast to the Arabian focus of the earlier Umayyads. (The first dynasty of Islam, called the Orthodox, also was pure Arabian, embracing four caliphs—Abu Bakr, Umar, Uthman, and Ali—each of whom was closely associated with the Prophet during his lifetime. The short-lived Orthodox dynasty, which lasted from 632 to 661, had ended with the founding of the Umayyad line by Mu'awiyah.) From 750 until 1258 the Abbasids reigned over Islam. To the outside world the most famous Abbasid caliph was Harun al-Rashid, the splendors of whose court have been described.

Never, however, were the Abbasids able to consolidate their hold over all Islam, despite the pious assurance of the Abbasids that their emphasis was to be on the establishment of a theocratic state, as opposed to the secularism of the deposed Umayyads. Full acknowledgment of the legitimacy of the Abbasids never was given by Spain and North Africa, by Egypt, nor by some eastern provinces of the empire. The Shiites, who had teamed with the Abbasids to overthrow the hated Umayyads, soon regarded the Abbasids themselves as usurpers of the throne, which, to the Shiites, belonged to the lineal descendants of the Prophet.

The great schisms of Islam, in other words, continued to widen, bringing in their train political and dynastic rivalries, nepotism and corruption. In particular, the cleavage between Shiite and Sunni Moslems, bred out of disagreement over caliphal succession, wrought havoc and brought bloodshed to Islam.

Gradually the structure of the Abbasid empire decayed. Independent dynasties sprang up where provinces had been before—dynasties called Idrisid, Tulunid, Tahirid, Samanid, Saljuq, and others. The Christian Crusades were a force of disintegration to Moslems in the west. In 1258 the Mongols of Hulagu, a grandson of Genghis Khan, sacked Baghdad and the Abbasid empire lay shattered.

As a world political power the Arab had fallen, never to rise. But the religion he had founded was destined to conquer the conquerers. The barbaric hordes of Saljuq Turks and of Mongols, the first in the eleventh century and the latter in the thirteenth, had swept down from the east to destroy the caliphs of Islam. Yet in the end they became Islamized themselves, and their last days were spent as champions of the faith.

So it was with the next great race to stalk across the stage of the Middle East—the Ottoman Turks. Descendants of Othman, a Mongolian Turk, and admixed with Iranian tribes of Central Asia, the Ottoman Turks gradually absorbed and displaced their Saljuq Turkish cousins in Asia Minor and swept east, south, and west to an empire of their own which, at its zenith, embraced almost as much territory as the Umayyads and Abbasids had held at their prime.

The beginning of significant Ottoman history, about 1300 A.D., found a small Turkish state centered in Asia Minor. Expansion of the Ottoman state was limited, and its existence even precarious, until the capture of Constantinople in 1453 by Mohammed II the Conqueror. From that day to this, Constantinople (now Istanbul) has been a Turkish city.

In 1515 the Ottomans spread eastward through Mesopotamia and part of Armenia, conquering a Shiite Moslem dynasty called Safawid. The following year, 1516, all Syria fell to the Ottomans when the latter conclusively defeated the armies of the Mamluk sultans of Egypt, a dynasty of slave warriors who had rebelled against their Arab caliphal masters in 1250 and founded their own empire, based on Egypt. In 1517 the Ottomans, under Sultan Salim I, invaded Egypt and crushed the Mamluk power. From Egypt, which now had become an Ottoman province, the Turks moved westward through North Africa, establishing over the years at least nominal Ottoman suzerainty over Tripolitania, Tunisia, and Algeria. Morocco, which had been Islamized by the Umayyads, remained independent of the Turks.

By sea the Ottomans moved south to the capture of Yemen, Aden, and Muscat, striking finally all around Arabia up to the head of the Persian Gulf on Arabia's east coast. Only in the sands of central Arabia, land of the Bedouins, was the Ottoman presence unfelt, though nominally the entire peninsula was under the Turkish flag. Europe also had not been neglected, for under Suleiman the Magnificent (1520–1566) much of Hungary fell to the Ottomans.

Under this sultan the zenith of Ottoman power was achieved. The rule of Constantinople "extended from Budapest on the Danube to Baghdad on the Tigris and from the Crimea to the first cataract of the Nile. This was the greatest Moslem state of modern times; not only that, but one of the most enduring Moslem states of all time. No less than thirty-six sultans, all in the direct male line of Uthman, reigned from 1300 to 1922."[5]

Through the centuries that followed the Ottoman conquest, the Arabs lay supine beneath the weight of the Turks whom they had Islamized. It was not until the nineteenth century that Arab nationalism again began to stir, and then but faintly. To the great powers of the West the Middle East had become the land of the Turks, and not of the Arabs. Only the desert Arabs, deep within the fastnesses of Arabia, retained their primal energy, but with no new call to galvanize them. Little disturbed by the Turks, as they had been untouched by every conqueror before, the Bedouins went on raiding each other's camps, grazing their sheep and camels, wandering ceaselessly across the sands. To the north of them the Arab world to which they had given their name and their language lay in torpor, unbroken until the gradual decline of Ottoman power gave nascent Arab nationalism an arena in which to work.

Many factors weakened the Ottomans, including nepotism and corruption, separatism and dynastic splits, the same conditions which earlier had struck down the Arabs. Contributing even more to the Ottoman decline, perhaps, was

[5] *Ibid.*, pp. 712-13.

the fact that the Turkish empire was organized to serve the interests of Constantinople, and not those of the subject peoples, most of whom felt kinship (if at all) to the Turks only through the tenuous tie of religion. Thus many of the far-flung Turkish provinces were held in allegiance only by the Ottoman sword.

Ottoman armies, in turn, were led in many cases by non-Moslems recruited as youths from among the subject peoples, taken to Constantinople, and trained up as Janissaries, or regular Ottoman infantry. More than once throughout the long Ottoman history an individual sultan was virtually the prisoner of his slave generals, or saw a province of the empire slip away from Constantinople under the leadership of such a slave. Notable was the mastery of Egypt by Mohammed Ali, founder of the line of which Farouk of Egypt was the latest king. Mohammed Ali began as a young Albanian officer in the Turkish army which drove Napoleon from Egypt in 1801.

Another symptom of decay in the Ottoman Empire was the millet system inaugurated by the early Moslems and continued by the Sublime Porte, as the Ottoman throne was called. Under the system of millets each religious minority —of which there were many of diverse kinds throughout the Ottoman realm—was allowed self-government in its religious and daily affairs. This comparative freedom in internal administration provided arenas in which local nationalisms might begin to work.

By the late nineteenth century the combination of these conditions had begun to toll the knell of Constantinople. Eyeing the decline of the Turks, the European powers, notably Britain, France, and Russia, began to stake out their claims to the lands of the Middle East. In North Africa the province of Algeria had been lost to the Ottomans when

France occupied Algeria in 1830 and later named it an integral part of metropolitan France. In 1881 the Ottoman province of Tunisia became a protectorate of France. The following year (1882) saw the British occupation of Egypt to protect Britain's Suez Canal lifeline to India. Centuries earlier European nationals had gained extraterritorial rights, similar in some respects to diplomatic immunity today, in the Ottoman Empire under a series of capitulations granted by Constantinople to the major Western powers. These capitulations formed the opening wedge which led to Western mandates over the eastern Ottoman lands after World War I when the Ottoman Empire, allied with Germany, finally collapsed, and Turkey was reduced to the relatively small nation it is today.

The Western powers rushed in to fill the vacuum left by the Ottoman collapse, and the age of Western colonialism in the area, looked back on so bitterly by Arabs today, had begun. Yet it was largely the very advent of the West, and in particular the influence of the schools and religious missions which Americans and Europeans brought with them, that enabled the Arabs gradually to awaken from their slumber.

On the one hand the European powers, with empires of their own to preserve or expand, were seeking to bend the Arabs to their will. On the other hand the teachers and missionaries of the West were struggling to impart some of their own intellectual vigor to the Arabs whom they taught. In the long run it was the teachers who, in a certain sense, were the victors. To them goes much of the credit for setting the Arabs once again on that long and difficult road, replete with revolts, upheavals, and confusion, which led toward the forefront of the world stage.

CHAPTER 6

Mandates and Their Heritage

Paradoxically, it was the system of independent reason and analysis introduced by Western schools which shaped the pattern of Arab resistance to the colonial activities of Western powers after World War I. The revolt of the Arabs against the Turks during the war had been nurtured at least partly in American, British, and French schools established under the Ottomans in Syria, Lebanon, and Palestine. With the collapse of the Ottomans during World War I, the tide of revolt swung almost unabated against the new masters of the Arab world—the mandate powers of Britain and France.

Late in the nineteenth century, as the power of the Ottomans waned, France had sought to establish cultural and economic influence through the Maronite Roman Catholics of Mount Lebanon, the dominant Christian sect of Lebanon. (Through the centuries the rugged heights of Mount

Lebanon had formed a sanctuary to which religious minorities, persecuted by Sunni Moslems, had fled. Under the Ottoman system of millets, many of these sects, including the Maronites, had preserved well-knit semi-independent communities of their own.) Russia, less successfully, had sought to exert the same kind of influence through the Orthodox churches of the area. The German Kaiser had dreamed of a Berlin-to-Baghdad railway that would plant Germany on top of the British Indian Empire.

Britain itself, however, had been the most adventurous of all. The opening of the Suez Canal, and the consequent need of protecting the "lifeline to India," had caused Britain to occupy Egypt militarily in 1882, though that land remained under nominal Turkish sovereignty until the outbreak of World War I. Overland, however, India still was vulnerable, through routes of commerce and possibly of conquest which led across Palestine and Iraq. Already the impending collapse of the Ottoman Turks was causing a scramble for control of those lands.

Britain's first move when Turkey allied herself with Germany in the war was to secure a revolt of the Arabs against their Ottoman masters. A groundwork for this revolt had been laid by the pan-Arab sentiment which increasingly was agitating educated Arab circles in Damascus, Beirut, Cairo, and elsewhere. Negotiating from Cairo with King Hussein of the Hejaz in western Arabia (where an Arab army could be formed without Turkish interference), the British promised the Arabs an independent kingdom in return for an Arab revolt designed to tie down Turkish troops in Arabia, Palestine, and Syria. Bolstered by secret intelligence that Arabs in Damascus were ready to revolt, Hussein sealed his agreement in a series of letters with Sir Henry McMahon, British High Commissioner in Cairo.

The result of this agreement was the Arab Revolt, launched when Hussein declared war against Turkey on June 5, 1916. Hussein's promise to Britain had been to raise an Arab army which would drive the Turks out of Arabia and continue north to assist the British in their military operations. In these tasks Hussein was aided by a corps of British officers, prominent among whom was T. E. Lawrence, later to be called "Lawrence of Arabia" for his part in the campaigns which followed. Under the leadership of Amir Feisal, third son of King Hussein, the Arab army cleared Mecca and Jidda of Turkish troops, left a portion of its force to lay siege to the Turkish-held city of Medina, and proceeded northward to concert its activities with the British.

Successively the Arabs under Feisal, and advised by Lawrence and other Englishmen, moved north to the capture of Wajh, Aqaba, Maan, and Deraa on their way to Damascus. On October 1, 1918, in a moment of great drama, Arab and British forces together entered Damascus, Feisal at full gallop at the head of a body of mounted Arab warriors. When the armistice brought an end to hostilities between the British and Arabs on one side and the Turks on the other, it was estimated that the Arab Revolt had tied down about 65,000 Turkish troops who otherwise would have been free to move elsewhere.

In return for their Revolt the Arabs now expected the granting of their promised kingdom with its capital in Damascus. This kingdom, as the Arabs understood it, was to include all of the Arabian peninsula except certain small territories with whose leaders Britain enjoyed special treaty relations; also Iraq, Palestine, and Syria, with the specific exception of the coastal regions of northern Syria (modern

Lebanon), which had been exempted by Sir Henry Mc-Mahon in his correspondence with Hussein.

The Arab dream, however, was not to be. France, with an eye to her own trade links with India and the Far East, also had been insisting upon a clear channel of influence across the Arab world; and Britain, allied with France in the war against Germany, was in poor position to cavil. Consequently, in the secret Sykes-Picot Agreement of 1916, Britain and France, together with Czarist Russia, privately planned the postwar division of the Arab world. France, generally speaking, was to enjoy unchallenged control of Syria and Lebanon. Britain was to have similar authority in Palestine and Iraq, while Russia was to gain Constantinople with some miles of hinterland on either side of the Bosporus, together with a large slice of eastern Anatolia.

The agreement did not long remain secret, however, for the Bolsheviks, having overthrown the Czars, published the details of the Sykes-Picot treaty. Consternation reigned in the Arab world. Not only was the Arabs' independence to be denied; but one of their new masters, apparently, was to be the same British with whom Hussein had negotiated in good faith.

Nor was this the end of complexity. The long and frequently harrowing travail of the Jews of the Diaspora (Dispersion) and their longing for a homeland of their own had culminated in a demand by the Zionists for a home in Palestine. Impelled by a complex of reasons, humanitarian and political (including a Zionist pledge to work for a British mandate in Palestine), the British Government issued the famous Balfour Declaration of November 2, 1917, in which Britain pledged herself to facilitate "the establishment in Palestine of a national home for the Jewish people," with the proviso that nothing would be done to prejudice the "civil and religious rights of existing non-Jewish communities in Palestine."

To the Arabs none of these commitments—the McMahon correspondence with Hussein, the Sykes-Picot Agreement, and the Balfour Declaration—was compatible with any of the others, especially in regard to Palestine. Again from the standpoint of the Arabs, the peace conference convened in Paris in January, 1919, paid remarkably little attention to the British correspondence with Hussein and a good deal to the Sykes-Picot and Balfour undertakings.

As the central pivot of this state of affairs, Britain was far from happy. She strove with France for a revision of the Sykes-Picot Agreement in order that Britain might honor her obligations to the Arabs. France's refusal was adamant; and, pressed on all sides, Britain finally urged Feisal, as representative of the Arabs, to come to terms both with the French and the Zionists. Though he finally signed an agreement with Dr. Chaim Weizmann, world Zionist leader, welcoming Jewish immigration to Palestine, Feisal refused to concede on the principle of Arab independence. At that time Feisal still was in possession of Damascus, under the over-all authority of General Allenby, Allied commander in the Middle East.

President Wilson, meanwhile, as head of the American delegation to the peace conference, rejected the wartime agreements as incompatible with the later Fourteen Points, promising national self-determination to subject peoples. When Britain and France refused to join the United States in an Allied investigating commission in the Middle East, President Wilson sent two Americans, Dr. Henry C. King, President of Oberlin College, and Charles Crane, a prominent industrialist, to the area to report their recommendations for the future of the Arab world.

Based on exhaustive investigations in Palestine, Syria, Lebanon, and elsewhere, the resulting King-Crane report recommended an American mandate for Syria, with a British mandate as a second alternative, and a British mandate for Mesopotamia. Constitutional monarchies under these mandates were recommended, with Feisal to be King of Syria. The report strongly opposed the establishment of a Jewish state in Palestine, but called instead for Palestine to become part of Syria and for the holy places to be internationalized. A feature of the report's findings was strenuous Arab opposition to France as a mandate power, except among certain Lebanese Roman Catholics.

The King-Crane report, unpopular with Britain and France, was ignored by the peace conference, and the question of mandates was shelved until the spring of 1920, at which time the Covenant of the League of Nations, which had to sanction any mandates, had been ratified. On April 24, 1920, the Allied peace conference met at San Remo where mandates were assigned. France was given Syria (including Lebanon), while Britain was assigned a mandate for Iraq and Palestine. These mandates, termed class "A," were designed to be temporary and to pave the way for complete independence of the mandated lands. The mandate for Palestine incorporated the Balfour Declaration calling for a national homeland for the Jews, though that area of Palestine east of the Jordan River (Transjordan) was excluded from this provision.

Immediate trouble came in Syria, where Feisal, in March, 1920, had been proclaimed King of Syria (including Palestine and Transjordan) by the so-called Syrian National Congress. On August 7, 1920, following clashes through the summer between French and Arab forces, General Gouraud of France entered Damascus and deposed Feisal, who fled to the British in Palestine.

Concurrently the British experienced difficulties in Iraq. Many Iraqi officers (including Nuri es-Said, present Premier of Iraq) had entered the Hejazi army of Feisal during the Arab Revolt, and these officers, backed by strong popular sentiment in Iraq, were opposed to any postwar solution save Arab independence. When the San Remo conference assigned Iraq to Britain, therefore, the country exploded in rebellion. More than 2,500 British soldiers lost their lives before the rebellion was crushed in October, 1920.

In Palestine, meanwhile, anti-Jewish disturbances had broken out in April, 1920, presaging a long and stormy period of conflict between Arabs and Jews until the State of Israel was proclaimed in May, 1948. The British mandatory government in Palestine under Sir Herbert Samuel, its first high commissioner, began the implementation of the Balfour Declaration by setting the first Jewish immigration quota at 16,500.

In the meantime, Amir Abdullah, elder brother of Feisal, had come up from Arabia at the head of an Arab force determined to march on Damascus and restore his brother to his lost throne. Anxious to prevent this and to achieve a stable arrangement in the Middle East, Britain, through Colonial Secretary Winston Churchill, offered the throne of Iraq to Feisal, and a new Amirate (Princedom) of Transjordan to Abdullah. Thus, it was hoped, both sons of King Hussein of the Hejaz would be appeased, the nationalist sentiments of Iraqis would be somewhat satisfied, and the mandate governments might settle down to stable control. On April 1, 1921, accordingly, Abdullah was established as Amir of Transjordan with his capital at Amman, and on

July 11, 1921, Feisal was proclaimed King of Iraq by the Arab Council of State in Baghdad.

In a separate development to the south, King Hussein of Hejaz, the disillusioned father of Abdullah and Feisal, continued to reign until he was driven from his throne in 1924 by Ibn Saud in one stage of the latter's expansion of his desert Kingdom of Saudi Arabia. It was Ibn Saud's expulsion of Hussein, founder of the Hashemite line, from the Hejaz that started a long enmity, extending to the present, between Saudi Arabia on the one hand and the Hashemite kingdoms of Iraq and Jordan on the other.

At this point, France was in possession of a mandate over Syria and Lebanon; Britain held mandates over Iraq and the new Amirate of Transjordan, and also over Palestine, where Britain was committed to the establishment of a national home for the Jews. Britain, in addition, was in military occupation of Egypt, as she had been since 1882. Only in desert Arabia, inaccessible to the outside world, were the Arabs, under Ibn Saud, truly independent. All the pent-up force of Arab nationalism, nurtured partly by Western schools, including the American universities of Beirut and Cairo; the nationalism fueled deliberately by the British in preparing the Arab Revolt—all this force, colored by the bitterness of what the Arabs considered their betrayal, now was turned against the mandate powers.

To the Arabs it meant little that in almost every way the government supplied by the mandate powers was superior to that of the Ottoman Turks whom they had displaced. The important thing, to the Arabs, was that they had been promised independence, a kingdom of their own. In return for this promise they had helped Britain by sending their own soldiers against the Turks in World War I. Their pact with Britain, in the eyes of the Arabs, had been a solemn undertaking, sealed in blood. Thus the secret plan of Britain and France to establish mandates in the Arab world was viewed by the Arabs as the betrayal of a sacred trust, against which their Semitic instincts, goaded by thwarted nationalism, rose in revolt.

Toward France their complaint was simple: they were a people occupied against their will. Toward the British, however, a special bitterness was reserved; the bitterness of the Arabs against a Western power whom they had regarded as a friend, and who (as the Arabs now saw it) had been plotting their division all along.

Arab reaction was pungent. Revolt against the French broke out in the Jebel Druze of Syria in July, 1925, and spread quickly to Damascus and other towns. Though this revolt itself was crushed, it was but the first of numerous insurrections against the mandate power which lasted until the French relinquished their mandate in 1945. Mounting nationalist pressure in Iraq forced the British into a series of increasingly more lenient treaties, culminating in the Anglo-Iraqi Treaty of 1930, which abrogated the mandate and acknowledged the independence of Iraq. In Palestine, terrorism launched both by Arabs and Jews brought conditions so near to anarchy that on May 14, 1948, Britain relinquished its Palestine mandate and thrust the Holy Land burden on the United Nations. Almost everywhere, in other words, the mandate period was marked by the rebellion of stiff-necked peoples against their rulers.

Within the mandated territories, a curious process developed under French and British rule. On the one hand both mandatory powers were striving to replace the Ottoman legacy of governmental corruption with Western standards of justice and administration. In addition, Arab nationalism, despite its threat to the security of the mandates, was in fact being encouraged by the very kind of Western education which the mandate powers sought to perpetuate and extend.

The American University of Beirut (AUB) was a case in point. Founded as the Syrian Protestant College under a New York state charter in 1866, and given its present name in 1920, the school's aim was the development of Arab leadership through the influence of Anglo-Saxon teaching, impelled by the spirit of free inquiry. Inevitably the thinking of many young Arabs, introduced by the university to new social and cultural patterns such as the concepts of freedom and justice for the nation as well as for the individual, chemicalized against the powers which ruled them, first against the Turks and then against the British and French. Thus the university, with no such intent, found itself a center of nationalist agitation.

AUB, though notable in this respect, was not alone. American colleges and secondary schools, working from similar standpoints and accommodating in some cases Arab girls as well as boys, dotted Lebanon in particular, but also Syria, Palestine, Egypt, and Iraq. These missionary schools, founded to leaven Arab thinking rather than to proselytize, perforce were a potent force in preparing the mental climate of revolt.

The Arabic press also, nationalistic and anti-Western though it was, enjoyed strange license under the mandate powers. British and French officials, whose governments at home championed press freedom, were loath to clamp down even on those journals whose attacks on the mandatory governments were extreme. Thus the whole tendency of the Arabic press, centered in Beirut, Damascus, and Jerusalem, was to set the people against the mandates.

Despite this leniency in some respects, however, there was

no mistaking the grip of the mandatory governments over every department of Arab life. The fact that the clamor for independence continued to grow and to manifest itself in demonstrations and revolts was a tribute, not to official laxity, but to the strength of the sentiment involved. The fact that the Arab lands were under mandate chiefly because they lay astride lifelines of empire made the humiliation even harder to bear.

Gradually the churning pressures of opposition forced the reduction and finally the liquidation of the mandates, beginning with the technical independence of Iraq in 1930 and continuing to the departure of the British from the troubled land of Palestine in 1948. The last French troops, symbolizing French control over Syria and Lebanon, withdrew from the Levant states in 1946.

A year earlier, following a series of tumultuous events, Syria and Lebanon had declared their independence of France, then led by General Charles de Gaulle. In this move the Levant states had been strongly supported by Britain, whose Prime Minister Winston Churchill at one point of tension in May 1945 had sent a virtual ultimatum to General de Gaulle, demanding that his troops cease fire against Syrians and Lebanese and return to their barracks. Faced with this ultimatum, France restored peace to the riot-torn lands agitating for independence, and on July 7, 1945, France formally assented to the transfer of final mandate powers to the Arabs.

Technically after World War II the Arabs were independent, for the first time since the collapse of the Arab Empire in A.D. 1258. Yet the end of the mandates left the Arab states so weak and divided among themselves that they could not stand alone, nor could they unify in a single Arab state.

Geographically and economically the area including Palestine, Lebanon, Syria, and Iraq was a homogeneous whole. The division of that area into mandated lands had set up economic and political barriers which down through the years had hardened into fixtures. At one point, indeed, those barriers had been increased when the British, to satisfy Hashemite ambitions and to stabilize the area, had carved out Transjordan from the Syrian desert east of the Jordan River and had given it to Amir Abdullah, older brother of Feisal. Because it could not support itself, the new Kingdom of Jordan had become an economic dependency of Britain. Political rivalries had been set in train throughout the area. Worse still, Palestine was in the process of being lost by the Arabs through Jewish conquest.

All this explains a curious bifurcation of Arab attitudes toward the West since the end of the mandates. On the one hand Arabs clamor for Western gadgets. Even in some cultured homes of Beirut the American refrigerator is placed in the dining room so that guests may see it. American cars throng Arab streets, often built wide enough for two donkeys to pass.

Deep within the Arabian desert, for example, so many princes and notables have switched from camels to cars that every day the Saudi Arabian capital of Riyadh is a bedlam of horns and traffic jams, with Arab policemen trying to direct traffic where traffic cannot go. To reach Riyadh, these cars must be brought in over hundreds of miles of desert on the king's single track railroad. Once there, there is no place for the cars to be driven, save in the oasis itself.

Arabs flock to see American films. Cairo's film studios grind out copies of Western musicals and dramas. British woolens, Italian neckties, American shirts, German cameras are featured in store displays.

Yet the same Arabs who seek these symbols speak bitterly of the West's political role in the Arab world. Even those Arabs who are shrewd and fair enough to acknowledge that the experience of the mandates, by introducing to the Arabs the methodology of Western political life, set the Arab world on the road toward parliamentary government—even those Arabs resent the fact that they had little choice in the matter, and that the tutelage was forced. Countless other Arabs, worked upon by Arab politicians seeking personal followings, seem aware only of the dregs of bitterness left behind by the mandates. As a surcharge to this bitterness is the Arab conviction that Israel would not exist today had it not been for the aid of the United States and Britain.

Such were the conditions which bred the political framework of the Arab world as it emerged after World War II and the end of the mandates. Egypt deserves a special word since, in the period between two world wars, she was not under a mandate, but under direct military occupation by the British. On December 18, 1914, in fact, Egypt had been proclaimed a British protectorate and served as the main Allied base for prosecuting the Middle Eastern war.

After World War I Egyptian nationalism came to the fore under the leadership of Saad Zaghlul Pasha, who in 1919 founded the Wafd Party, destined to spearhead Egypt's struggle for independence. In March, 1919, Zaghlul was deported to Malta by the British, and revolt against British rule broke out in Cairo. So bitterly was the nationalist campaign pressed from that time on that on February 28, 1922, Britain abolished Egypt's protectorate status and proclaimed the country's independence, though reserving real control for the British crown. Subsequent to this move Sultan Faud (a descendant of the Albanian Mohammed Ali) became King of Egypt, a Western-style constitution was promulgated, and elections were held in January, 1924, in which Zaghlul's Wafd Party won 188 seats against the opposition's 27. Restored to Egypt, Zaghlul became premier and worked for a revision of the 1922 treaty of independence, which had been unilaterally proclaimed by Britain and to which the Wafdists did not adhere. Main Anglo-Egyptian differences narrowed down to British control of the Sudan, which London was not willing to give up, and to the presence of British troops in Egypt. A struggle to resolve these differences and to obtain a new bilateral treaty dominated Egyptian affairs until 1936. Also marking this period was a growing cleavage between the palace and the Wafd.

In an effort to curb the influence of the Wafd, King Fuad engineered the creation of a number of rival political parties, none of which, however, rivaled the Wafd in popular support. Even a split within the Wafd, resulting in the formation of the splinter Saadist Party, did not reduce the mass following of the Wafdists, led by Mustafa Nahas Pasha since the passing of Zaghlul in 1927. Early in 1936 King Fuad died, to be succeeded by his sixteen-year-old son, Farouk.

On August 26, 1936, a new Anglo-Egyptian treaty was signed in London, binding on both parties for 20 years. Under the terms of this treaty Britain agreed to evacuate its troops from Egypt, though the latter agreed to a strong British garrison in the Suez Canal Zone to protect Britain's lifeline to India. In other concessions Britain replaced its high commissioner with an ambassador, and allowed Egyptian troops to return to the Sudan, nominally ruled by Britain and Egypt together under an Anglo-Egyptian Condominium.

After the signing of the treaty and until World War II Egyptian politics reverted to their familiar pattern. The Palace, now headed by King Farouk, strove, generally with

British support, to reduce the Wafdists, who continued to dominate popularly-elected parliaments. During World War II, however, the British felt it necessary to placate the Wafd, still the most influential political factor in Egypt. To this end Britain reversed its policy and forced Farouk, on February 4, 1942, to accept his old enemy, Nahas Pasha, as Wafdist premier.

During its 20 years of existence the Wafd had become dominated by a system of political patronage which led to large-scale corruption and abuses. Though the public gradually had become aware of these practices, they were exposed to the full glare of publicity by the publication of a Black Book, compiled by Makram Ebeid Pasha, a former Wafdist who had split with Nahas. From that time on the taint of corruption never left the Wafd.

As the Wafd began to lose its popular following, extremist organizations assumed new importance. Principally these were the Communists on the left and the xenophobic Moslem Brotherhood on the right, founded by Sheikh Hassan el-Banna in 1929 and dedicated to the establishment of a theocratic Moslem state with foreign influence expelled from Egypt. As extremist sentiment spread, terrorism began to mark the Egyptian scene, including finally the assassination of El Banna in 1949.

Agitation against the British continued to mount, and on October 8, 1951, Wafdist Premier Nahas Pasha unilaterally abrogated the 1936 Anglo-Egyptian treaty; called for the eviction of British troops from the Suez Canal Zone, and for the uniting of the Sudan and Egypt; and proclaimed Farouk "King of Egypt and the Sudan."

Though the Canal Zone issue was the more dramatic, Egyptian leaders were even more fundamentally concerned about the Sudan. To Egyptians it was not "union" of the

Sudan with Egypt, but "reunion," since Egypt had controlled the Sudan before it was occupied militarily by the British in the late nineteenth century. Of paramount importance to Egypt was the fact that the Sudan, embracing the southern reaches of the Nile valley, controlled the waters of the Nile on which Egypt depended for life, and also the fact that in the Sudan's vast plains might be settled surplus fellahin (peasants) from overpopulated Egypt.

Britain refused to budge, either from the Suez Canal or from the Sudan, and on January 26, 1952, the explosion came. Cairo was sacked by angry mobs, demonstrating ostensibly against the British, but whipped up by Communist and other agitators aiming at anarchy. Thus, the stage was set for the Army revolution of July 23, 1952, when a group of young officers led by Lieutenant Colonel Gamal Abdel Nasser seized power, forced King Farouk to abdicate and abolished the monarchy.

Differences between Nasser and Major General Mohammed Naguib, the regime's older and respected "front man," led finally to the assumption of open power by Colonel Nasser, who assumed the title of premier. Governing as a junta through the so-called Revolution Command Council (RCC), Colonel Nasser and his young officer cohorts obtained British agreement to evacuate the Suez Canal Zone, with permission for British troops to return should the Arab states or Turkey be attacked, and obtained also the dissolution of the Anglo-Egyptian Condominium over the Sudan.[1]

Egyptians were jubilant over the Canal Zone agreement, which removed the last symbol of British control of Egypt. Egypt's joy over the Sudan agreement, however, was short-

[1] On June 23, 1956, Nasser was elected President of Egypt in a nationwide plebiscite in which a new Constitution was approved, and the Revolution Command Council officially was dissolved. None of these surface changes, however, dilute the absolute control of Colonel Nasser's military junta over Egyptian life (see pp. 73-74).

lived. In a reversal of form, the formerly pro-Egyptian political parties of the Sudan rejected union with Egypt and voted for independence for their country. As a result the Sudan now is an independent Arab state, and water rights, settlement of Egyptian peasants on Sudanese land, and other questions must be negotiated between equals instead of being legislated from Cairo, as the Egyptians had hoped.

Internally, Colonel Nasser abolished political parties, including the Wafd, crushed the Communists, and finally the Moslem Brotherhood, in order to give his regime a free hand in the implementation of its land reform program and other social reforms designed to uplift the lot of Egypt's depressed peasantry. This, indeed, is Nasser's greatest task, for Egypt's population of 22,000,000, already overtaxing the country's meager arable land, doubles itself every 50 years. To win the race against expanding population, or even to maintain the status quo, Colonel Nasser's government has outlined a giant program of land reclamation and industrialization, dominated by plans for a new High Dam on the Upper Nile, for which Egypt has obtained promises of United States and British aid.

Externally, Nasser has made clear to the other Arabs that Egypt intends to maintain her leadership of the Arab world. Cairo's chief and determined rival for this honor is Iraq, bolstered by expanding income from oil. Thus the Arab scene is marked by hostility between Egypt and Iraq as each tries to draw the other Arab states into its orbit. Egypt's importance now has been magnified in Arab eyes by Colonel Nasser's ability to get large quantities of arms from the Soviet bloc, thereby creating anxiety in Israel, and in the West as well.

Nasser has proclaimed a new draft constitution for Egypt, which bars political parties, and calls for a nonparty parliament made up of representatives of agriculture, religion, the liberal professions, trade, industry, and the provinces. Though Egypt's first parliament under this constitution is scheduled to be elected in 1956, it is not expected that the grip of Colonel Nasser's military junta thereby will slacken. This, Nasser cannot afford until sufficient progress has been made in social reform to ensure that removal of the dictatorship would not bring back into power the old discredited politicians, led by the Wafdists.

North of Egypt, across the Sinai Peninsula, lies Palestine, forming the western horn of the so-called Fertile Crescent. (The name "Fertile Crescent" is applied to a crescent-shaped belt of fertile land starting at the Mediterranean Sea on the west, extending north through Palestine and Lebanon, then east across Syria, and finally south through Iraq to the Persian Gulf. Cupped between the Crescent's horns is the arid Syrian desert, merging southward into the great deserts of the Arabian peninsula.)

In her mandate over Palestine, Britain sought to establish a national home for the Jews, while at the same time preserving the rights and prerogatives of the Arabs who formed Palestine's indigenous population. The task of juggling the two sides proved impossible, and the latter years of the mandate, after World War II, found British troops and administrators the target of terrorism launched both by Arabs and Jews. Faced with near chaos, Britain ended her Palestine mandate on May 14, 1948, and shifted the problem to the United Nations. Earlier the UN, struggling to find a modus vivendi between Arabs and Jews, had voted partition of the Holy Land, recommending the creation of separate Arab and Jewish states in Palestine, with an internationalized Jerusalem.

On May 14, 1948, the same day the British withdrew, the Zionists proclaimed the state of Israel. Promptly the surrounding Arab lands invaded Palestine and war, broken by two UN-arranged truces, raged throughout the year. The result was defeat for the Arabs and an expanded Jewish state, since Israel had won by conquest more land than that assigned to her under the partition plan. Nearly 1,000,000 Arabs fled their Palestinian homeland and sought refuge in neighboring Arab lands.

Palestine no longer was Arab. It had become a homeland for the Jews, and had been given a new name—Israel. The new state faced grave problems which continue to the present. Not the least of these is the fact that the Arab states, technically still at war with Israel, have imposed an economic boycott on Israel which has closed the Suez Canal and the Gulf of Aqaba to shipping bound to and from Israel. Added to this restriction of normal trade relations with the outside world is the fact that Israel's land, except for select portions, needs extensive development before the country's economy can be called viable. Finally, Israeli leaders seek to absorb in their tiny land a continuing influx of immigrants, many of them Oriental Jews poorly adapted to the Europeanized outlook of their adopted homeland.

Directly east of Israel lies the Hashemite Kingdom of Jordan (formerly Transjordan), which emerged from mandate status under Britain on March 22, 1946, in a treaty signed in London recognizing the political independence of Amir Abdullah's realm. Economically, however, Jordan could not become independent. Carved out of desert land east of the River Jordan in 1921, the amirate was largely a Bedouin land with few sources of income. From the beginning, therefore, Amir Abdullah (who changed his title to King in 1946) was utterly dependent on British subsidy,

both for his country's administration and for the maintenance of the Arab Legion which, under British training,
became the best army in the Arab world.

Despite the poverty of his land, King Abdullah was ambitious to link the northern Arab world—Jordan, Iraq, Syria,
and Lebanon—in a so-called Greater Syria under his own
rule. As a first step toward this end, he unilaterally annexed
to Jordan, after the Arab-Israeli war, that part of Palestine
not occupied by Israel. Though this increased Abdullah's
realm, it added greatly to his economic problems, for Jordan's population was thereby trebled, counting the 475,000
Palestine refugees to whom Abdullah gave Jordanian citizenship.

Politically also the move was portentous, as became apparent after Abdullah's assassination in 1951 and the assumption of the throne by his young grandson, King Hussein.
(Between Abdullah and Hussein was the short reign of
Abdullah's son, Talal, who was removed from the throne
because of mental instability.) Jordan's new citizens from
Palestine were well-educated by Arab standards and found
themselves in sharp conflict with the patriarchal, conservative outlook of the old Transjordanian ruling class. This
caused a sharp cleavage in Jordan, with the new citizens
from Palestine tugging in general toward union with oil-
rich Iraq, which would remove the necessity for British
subsidy, and the Jordanian Palace backing away from such
merger lest its own throne be lost in favor of Iraq's. Thus
Jordan, which must depend on someone else's aid, finds herself pulled toward Iraq on the one hand and toward the
rival Egyptian camp on the other, since Egypt sees therein
a way to frustrate Iraq. In the meantime, though the Arab
Legion no longer is British-commanded, the British subsidy
to Jordan continues.

East of Jordan, across the Syrian desert, lies Jordan's sister Hashemite Kingdom of Iraq. On Iraq's throne sits young King Feisal, grandson of the Feisal who led the Arab Revolt, and cousin of King Hussein in Jordan. Beyond this family relationship, however, the two kingdoms have little in common. Iraq is wealthy, due to oil. In addition, her broad plains watered by the Tigris and Euphrates Rivers form a potential granary for the entire Middle East. To the irrigation and cultivation of these plains, the Iraqi Government is devoting substantial income from oil. In Iraq, therefore, lies the hope of agricultural abundance sufficient to supply the entire Arab world.

Iraq also is the most pro-Western of all Arab states, and the only Arab land to have joined the Western-sponsored Baghdad Pact, designed to protect the Middle East from the Soviet threat to the north. These pro-Western leaders of Iraq, led by Premier Nuri es-Said, are ambitious. With Iraq's oil wealth and agricultural potential to back them up, they seek to unite at least Syria and Jordan, and possibly Lebanon, in a Greater Syria similar to Abdullah's, but under the leadership of Iraq. Poised against them in this effort is Egypt, fearing in Greater Syria a diminution of her own leadership of the Arabs.

North of Iraq and Jordan lie the republics of Syria and Lebanon, which are treated as a unit because geographically they form one. Lebanon is the mountainous coastal strip of the great hinterland of Syria. To the mountains of Lebanon, during the ages, fled minority sects persecuted by the Sunni Moslems of the Arab and Ottoman empires. Prominent among these sects were the Maronite Roman Catholics, who, under the Ottomans, formed a semiautonomous community clustered on Mount Lebanon, overlooking the Mediterranean Sea.

When she assumed her mandate over Syria, France formally detached Mount Lebanon, added to it several Moslem districts of Syria, and formed the new state of Lebanon. The French object was to create a predominantly Christian Arab state which would be friendly to France after the mandates had ended. To this end France supplied Lebanon with a constitution preserving the Christian character of the state by requiring the president of the republic to be a Christian. A sectarian breakdown was required in each government department, with Christians in the ascendancy. Basis for this structure was a French-controlled census of 1932, which found the Christians in a 55 to 45 per cent majority over the Moslems.

Since that time, however, the Moslems claim that their higher birth rate has placed them in a majority and that the constitution should be rewritten to accord. This the Lebanese Government refuses to do, nor will it hold a new census. As a result Lebanon teeters on the verge of sectarian strife.

Externally, Christian Lebanese fear that Syria desires to absorb Lebanon within the Syrian land mass. Dominated by this fear, and by the more general fear of persecution should their country be engulfed in the surrounding Moslem sea, Christian Lebanese warily tread a neutral path in Arab affairs.

Syria, also a republic, has found its politics dominated by violence since the country achieved independence in 1945. Basically the violence has stemmed from the inability of Syrian political parties—led by the National Bloc and the People's Party—to formulate programs satisfactory to the country at large, and to the Syrian Army in particular. Four times since the beginning of 1949 the Syrian Army has intervened, ostensibly to launch new programs of reform.

Each of the first three *coups d'etat*—led successively by Colonel Husni Zaim, Colonel Sami Hinnawi, and Lieutenant Colonel Adib Shishakly—finally failed. The fourth *coup* in February, 1954, removed Shishakly from power and installed in his place the old-time civilian politicians of Syria. To date rivalries among these politicians have prevented any forward-looking program, and the result is the same kind of governmental stagnation which led to the former *coups*.

Externally, republican Syria fears Iraq's desire to unite Syria with Iraq and Jordan under the leadership of the Hashemite crown. This fear has led Syria to side strongly with Egypt in the latter's anti-Iraq campaign. As a display of their solidarity, Egypt and Syria have merged their armed forces under over-all Egyptian command.

At the southern end of the Arab world lies the vast Arabian peninsula, nine-tenths of which is controlled by Saudi Arabia. Never under a mandate, Saudi Arabia has been left free to her own development, which began in 1901 when Ibn Saud captured the Arabian city of Riyadh and began the founding of his kingdom. During the expansion of his realm, Ibn Saud deposed King Hussein of the Hejaz, and since that time there has been distrust and even enmity between the House of Saud and the Hashemite kingdoms of Iraq and Jordan, whose thrones are held by the family of the exiled Hussein. In particular King Saud, son and successor of the late Ibn Saud, fears the growing strength of Iraq. To this end King Saud has merged his country's armed forces with those of Syria and Egypt, in an anti-Iraq bloc.

Internally, Saudi Arabia's major problem is the distribution of its vast income from oil, which now totals about $250,000,000 a year. This income goes directly to King Saud, one of the few remaining absolute monarchs on earth. Unrest is springing up within the kingdom, particularly among those Saudis who have gained some education through working for the Arabian American Oil Company, at the manner in which the King spends his wealth. Most of the money, in one way or another, enriches the royal family and its hangers-on. Little of the money flows back into the country in the form of public services, such as schools, roads, sewage systems, and the like. So widespread has unrest become that observers estimate King Saud might lose his throne should the income from oil stop. Under such circumstances the Arabian American Oil Company, wholly American-owned, feels its own position increasingly uncertain and strives to maintain neutrality between the King and the people at large.

Along the eastern and southern fringes of the Arabian peninsula are a number of hot and sandy sheikhdoms and amirates whose defense and foreign relations are controlled by Britain. These tiny principalities make up a world of their own, including tribal intrigue, the lassitude of extreme poverty, and, in some cases, fantastic development as a result of oil. Starting at the head of the Persian Gulf and working clockwise down the east coast of Arabia, these sheikhdoms are Kuwait (enormously rich from oil), Qatar, the island of Bahrein, and the Trucial Oman, which includes the six sheikhdoms of Ras al-Khaima, Umn al-Qawayn, Ajman, Sharja, Dibai, and Abu Dhabi. The last named sprang recently into prominence because of its jurisdictional claim over the inland oasis of Buraimi, claimed also by Saudi Arabia.

From the southern tip of the Trucial Oman the coastline of the Sultanate of Muscat and Oman stretches down to the mouth of the Persian Gulf and then westward along the Arabian Sea, 1,000 miles in all. West of Muscat and Oman, still running along the coast, lie the Aden Protectorates, whose tribal population is divided into some 30 sultanates, sheikhdoms, and other tribal units. Of chief importance here is the British Crown Colony of Aden, which was an important Allied base during the East African campaign against the Italians in 1941.

To the west of Aden, occupying the mountainous southwest corner of the Arabian peninsula, stands the independent Imamate (Kingdom) of Yemen, a Moslem kingdom even more strictly isolated from the outside world than Saudi Arabia to the north.

These were the countries and the relationships which emerged from the mandate period at the close of World War II. Even had the Arabs been granted their kingdom after the first World War, as promised by the British, some of their rivalries would have sprung up. It is doubtful, for example, that either Saudi Arabia or Egypt would have looked with comfort at a powerful Arab kingdom ruled from Damascus. Indeed, the followers of Feisal, who was to rule the Arab kingdom, assumed that the territory of Saudi Arabia would be controlled by the Damascus throne.

Nonetheless, the divisive roles of Ottoman nepotism and mandate machination in splitting the Arab world cannot be denied. The world of the Arabs had been truncated, economically and politically, and today the Arab states face one another and their problems in a state of uneasy truce.

CHAPTER 7

Search for Unity
Among the Arabs

Against the background of original ethnic and cultural integrity, dissipated through centuries of dynastic rivalries and the divisive tendency of Ottoman and mandate rule, the Arabs present a picture of contradiction before the world. On the one hand they proclaim their unity in the face of Israel. On the other hand they indulge so openly in quarrels among themselves that the observer is left bewildered as to the real meaning of relationships among the Arabs.

The fact is that Arab unity today, despite a common religion and language, is largely a myth. Except in certain cultural, commercial, and technical fields, the drive toward pan-Arabism is defeated by political ambitions at the top. Even toward Israel, considered by most Arabs to be an enemy, the quality of their opposition varies. Some Christian Arabs of Lebanon, fearful always of an engulfing Moslem sea, privately are relieved to see in Israel another non-Moslem element in the Arab world. Shiite Moslem farmers of south Lebanon complain bitterly that the Arab economic boycott of Israel has deprived them of a natural market for their produce.

Saudi Arabia's ruling class, though it fulminates against Israel its full share, demonstrates far more interest in its continued income from oil and in weakening its old enemy Iraq than in practical measures designed to injure the Jewish state. King Saud's much-quoted statement that Israel is "a cancer on the body Arab, which must be removed at the cost of 10,000,000 Arab lives, if necessary," was made before a group of Arab journalists flown into Arabia for an audience with the King. There is reason to believe that the monarch intended his statement for local Arab consumption and had little idea that some of those reporters represented news agencies which would flash his words around the world. Having made the statement, the King, as an Arab, was stuck with it, and his words have been quoted many times by Israelis as "proof" of Saud's intransigeance toward the Jewish state.

Jordan, though its border villagers have suffered more than other Arabs from the presence of Israel, might welcome an equitable peace if it could persuade its Palestinian citizens to accept it. Then the port of Haifa, Jordan's natural outlet to the sea, would be opened, and Amman would be freed of the onerous import and export duties levied on Jordanian goods in transit through Damascus and Beirut. Egypt, too, with enough internal problems to occupy its entire attention, might move toward peace if it were possible at the same time to maintain its leadership of the Arabs, and if the need for a possible scapegoat were not felt should internal policies fail.

Only Iraq and Syria exhibit little margin for compromise so far as Israel is concerned; and in the case of Syria, at least, a part of this tenacity may stem from the conviction of some Syrian leaders, plagued by chronic instability and the threat of *coups d'état*, that they would have little to lose and possibly much to gain through adventure against Israel.

Shortly after he came to power in Egypt, Colonel Nasser put his finger on a basic Arab ill when he said that the Arabs lost the Palestine war in 1948 because they had "seven armies instead of one." Nasser then called for a unified Arab command, declaring that the Arabs never would defeat the Jews until they unified their armies. "These (Arab) armies are stronger than the Israeli Army," the Egyptian leader said, "but they are scattered. A solution of the Palestine problem will not be achieved except by the collaboration of the Arab countries in a true union."

The truth of the Egyptian's words was acknowledged by most Arabs. Because of Nasser's position as leader of an ambitious Egyptian state, however, his words immediately were suspect in the same Arab eyes. Who, it was asked, would lead this all-Arab command? Presumably Colonel Nasser meant that Egypt, as the most powerful and populous of Arab lands, should be entrusted with the task. Iraq, however, as Egypt's arch rival within the Arab League, scarcely would allow its soldiers to be commanded by an Egyptian. Egypt held the same sentiment so far as an Iraqi commander was concerned. Syria also, suspicious always that Iraq intended to swallow her, never would consent to Iraqi command. Jordan's army, qualitatively the best in the Arab world, at that time was commanded by a Briton; and no Arab state, least of all Syria and Egypt, could persuade its people that an over-all British commander meant anything but surrender of Arab independence.

So it was that Colonel Nasser's thesis fell victim to Arab divisiveness. Late in 1955 Egypt did sign bilateral military pacts with Syria and Saudi Arabia, and later with Yemen, placing the armed forces of the four countries under joint command, headed by an Egyptian. Even this departure, however, was motivated not so much by an impulse toward unity as by the determination of the states concerned, each for its own reasons, to isolate and weaken their sister nation of Iraq.

Besides, it is too early to tell what practical effect the Saudi-Syrian-Yemenite-Egyptian merger would have in the event of fighting against Israel. It is hard to envisage, for example, Saudi Arabian troops moving across hundreds of miles of difficult desert terrain to go to the aid of Syria, particularly if the latter launched an attack against the Jewish state. Indeed, the four Arab states, in striving to isolate Iraq, may have signed themselves to a larger commitment than they realized in the event of fighting between one of them and Israel.

Thus even as regards Israel, where Arab unity is proclaimed the loudest, agreement among the Arabs is a façade, with deep fissures underneath. In the realm of political competition among the Arabs, not even a façade of unity is offered. This separatism is due in part to the conscious effort of European powers to divide and rule in the Middle East. In part it is the result of Egypt's being ethnically more Hamitic than Semitic; in other words, being related to the other Arabs more by history than by blood, though their religion and language are common. This causes Egyptian leadership to be resented by many Arabs in Lebanon, Syria, and Iraq, who look upon Egypt as an African rather than as an Arab state. In part also Arab separatism is the result of dynastic rivalries which, in one form or another, have characterized the Arabs from their desert days down to the present.

Whatever its causes, separatism has left the Arabs weak and divided in a geographic locale demanding unity if maximum strength is to be achieved. Geographically the area inhabited by Lebanon, Syria, Iraq, and Jordan (as well as Israel) is a unit, with so few natural resources that ideally there should be close cooperation between the peoples of the desert and those of the settled lands. As it stands, however, there is suspicion of each other among these states, with the result that Jordan, poorest of them all, must depend almost entirely upon outside subsidy to exist.

Basically, Arab separatism revolves around two poles, Iraq on the one hand and Egypt on the other. These two states, the most powerful among Middle Eastern Arabs, strive with each other for dominance. Egypt, with 22,000,-000 persons, is by far the more populous. Her army is larger, and her land still yields up more wealth than does Iraq's. The latter, however, has vastly greater agricultural potential in her underdeveloped plains watered by the Tigris and Euphrates than does Egypt, and Iraq now has the income from oil to go about systematic development of her land. With the influence these factors give her, Iraq presses steadily to group the northern Arabs (Syria, Jordan, and Lebanon) beneath her wing. This Egypt resents, for a grouping of the northern Arabs would reduce Egypt to a secondary role.

This rivalry, fought out within the Arab League, was kept partly from public view until February, 1955. At that time, however, Iraq joined the Baghdad Pact sponsored by Britain and the United States. To Egypt, this was a direct affront to her leadership, for Cairo's view, influenced by the long British occupation of Egypt, was that the Arabs should eschew Western alliances and build their own collective security system within the Arab League. In such an arrangement Egypt, with the largest Arab army and population, would play the dominant role. Iraq, on the other hand, conscious of the Soviet threat to her oil fields in the north, welcomed the protective shadow of the West cast by the Baghdad Pact.

To halt any gravitation toward Iraq, now to be strengthened by Western arms, Egypt worked swiftly to draw other Arabs to her side. In this campaign Syria and Saudi Arabia, each distrustful of Iraq, proved ready allies, and by the end of 1955 Egypt had secured a merging of Syrian, Saudi Arabian, and Egyptian armed forces under over-all Egyptian command. Only Lebanon and Jordan remained outside the two camps, ostensibly neutral.

Lebanon, wary of entanglement with the Moslem East, has maintained an attitude of watchful waiting. In December, 1955, however, Jordan was drawn into the fray. Early that month Britain sent General Sir Gerald Templer, Chief of the British Imperial General Staff, to Amman to promise Jordan jet planes and heavy arms for the Arab Legion if the desert kingdom would join the Baghdad alliance. Split sharply on the issue, the Cabinet of Premier Said el-Mufti resigned, to be replaced by the government of Hazza el-Majali, reportedly willing to enter Jordan in the controversial pact.

Beginning in December four days of demonstrations and riots rocked Jordan's cities, including Jerusalem, Amman, Nablus, Hebron, and Bethlehem, as angry crowds denounced El Majali and the Baghdad Pact. Chiefly the protestors appeared to be Palestinians, people of Jordan's "west bank," who became Jordanians following the Palestine War of 1948 when King Abdullah annexed that part of Palestine not occupied by Israel. Preoccupied with the division of their homeland, these new citizens of Jordan feared that Jordan's adherence to the Baghdad Pact would divert attention from the Palestine problem and engage Jordan's energies in Western plans for defending the Middle East against the Communist threat from the north.

In office less than a week, El Majali resigned. King Hussein dissolved Parliament and announced that the Jordanian people could express their views on the Baghdad Pact in early national elections. On January 4, 1956, however, the Jordanian Supreme Council for Interpretation of the Constitution ruled that the dissolution of Parliament had been unconstitutional, leading to reports that the King had abandoned plans for early elections. Then, despite reports that a premier opposed to the Baghdad Pact had been named, fresh rioting broke out January 7 and continued for three days, threatening the stability of the Jordanian throne, and sinking beyond early recall Britain's effort to enlist Jordan in the Baghdad Pact.

This time also the demonstrations were led by Palestinians. In both sets of rioting, however, it was obvious that extraneous elements had helped to stir up the people. The British Foreign Office officially charged that Communists had helped foment the rioting, and declared also that the demonstrators had been paid "a certain amount of money . . . not only from Communist sources." Though the Foreign Office spokesman refused to identify the latter instigators, informed British officials said he undoubtedly was referring to Egyptian agents and money from Saudi Arabia.

A British document handed later to the United States government is believed to have alleged that Saudi Arabian payments totaling $8,400 were divided among three Cabinet ministers whose resignation led to the collapse of the Said el-Mufti government in Jordan prior to the December riots. The British also alleged that editors of five Jordanian newspapers each received $560 in Saudi Arabian money November 7, and that each accepted four to five times that amount later in the month.[1] It is known that the newspapers involved consistently printed articles favoring the Saudi point of view and opposing the Baghdad Pact.

Cairo had won its battle to keep Jordan out of the Baghdad alliance, and within a few days reports were current that Egypt, Saudi Arabia, and Syria were offering Jordan $280,000,000 over a 10-year period to replace British subsidies to the barren little land. If accepted, this offer, thus far shelved by Amman, would place Jordan under the effective control of Egypt.

Cairo's battle had been won but at considerable cost to itself and to the Arabs at large. Iraqi-Egyptian hostility had deepened to the point that early in January, 1956, Said Gazaz, Iraqi Minister of the Interior, reported to Parliament in Baghdad that police had uncovered subversive activities in Iraq, aimed at assassinating leading Iraqi statesmen, under the direction of another Arab state. Clearly this meant Egypt, and the report was followed by Iraq's demand that the Egyptian military attaché in Baghdad be recalled.

In another way Colonel Nasser endangered himself in seeking to frustrate Iraq. When Syria and Saudi Arabia placed their armed forces under Egyptian command, Egypt theoretically became responsible for the security of those states as well as for her own. What this might mean became clear in December, 1955, when the Israeli Army attacked Syrian outposts east of the Sea of Galilee, killing more than 50 Syrians. Though Egypt did not intervene at the time,

[1] For details of the Saudi campaign of bribery see *The New York Times* of January 27, 1956.

Premier Nasser felt compelled to warn Dag Hammarskjold, Secretary-General of the United Nations, that any further Israeli attack against the Arabs would involve full-scale Egyptian retaliation. This may have been further than Colonel Nasser wished to go at the time. He was virtually forced to his declaration, however, by the terms of the pact he had concluded with Syria, a pact intended primarily to frustrate the Baghdad alliance rather than commit Egypt to go to Syria's aid when attacked. It was this fact which caused Iraqi Premier Nuri es-Said to declare that Egyptian opposition to the Baghdad Pact had exposed the Arabs to danger vis-à-vis Israel, where unified action was needed most.

In effect the Baghdad Pact did not create new hostilities among the Arabs; it merely crystallized existing ones. Syria and Saudi Arabia long had practiced anti-Iraq policies, and Egyptian opposition to the pact caused them to fall naturally into line. Most Syrian leaders are dedicated to the principle of republicanism and reject any alliance with neighboring Iraq under the latter's Hashemite crown. These same Syrians, however, are aware that Nuri es-Said and other Iraqi leaders long have worked, and still desire, to link at least Syria and Jordan with Iraq under the leadership of Baghdad.

At times of political crisis in Damascus, Western diplomats have been convinced that Nuri es-Said was ready to march on Damascus to achieve his aims. The British-trained Iraqi Army of 40,000 men is a greatly superior force to the Syrian Army of half that number, or less. Of late, however, Nuri es-Said, himself an army officer before he became a politician, has indicated to diplomats that he no longer considers overt force the best method of achieving his goal, at least at present. Instead he is concentrating on a campaign of propaganda, via radio, pamphlets, and other means, to convince Syrians that they should replace their government with one sympathetic to union with Iraq. Under these circumstances it is not surprising that Syria has subscribed to the anti-Iraq policies of Saudi Arabia and Egypt.

The House of Saud's reasons for opposing Iraq are different. In 1924, as has been seen, Ibn Saud of Arabia chased King Hussein, head of the Hashemite line, out of Mecca and subsequently out of Arabia into exile. Since that time the Sauds, including King Saud, the present ruler of Saudi Arabia, have been obsessed with fear that Iraq, ruled by the Hashemite descendants of Hussein, might become strong enough to attempt seizure of Mecca, holiest city of Islam, or at least to isolate Saudi Arabia and weaken her influence in the Arab world. As Iraq has grown stronger through income from oil, Saudi fears proportionably have increased.

The result has been a campaign by King Saud to oppose Iraq generally, and specifically to keep alive Iraqi-Egyptian jealousy, lest there be a *rapprochement* between the two most powerful Arab states, to the detriment of the Sauds in Arabia. Thus Saudi Arabia, like Syria, became a natural ally of Egypt when the latter sought to frustrate the Baghdad Pact.

Made enormously rich by oil, King Saud has employed the weapon of bribery to weaken Iraq. His alleged payments to three Jordanian Cabinet ministers have been mentioned, as well as his doles to the editors of five Jordanian newspapers. For some time Jordan's three major newspapers have carried articles advancing the Saudi line, and have refused even at the Jordan Government's insistence to publish anti-Saudi material. At least one Jordanian editor has admitted to Western sources that his paper is paid regularly by Saudi Arabia. In Cairo the Sauds bought outright a small weekly magazine called *Al Kahira*. Like all Egyptian publications, however, *Al Kahira* is under strict internal censorship, and prints nothing inimical to the military junta of Colonel Nasser. In addition, of course, Saudi and Egyptian policies currently are hand-in-glove.

Suspicion on the part of Saudis that President Camille Chamoun of Lebanon favors the Baghdad Pact allegedly has caused Riyadh to offer money to all of Beirut's 37 dailies which would accept it. On a state visit to Lebanon while the author was in Beirut, King Saud reportedly offered large gifts of money to Lebanese editors. One Beirut editor told a Western businessman that he had refused such a gift. In this connection George Akl, Lebanese Minister of Information, recently warned newspaper editors to halt their attacks on the Lebanese Government. The minister declared these attacks were financed by payments from a foreign power. Leaders of Palestine Arab refugees have told United Nations officials that some refugees, including pro-Communists, have been paid by the Saudis to stir up trouble, especially in Lebanon against President Chamoun.

The irony of it is that the Saudi Arabian Government, anti-Communist though it is, is paying to push the same propaganda line now being advanced by the Soviets in the Middle East; namely, that the Baghdad Pact is a colonial device of the West designed to perpetuate Western influence in the area. Newspapers and other agencies which might reject outright Communist advances nonetheless are serving Soviet ends by advancing the Saudi line.

Saudi Arabian bribery extends to fields apart from Iraq. Britain and the Sauds long have disputed ownership of the tiny Buraimi Oasis in southeastern Arabia, lying in a poorly-mapped district where the Empty Quarter fringes out into the border lands of Oman and Muscat. Britain claims that six of Buraimi's nine villages belong to the Bani Yas, a dominant tribe of the Sheikhdom of Abu Dhabi, and that the other three belong to the Sultan of Muscat. Both Abu Dhabi and Muscat are in special treaty relations with Britain. Saudi Arabia claims jurisdiction over all of Buraimi, basing its claim on old records of tax payments from Buraimi to the House of Saud, and on the visits of Buraimi tribal delegations to the late Ibn Saud, placing their tribes under his suzerainty.

Oil interests rest at the base of the conflict. As one American diplomat put it, subsidiaries of the British-owned Iraq Petroleum Company and the American-owned Arabian American Oil Company (Aramco) have "bumped into each other" in the Buraimi area. Should King Saud gain sovereignty over Buraimi, its oil, exceedingly important to Britain, would fall under the concession of the American-owned Aramco.

Of late, however, the Buraimi dispute has acquired a political flavor as well. The Saudis fear that Britain is planning to delimit all the boundaries between Saudi Arabia and the Trucial Coast, and thus Saudi Arabia would find herself surrounded on the south and east by British-controlled possessions, and on the north by the British-influenced Hashemite Kingdoms of Jordan and Iraq, traditionally hostile to the Sauds. Britain, on the other hand, is believed to be watching closely the growing influence which the United States inevitably exerts in the Persian Gulf area as a result of Aramco's oil investment, estimated at three-quarters of a billion dollars. Britain also fears Saudi expansionist pressure aimed at amalgamating some or all of the Persian Gulf territories under the Riyadh throne.

International arbitration of the Buraimi dispute broke down in September, 1955, when Sir Reader Bullard, the British representative, charged Saudi Arabia with "deliberate, systematic, and persistent" bribery of Buraimi tribes in an attempt to win control of the oasis. Subsequently, British-backed Arab levies occupied Buraimi after a clash with Saudi forces. Powerless to evict these British-led troops by herself, Saudi Arabia looks to the United Nations for help should her campaign of tribal "persuasion" fail.

In allying herself with Egypt in general Middle Eastern policy, Saudi Arabia may be courting a danger unrealized by King Saud. He is a monarch clinging to a patriarchal authoritarian mode of rule, and many of his subjects are gravely discontented at the percentage of oil income reserved for the royal family. Among these malcontents are officers of the Saudi Army, upon which the King depends to ensure order in his land. Egypt, Saud's chief ally in the Middle East, is led by officers who overthrew their own king because of conduct not unlike that of Saud in some respects. Consciously or unconsciously, some of this revolutionary zeal may rub off on officers of the Saudi Army, now that the forces of the two countries have been merged.

Basically, then, the pattern of alignments in the Arab world finds Iraq on one side and Egypt, Syria, and Saudi Arabia on the other, with Yemen generally following the Egyptian-Saudi lead, and Jordan and Lebanon vacillating somewhere in between. Even within this pattern, however, subdivisions exist.

Jordan, torn over the issue of the Baghdad Pact, is split even more deeply on the whole question of federation with Iraq. Early in 1954 Fadel el-Jamali, then Premier of Iraq, urged Jordan to federate with her wealthy Hashemite sister, arguing that Jordan's economy thereby would be benefited. "West bank" Jordanians from Palestine in general agreed, declaring that British subsidy then could be rejected and

Jordan's prosperity would be assured as part of an oil-rich Hashemite kingdom.

Opposition came from elements surrounding King Hussein, who foresaw in the event of a merger the disappearance of Jordan's throne in favor of the Iraqi throne of King Feisal, cousin of Hussein. Dr. Jamali then made a hurried trip to Amman, capital of Jordan, in a reported attempt to convince the palace of the wisdom of Jordanian-Iraqi union, stressing that both kingdoms were ruled by the Hashemite family. Dr. Jamali is believed to have expressed to King Hussein Iraq's readiness to offer Jordan all necessary material and military aid, and is believed further to have hinted that Iraq "could not remain inactive" should the Jordanian palace continue its present "hostile" policy toward Iraq. Dr. Jamali is reported to have claimed that a majority of Jordanians favor union with Iraq, and that for the palace to frustrate this aspiration would be "a serious matter," since Iraq "could not overlook" what was termed the Israeli threat at the Jordan border.

The Jordan-Iraqi clash found reaction outside the Hashemite fold, with King Saud of Saudi Arabia doing his best to prevent any union of the two Hashemite lands. At a subsequent meeting of King Saud and King Hussein at the Saudi border town of Badanah, the Saudi monarch gave Jordan 50,000 Jordanian pounds ($140,000) for the strengthening of Jordan's national guard, and observers believe it not unlikely that King Saud offered Hussein assurances of further financial aid should Jordan successfully resist pressure for union with Iraq.

At the time many independent Arabs expressed their conviction that nothing could be better for Jordan's welfare than union with oil-rich Iraq, which presumably would be willing to extend the benefits of her economic development plan to include less-favored Jordan. The Arab press in general, or at least that portion of it not influenced politically by the matter, appeared to deplore what was termed the attempt of the Jordanian royal family to preserve itself at the expense of the country's welfare, a sentiment which apparently agreed with Dr. Jamali and "west bank" Jordanians that the majority of the country's 1,400,000 citizens lean toward union with Iraq.

Today Dr. Jamali is out of office, and "west bank" Jordanians are in the forefront of those protesting any move by Jordan to join the Baghdad Pact, reportedly favored by King Hussein. Dr. Jamali, however, was merely the spokesman of a wide segment of leading Iraqi opinion, and "west bank" opposition to the Baghdad alliance is directed not so much toward Iraq as toward the Western powers. In other words, the basic question of relations between the Hashemite kingdoms is destined to outlast the current furor over the Baghdad Pact, and sentiment for a federation of the two lands appears to be growing rather than declining.

Lebanon, carved by the French out of the Syrian hinterland to preserve its Christian character, almost always is in uneasy relationship to the Moslem world at large. In particular, Lebanon's relations with Syria are made difficult, since Christian Lebanese sense the very real desire of many Syrians to reabsorb this sliver of land which forms Syria's natural outlet to the sea. This suspicion finds expression in the inability of the two countries to form a permanent customs union, which both of them sorely need. Lebanon is a trading nation, with imports greatly exceeding exports, and with at least a part of the deficit made up by middleman services rendered the goods of other nations flowing through the free port of Beirut. During the French mandate Syria received her imports through the port of Beirut and exported her agricultural products via the same route, supplying Lebanese traders with one of their chief customers. When independence came, however, Syria and Lebanon replaced the French customs union with a hasty arrangement which satisfied neither party over the long run. A series of disagreements led to the dissolution of economic union in March, 1950.

Since that time the two states have made sporadic attempts to get together again, but to little avail. In the meantime both countries have suffered from the break. Syria lost a natural market for her produce, and also her most convenient outlet to the sea. Lebanon's citrus growers lost an important market in Syria, some Lebanese industries were curtailed or even shut down, and the middlemen themselves experienced a sharp drop in trade.

Both states have tried to cushion these economic bumps, Lebanon by expanding her middleman trade elsewhere, and Syria by building a new port at Latakia on the Mediterranean, a more natural outlet than Beirut for the agricultural and industrial goods of northern Syria. In addition, through drastic import and export controls, Syria has striven to achieve a balance in foreign trade. To this end Syrian agriculture and industry both have been expanded, and imports into Syria have been limited largely to capital goods and machinery. A not insignificant item for both Syria and Lebanon have been the heavy customs duties slapped on Jordanian goods in transit through Beirut and Damascus, ever since the port of Haifa was closed to Jordan as a result of the Arab economic boycott of Israel.

Several times Syria and Lebanon have achieved temporary agreements whereby local agricultural produce was allowed free transit back and forth, and tariffs were reduced on a restricted list of other goods. Syria also has offered a

plan leading to a genuine customs union, including unification of currency, uniform taxation, and common legislation on matters affecting the union.[2] Though Lebanon has
accepted the plan as a basis for study, its implementation
has hung fire, largely because important Christian elements
in Lebanon fear that a customs union would be the opening wedge leading finally to complete political union and
the submergence of Lebanon within the Syrian state.

This fear is increased by the fact that irredentism is strong
in some areas of Lebanon which are predominantly Moslem, and which were taken away from Syria by the French
to make the new state of Lebanon economically viable.
There have been times in the past when the Lebanese-Syrian border was closed over some transient quarrel that a
visit to the President of Lebanon by Moslem leaders from
Tripoli in northern Lebanon, threatening secession to Syria,
has been enough to open the border through Lebanese concession. It has not been enough, however, to outweigh the
Christian distrust which still blocks economic union.

In some ways the two countries appear to be drifting
even further apart. Lebanese currency now is worth about
10 per cent more than Syrian currency, and Lebanon sees
no reason to devalue her pound to achieve unity. Over the
past few years Beirut has developed rapidly as a free-trade
center and world money market, and many Lebanese fear
that economic union with Syria would restrict their activities. Syria, on the other hand, points to the fact that
Latakia increasingly competes with Beirut, particularly as
a port of entry for the northern hinterland of Syria and
Iraq, formerly supplied through Beirut alone. Latakia is

[2] For a more complete discussion of this development, see Nejla
Izzeddin, *The Arab World* (Chicago: Henry Regnery Co., 1953), pp.
181-85.

bound to boom further when the new port is linked to Syria's rail network.

The most serious Lebanese objections to union, however, remain political. At the end of 1954 political opponents of Rashid Kerame, at that time Lebanese Minister of National Economy, charged that his own plan for economic union had been submitted to, and rejected by, the Syrian Government before the Lebanese Cabinet even had seen it. Mr. Kerame is the leading politician of Moslem Tripoli (Lebanon's second city), and irredentist sentiment is perhaps stronger in Tripoli than anywhere else in Lebanon. Thus the same kind of divisiveness found elsewhere in the Arab world keeps apart two Arab lands whose economies, as viewed by neutral observers, are interdependent.

Despite the evidence, attempts at Arab unity have not been wholly lacking, though most of these attempts have been politically inspired. We have seen the persistent efforts of the Hashemites, first under King Abdullah of Jordan and later under the governments of Iraq, to achieve a Greater Syria. During World War II Britain sponsored a somewhat similar arrangement, hoping for eventual Arab union under the pro-British leadership of Iraq. To this end Nuri es-Said, perennial premier of Iraq, called for a union of northern Arab lands (Greater Syria under another name), exclusive of Egypt and the Arabian peninsula. These plans came to naught, partly because of Egyptian and Saudi opposition, and partly because Syria and Lebanon suspected that their newly-won independence would be obscured in an Iraqi federation.

At this point initiative was seized by Egypt, and on March 22, 1945, after two years of wrangling and consultations, a new organization of Arab states was born in Cairo. Signatories of this Pact of the Arab League were Egypt,

Iraq, Jordan (then Transjordan), Lebanon, Saudi Arabia, Syria, and the Yemen. (On March 28, 1953, Libya became the eighth member of the Arab League, followed by the Sudan on January 19, 1956.) Political center of the League was Cairo, and, because of the Egyptian struggle to oust the British from the Suez Canal Zone, the Arab League tended to become anti-British rather than pro-British, as London originally had hoped.

The new organization, in the claim of its founders, was designed to strengthen relations among the Arab states, to promote their several interests, and to protect Arab independence and sovereignty. Under the terms of the Pact, each member had one vote. Unanimous decisions of the League were binding on all members, as were majority decisions in specified cases. A Council, six permanent committees, and a permanent Secretariat-General were set up. Machinery was provided for pacific settlement of disputes between member states and between them and outside countries. In the event of aggression or its threat, the member states could call for an immediate meeting of the League Council, which was to decide by unanimous vote the measures to be taken against the aggressor. The only sanction specified for failure to abide by League decisions was expulsion from the League.[3]

Though adequate on paper, this machinery fell down in practice, chiefly because the League became in part an arena for the Arab rivalries already operating in the Middle East. Egypt saw to it that the first two secretaries-general (and the only two so far) were Egyptians. This could be explained in part, but only in part, by the fact that Egypt

[3] For a detailed study of the organization and operation of the Arab League, see B. Y. Boutros-Ghali, "The Arab League, 1945-1955," *International Conciliation*, No. 498 (May, 1954).

supplied upward of 40 per cent of the League's budget, while Iraq, its chief Arab rival, supplied 20 per cent or less.

Acid test of the League's solidarity came over the Palestine problem. Meeting at Sofar, Lebanon, on September 19, 1947, the Political Committee of the League decided secretly to send troops into Palestine should the United Nations vote a partition of the Holy Land. On November 29 the UN General Assembly passed its partition plan, and within a week open fighting between Arabs and Jews began. An Arab Liberation Army was formed, and on May 15, 1948, the day after the British mandate ended, the Secretary-General of the Arab League informed the UN that the Arab League had intervened in order to restore Palestine to its Arab inhabitants.

The question then arose of a commander-in-chief for the Arab armies invading Israel. Several nations demanded the honor, and none would cede it to the other. In the end the Arab armies, uncoordinated and pursuing separate battle plans, fought each on its own. The result was defeat, from which Arab pride and self-confidence has yet to recover.

Politically, also, the members of the Arab League disagreed on the status of the future Palestinian state. Iraq and Jordan favored the annexation of Palestine as a first step toward Greater Syria. Egypt, on the other hand, pushed for an independent Palestine republic headed by the Grand Mufti of Jerusalem, arch foe of King Abdullah of Jordan. Separate phantom governments were formed by the proponents of each side, until Israel settled the question by driving Arab armies out of all Palestine except in the east. This portion Abdullah promptly annexed to his Transjordanian kingdom, an act which nearly caused his expulsion from the Arab League. Finally, however, faced with Abdullah's *fait accompli*, the League recognized the new situation by entrusting the annexed portion of Palestine to Abdullah's administration.

The lessons of Palestine burned deep, and to correct some of their mistakes the Arab states supplemented the Pact of the Arab League with a Treaty of Joint Defense and Economic Cooperation, which came into force August 23, 1952. This treaty provided for an automatic collective security system, under which member states would come to the aid of an attacked Arab state. A Joint Defense Council was created, composed of the defense and foreign ministers of the member states, and also a Permanent Military Commission, representing the general staffs of the countries concerned. To coordinate affairs in the economic field the treaty called for an Economic Council, made up of Arab ministers of finance.

For a time, possibly because the treaty never was put to a test, the member states maintained a façade of unity through the collective security system, though still there was no commander-in-chief, and no unified Arab army. Egypt, preoccupied with removing the British from the Suez Canal Zone, had caused to be included a stipulation that no member state might join an international agreement which would contradict provisions of the League's treaty. This clause was intended to prevent any Arab state (in particular Iraq) from giving comfort to the West by joining any such organization as the "northern tier," or Baghdad, alliance. It was intended also to leave with Egypt the initiative to decide at what point the Arabs should enter Western pacts.

Until the British left the Suez Canal Zone, Iraq remained obediently within the fold. Then, on its own initiative, Iraq joined the Baghdad Pact in February, 1955. The veil was rent, and Iraqi-Egyptian hostility emerged fully into public view. Cairo's subsequent attempts to keep the other Arab states firmly on its side already have been described. In matters of substance the Arab League was shown to be a shell; the League's efforts at unity broke whenever they encountered the rock of Arab rivalries.

In peripheral matters, however, even concerning Palestine, it cannot be said that the Arab League has been wholly ineffective. The League's economic boycott of Israel is perhaps the most successful Arab tactic. Purpose of the boycott, according to League officials, is to bring about the eventual economic collapse of Israel by excluding her from her natural markets in the Middle East and by preventing Arab goods, at least, from flowing to the Jewish state.

To this end a general boycott office has been established by the League in Damascus, with branches in all the Arab states. Close liaison is maintained by these offices to enforce the boycott and punish smuggling. In addition, the Arabs threaten foreign nations and companies with economic reprisal if trade with Israel is not stopped. B. Y. Boutros-Ghali quotes a 1954 report of the Arab Regional Offices for the Boycott of Israel to the effect that 50 leading foreign companies had severed their business connections with Israel at the time the report was written, preferring to maintain trade relations with the Arab states. "Seventeen companies were blacklisted in the Arab countries for not having submitted written guarantees of their intention to cease business with Israel," Mr. Boutros-Ghali said. "Up to the end of December 1954, there were still 84 ships on the blacklist, but 14 ships had been struck off as a result of complying with Arab boycott regulations."[4]

Egypt seeks to close the Suez Canal to ships bound to and from Israel, despite a United Nations condemnation of

[4] *Ibid.*, p. 419.

her action. To build up trade with South Asia and the Far East, Israel has been forced to develop the poor port of Elath at the head of the Gulf of Aqaba, separated from the heart of Israel by the barren Negev. To date, however, Elath also has been blockaded effectively by Egyptian gun positions on small Egyptian-held islands at the entrance to the Gulf.

Though the boycott seems unlikely to threaten Israel with extinction so long as her economy is artificially bolstered by foreign aid, including that from world Jewry, the boycott remains a distinct annoyance from the Israeli point of view. From the Arab point of view, it is the chief example of cooperation through the Arab League.

Apart from politics and matters of substance, the record of the Arab League has been reasonably impressive on paper, less so in practice. Mr. Boutros-Ghali lists several non-political fields in which the League has laid groundwork for possible future cooperation. These include efforts to reach agreement on direct telephone communication between Arab countries; discussions on the establishment of an Arab shipping company and on a draft treaty for civil aviation; also resolutions on the integration of land and air communications among the Arab countries, the putting back into operation of the Hejaz Railway line, and the promotion of inter-Arab river navigation.

Lebanon, perhaps the most commercially minded among Arab states, has been a leader in these and other discussions to promote economic cooperation among the Arabs. A few agreements, notably on currency exchange and the exchange of goods and services and the lowering of tariff barriers, have been put into limited practice. Progress has been made in dropping visa requirements for Arab citizens traveling from one member state to another. An Arab

Postal Union and an Arab Telecommunications and Radio-communications Union have been established, each with a permanent office at the League Secretariat.

The list of such agreements in cultural, judicial, and commercial fields might be expanded. Yet even those few which have progressed from paper into practice make barely an imprint on the whole field of Arab nonpolitical cooperation; and even those few are subject to overriding political warfare.

An example was the announcement in Cairo on February 22, 1956, that the establishment of an Arab financial organization for economic development, with a proposed capital of $56,000,000, had been approved by the Arab finance ministers' Economic Council of the Arab League. Main object of the organization, the announcement said, was to take part in financing development projects of Arab states, thereby promoting economic solidarity among the Arabs. Funds would be provided for needy member states (Jordan would appear to be the only country in this class) for development schemes, with the understanding that these amounts would be repaid with ample interest. Arab League members would subscribe to the organization in proportion to their shares in the League budget.

Yet Iraq, with ample capital and perhaps the most extensive Arab experience in economic development, refused to enter the compact, claiming that she already was fully occupied with her own internal plans. A more important reason was Iraq's current battle with Egypt, which some Arabs fear may wreck the Arab League. It remains to be seen whether the new financial organization is a sincere plan to foster unity, worked out by unbiased technicians, or a veiled attempt to bring Jordan more firmly under Egyptian control. In the former case, its effectiveness would appear to have been spiked in advance by the rivalry dividing the two most powerful members of the parent League.

On balance, the Arab League is the most ambitious recent attempt to achieve unity among the Arabic-speaking peoples. But it has been a failure because from the beginning it became a vehicle for inter-Arab rivalries, rather than the forum where these rivalries might be threshed out and subordinated to the general good.

Apart from the Arab League, the search for unity among the Arabs is further confused by the presence in Syria and Lebanon of an outlawed political party called the Syrian Socialist National Party. Popularly known as the PPS, this party operates apart from the Hashemite drive to achieve a Greater Syria, and also apart from the People's Party of Syria, which desires unification with Iraq under certain conditions.

Top echelon members of the PPS are well-educated Syrians and Lebanese, many of whom received their training at the American University of Beirut. These men, whose politics are a major concern both to Syrian and Lebanese authorities, are among those Westernized Arabs who have become extremists because of their frustration over the slowness of Arab reform.

Before I went to the Middle East, a respected Arab diplomat in Washington gave me a letter of introduction to a former student of his at AUB. Still in his late twenties, this young man already was a leading politician in Lebanon, operating as a political independent. In reality he was a leading member of the PPS and the party's chief representative in Parliament. Because of my letter of introduction, he treated me with the utmost friendliness during my years in Beirut, never deviating from party discipline when talking about the PPS, but otherwise briefing me objectively on

Arab affairs, even when they cut directly across his party's line.

One afternoon in his apartment he gathered for me Lebanon's leading members of the PPS. Among them were lawyers, doctors, pharmacists, and other professional men, respected in their fields and comprising perhaps the best-disciplined and best-educated leadership group in Lebanese politics. Every one of them was Arab, yet all of them, as I recall, spoke English and French in addition to their native Arabic. They made a point of telling me that there were Moslems, Druzes, and Christians of various sects among them. Only one thing they would not tell me about their party, and that was the identity of their top leader, now that Anton Saadeh, founder of the PPS, had been executed by the Lebanese Government.

The subtlety of PPS operations was illustrated early in 1953 when a handbill in English was distributed in Beirut to American sailors of the visiting United States Sixth Fleet. On the surface, the handbill, published by the Beirut newspaper *Sada-Loubnan*, was a more or less straightforward attempt to present the Arab side of the case in the Palestine dispute. It reminded its readers that the establishment of Israel not only gave homes to 1,000,000 Jews, but also uprooted nearly the same number of Palestinian Arabs, still living as refugees in the surrounding Arab lands.

"Go ahead and visit some of these (refugee) camps," the American sailors were urged. "There are two of them right here in Beirut. If you have not been urged to see all that misery, then someone has pulled some very thick wool over your Navy eyes."

The pamphlet, signed by M. Baalbaki, editor of *Sada-Loubnan*, then sought to persuade its readers that "Jewish Americans, who through advertisers control some of your press and through their votes can influence your politicians, went to work," with the result that "your diplomats at the UN cajoled and intimidated a majority of other nations into creating the State of Israel."

This concept, undoubtedly somewhat strange to many of its readers, was carefully prefaced by a profession of friendship for the American people, and by an account of the part played by Protestant educators and missionaries in building friendly relations between the Lebanese and American peoples. The handbill also included a statement which is largely true, that Lebanon accords its Jews "the same rights it grants all its citizens. They peacefully live in homes and go about their business like everybody else."

Up to this point few Lebanese would have found anything to disagree with in *Sada-Loubnan*. But the fact is that most Lebanese read the pamphlet on a second and deeper level, which would have escaped the newcomer to the Arab scene. In the first place, it was written not by M. Baalbaki who signed it, but by Said Taky Din, prominent member of the PPS (and one of the conferees in my friend's apartment that afternoon), and was published by *Sada-Loubnan* solely because this paper is one of the principal mouthpieces of the party.

The PPS aims at the political union of Lebanon and some other Arab lands—plus what now is Israel—within a "natural Syria," and thus has been outlawed by the Lebanese Government for what are termed "subversive activities." Thus the pamphlet contained statements along the party line with which many Arabs sharply disagree, such as the sentence that "Palestine has always been an integral part of Syria, as New Jersey is of the U.S." Few Palestinians, as a matter of fact, have given any evidence of agreeing that their country lies within Syria.

The handbill also included a charge with which many Lebanese would disagree that American "oil interests" are indirectly fostering communism by "milking" the Lebanese people out of royalties rightfully due them, and by "browbeating" Lebanese labor. "You, of course, remember," the handbill remarked, "that your Treasury is prosecuting (the oil interests) for doing the American people out of $60,000,-000 in income tax evasions." (At the time the pamphlet was written, the United States Government was prosecuting an antitrust suit against seven American oil companies, including the parents of Aramco.)

"Well, some of these gents are operating here in a big way," the handbill went on. "The corrupt few amongst them have formed an alliance with some of our corrupt. . . . They have dummy corporations, hush money, collusions, cherchez-la-femme, the kick-back, and a byproduct of oil which whitewashes everything." This last was a reference to the claim of the Lebanese Government, that the Trans-Arabian Pipe Line Company (under the same ownership as Aramco) was underpaying Lebanon for the privilege of carrying oil through its pipeline to the Lebanese city of Sidon, though Tapline only eight months before had negotiated a new agreement with the last Lebanese government, under which royalty rates had been substantially raised. PPS supporters in Parliament had been active in pressing the government's claim, more to whip up popular feeling on the subject, it was felt, than to help the government. Indeed, a consistent PPS device has been to force whatever Lebanese government was in power to adopt positions on popular issues which the government could not sustain, thereby threatening its downfall, possibly in the wake of street riots.

These tactics are directed toward the ultimate aim of PPS, the union of "natural Syria" within a disciplined socialist state. "Natural Syria," according to party tenets, includes present-day Lebanon, Syria, Israel, Jordan, parts of Iraq, and those lands ceded to Turkey by Britain and France after World War I. All this territory, it is claimed, comprises a geographic, economic, and cultural unit, or Arab nation, which has been artificially divided by the Western powers.

Founded in 1932 by Anton Saadeh, a political zealot executed by the Lebanese Government in 1949, the party grew rapidly into a sizable semisecret group built around the personality of "the leader," as Saadeh came to be called. Its aims seemed closest to fruition with the seizure of power in Syria in 1949 by Colonel Adib Shishakly, whom party leaders termed "sympathetic" to the party's aims. Soon, however, foreseeing a threat to his own program and position, Shishakly excluded the PPS from his Arab Liberation Movement, and finally outlawed the PPS in Syria. Though the party is similarly outlawed in Lebanon, many observers believe the PPS is correct in claiming the strongest and best-disciplined political force in Lebanon today.

Though a Christian himself, Saadeh early alienated many Lebanese Christians who feared that the merging of Lebanon into a "natural Syria" would drown the Christians in a Moslem sea. His program, on the other hand, antagonized orthodox Moslems by calling for the franchise for women and the exclusion of both church and mosque from any voice in political events. Both Egypt and Saudi Arabia have remained bitterly opposed to the PPS since its inception, since any "natural Syria" as the party sees it would gravely overshadow both those lands.

A career marked by jailings and exile—as well as by the steady growth of his party—came to an end when Saadeh was surrendered by Syria to the Lebanese Government, which executed "the leader" July 9, 1949, after what observers agreed was a mock trial. Two of the principal actors in this drama, dictator Husni Zaim of Syria and Premier Riad Solh of Lebanon, were assassinated soon afterward, the latter by a PPS member and Zaim, it is believed, through party complicity.

Since that time the party has been governed by a "supreme council," membership of which is secret (presumably some members were included in the afternoon get-together in my friend's apartment), and the orders of which are implicitly obeyed by the party rank and file. It is this quality of absolute discipline, when coupled with the party's aims, which has caused much distrust and opposition to the PPS among political leaders in the Arab world.

In its "natural Syria" the party would nationalize public utilities and limit land ownership to about 1,000 acres, a feature abhorrent to many great landowners of Syria, Lebanon, and Iraq. Within these partial limits, however, party leaders say, the individual would be allowed as much income as his talents—and a graduated income tax—would allow. A slight majority of PPS members is believed to be Christian, though party membership cuts across religious lines perhaps more successfully than in any other political grouping, particularly in Lebanon. Observers credit the PPS with being the only modern party, apart from the Communists, which has been able to transcend religious as well as family loyalties in the Arab world.

Party leaders claim there is no "shock troop" formation within the party to enforce discipline, but that it is based on members' mutual trust and confidence in each other and on unquestioning obedience to "the leader's" party constitution. PPS leaders admit, however, that force might be necessary to carry out some of their decisions during the early days of power, and they speak freely of a strong army for "natural Syria."

Some observers see in the PPS platform—with its abolition of feudalism and sectarianism in government, its offering of the vote to women, and its equality of all citizens before the law—a ray of hope for an Arab world still largely bound by feudal land practices and nepotism in government. Other observers distrust the burning cult of "the leader," the subordination of the individual to "society, or the state," and the determination to brook no opposition to PPS aims and objectives.

PPS leaders claim, for example, that the party, bolstered by armed cadres throughout the country, was poised to revolt against the Lebanese Government during September, 1952, had not embattled President Bishara el-Khoury resigned when he did, paving the way for a "reform" government under President Camille Chamoun. It is the presence of these armed cadres of the PPS, plus the determination and discipline to use them, that strikes uncertainty into Arab hearts generally concerning the PPS.

On the whole, however, the leaders of the party appear to feel it currently impossible to unify "natural Syria" politically, and seem willing to work for cultural and economic union among the affected lands. To this end, the party claims to be organized in each one of the countries—with the exception of Israel—which would be included in "natural Syria," as well as having active cells among Syrian and Lebanese migrants in Brazil, Argentina, Liberia, the Gold Coast, the United States, and elsewhere.

Eventually, however, it is political union of a vast area which the party is seeking, despite the apparent difficulties in the way, including the presence of Israel, Turkish control of certain northern districts, and the imposition of PPS will on the Arab lands. In the meantime the outlawed party is forced to operate chiefly underground, making it difficult for observers to gain a true measure of its strength and aims. Recently there has been a recrudescence of overt PPS activity in Syria, reflecting the political uncertainty prevailing in that country since the overthrow of dictator Shishakly. On February 21, 1956, military court sources in Damascus announced the arrest of seven PPS members on a charge of conspiring to assassinate three high military officers and a member of parliament.

Scheduled victims of the alleged plot were said to have been Brigadier Shawkat Shukair, Syrian Army chief of staff; Major Abdul Hamid Sarraj, chief of Army intelligence; Captain Mohammed Jarrah, military prosecutor; and Akram Hourani, leader of the Arab Socialist Resurrection Party which is sympathetic to Communist aims. Major Sarraj had been singled out, it is believed, because he had come to be the leader of a loose "young officers" group in the Syrian Army, occupying somewhat the same position as Colonels Zaim, Hinnawi, and Shishakly respectively before they launched their *coups*.

The February arrests followed another flurry of PPS activity in Syria when Colonel Adnan Malki, Syrian Army deputy chief of staff, was assassinated by the PPS on April 22, 1955. At that time a military court sentenced seven PPS leaders to be shot and 40 others to prison terms, though a Syrian official later reported that the Syrian Supreme Court had reversed the decision. Apart from anything else, the arrests showed that the PPS continues actively to pursue its aims.

By and large the major movements seeking some kind of unity in the Arab world—namely, the Hashemite desire to link at least Syria, Jordan, and Iraq in a Greater Syria; Egypt's consequent efforts to line up Syria, Saudi Arabia, Yemen, and possibly Jordan in a counter pact; and the clandestine operations of the PPS—are sparked by partisan motives, and show how remote true unity is in the Arab world. Indeed, unity in the sense of kindred nations striving toward a common goal, and coordinating their individual programs toward that end, appears beyond achievement at the present time.

The best hope in the Arab mélange, at least from the outsider's point of view, would seem to be the potential of Iraq. Assured of adequate income from oil, and with a concrete development program already under way, Iraq may offer the Arabs an example of orderly progression from backwardness to modern statehood. The danger even here is that the development program may benefit primarily the holdings of feudal landowners, thereby separating further top and bottom layers of society and in the long run hastening revolution of some sort.

A hopeful sign was the cabinet formed by a recent premier, Fadel el-Jamali, in which several young Western-educated Iraqis of progressive bent were included. The penetration of enlightened social thinking, however, must extend more widely throughout Iraq's governing circles if the maintenance of law and order is to be assured.

A merger of Syria and Jordan under general Iraqi hegemony would seem to promise benefits to both those states, given reasonably fair-minded elements in power in Iraq. This again, however, is an outsider's point of view, and the advantages or otherwise of such a move would depend upon the kind of leadership Iraq was able to provide, and upon the sharpness of Egyptian reaction.

Another element of presumable stability in the area is the government of President Gamal Abdel Nasser in Egypt, particularly if Nasser, through economic and social progress, is able to spike unrest both in his Army and throughout the country at large. The more completely Colonel Nasser becomes committed to the building of the High Dam, thereby tying up almost all of Egypt's resources, the better the chances for peace between Egypt and Israel, it would seem.

Israel itself, committed to a program of constructive development within a Western parliamentary system, theoretically is an element of major stability in the Middle East, despite the paradox that currently Israel is the cause of great unrest in the area and of fundamental readjustments among the Arab states which surround it.

Though true unity among the Arabs glimmers only on the far horizon, the nearer goal of stability can be approached. Toward the end of stability recent Western policy has been directed, though so far with minor success. Chief elements of current Western policy include the 1950 Tripartite Declaration guaranteeing Arab-Israel borders, the denial of large-scale Western arms to either side, and the building up of the Baghdad Pact, or "northern tier" alliance.

The effects of the Baghdad Pact have been quite the opposite of those intended. In the first place, Secretary of State John Foster Dulles foresaw a useful unity merely among those countries bordering on the Soviet Union and facing an immediate Soviet threat. These countries included primarily Turkey and Iran, nations not preoccupied with Israel. The British view, on the other hand, was that the "northern tier" alliance should extend southward in depth. To this end Britain persuaded Iraq to join, and offered inducements to Jordan also. The result was to weaken the Middle East, rather than to strengthen it.

Egypt immediately negotiated counter-pacts embracing Syria, Saudi Arabia, and Yemen, and the end of deterioration of relations between Britain and Jordan is not yet in sight. In her eagerness to frustrate the Baghdad Pact, Egypt may have threatened her own security by committing herself to go to the aid of Syria should the latter be attacked by Israel. Such divisive results hardly were foreseen by the West when it promoted the Baghdad Pact.

In another respect also the Baghdad alliance has boomeranged, since it served as the signal for the Soviets to launch their carefully prepared campaign to infiltrate the Middle East. At one blow—through her sale of Communist arms to Egypt and Syria and through trade and aid agreements with the Arabs—the Soviet Union vaulted the "northern tier" arrangement into the heart of the Arab world.

At the same time these Soviet moves undercut the 1950 Tripartite Declaration and the carefully fostered Arab-Israeli balance of arms. The acquisition by Egypt of $80,-000,000 worth of Communist arms, including jet fighters and bombers, caused Israel to request urgently from the United States the right to purchase $50,000,000 worth of "defensive" arms. No matter to what extent Washington yields to the Israeli demand, the arms balance concept already has been sunk, and in its place looms a possible arms race.

To counteract this dangerous trend, the United States, Britain, and France have sought ways to put teeth into their guarantee of Arab-Israeli borders. In this context the use of the United States Sixth Fleet and British paratroopers on Cyprus is a possibility, should Palestine fighting break out. The Soviet Union, in reprisal, has warned the West strictly not to intervene in the Middle East, and the effect of this warning might be to cancel out both Soviet and Western intervention, leaving the field to Arabs and Israelis. The chaos resulting from such fighting, whatever its specific outcome, would benefit the Soviets, not the West.

Apart from the Soviet warning, the difficulties of Western intervention cannot be minimized. American pilots from Sixth Fleet carriers might find themselves shooting one day at Israeli planes and the next day at Egyptian, in efforts to halt "aggression." American and British ships might be forced to bottle up both Arab and Israeli ports. The diplomatic dangers of such action would be increased by the fact that very likely the action would have to be taken outside the United Nations, to avoid the Soviet Security Council veto.

American policy, at least, has been further undermined by Arab distrust of United States motives since the establishment of Israel. Egyptians like to point out, for example, that from 1945 through 1955 Washington gave Cairo a total of $27,000,000 in grants and credits, while Israel received $376,000,000 during the same period. Although the balance has been somewhat redressed since President Eisenhower came into office (Washington and London now have promised Cairo at least $70,000,000 for the High Dam), the earlier suspicion lingers.

Washington red tape is another deterrent to American policy in the Middle East. An instance of this was recounted by Don Cook in the New York *Herald Tribune*, where Egypt's need of diesel locomotives was cited.

The Egyptians said they wanted diesel-hydraulic locomotives. The United States aid authorities said diesel-electric would be better. The Egyptians said they had some British diesel-electrics that were no good and they preferred diesel-hydraulic. The United States said they would only give diesel-electric locomotives, and anyway American diesel-electrics were better than British diesel-electrics.

So the Egyptians, after weeks of such exchanges, agreed to take the diesel-electrics. Then bids went out in the United States, but when the bids closed it was found that they had not been distributed widely enough under the law. So the bids were canceled and the contract reopened. The same thing happened a second time, this time the cancellation resulted from the writing of the specifications.

Three times the contract verged on completion. Meanwhile, the Hungarians entered the picture with an offer to supply locomotives in a cotton-barter deal. Less than three weeks ago, the Egyptians announced that they were obtaining eighty locomotives from Hungary—no strings attached, no argument over specifications, and a chance to unload surplus cotton.[5]

Cotton itself is a major thorn in American-Egyptian relations. Since cotton is a home-grown surplus in the United States, American and Egyptian cotton are in sharp competition throughout the world. On February 28, 1956, furthermore, Secretary of Agriculture Ezra Taft Benson announced that the United States government would put all federal-owned surplus cotton on the world auction block at competitive prices, effective August 1, 1956. The aim would be to double American cotton exports, from the present level of about 2,500,000 bales to 5,000,000 bales yearly. An immediate protest came from the Egyptian Embassy in Washington, where a spokesman declared that his government considered it "a very unfortunate step at this time."

A key to the kind of new policy needed by the Western powers is afforded by the Soviet Union herself. In the

5 New York *Herald Tribune*, December 26, 1955.

Middle East the Soviets have turned from their classic world revolutionary aims—i.e., working through local Communist parties—to traditional diplomatic channels. That is, they are working to increase their prestige through economic and technical aid, offering this freely to Arab rulers who have outlawed the Communist party internally in their lands.

A program equally bold, imaginative, and daring must be evolved by the West if the Soviet policy is to be successfully opposed. First, however, the Western powers must agree among themselves as to what their policy should be. British and American differences on the Baghdad Pact have been cited, as well as the Anglo-American conflict of interest in the oil-rich Persian Gulf. In addition, both Britain and France are gravely disturbed at the stream of anti-Western propaganda broadcast by the Egyptian State Broadcasting System to British and French colonial possessions throughout Africa, already greatly inflamed by nationalist sentiment.

These broadcasts—in Arabic, Swahili, and Amharic—all stress the theme that the subject peoples should cast off their colonial yokes and follow the lead of Colonel Nasser in "positive neutralism" between East and West. One apparent attempt is to project Egypt into a leading African role as well as among the Arabs. The broadcasts are particularly troubling to the French, engaged in a desperate rear guard action to preserve their North African empire in Tunisia, Morocco, and Algeria. In addition to the broadcasts, the French charge Egypt with channeling arms and training to the "Arab Liberation Front" of anti-French nationalists in North Africa.

A recent *New York Times* summary described government-controlled Egyptian broadcasts as reaching out "as far as Zanzibar and Pemba, British island protectorates off East Africa, to Algeria, Morocco, and Tunisia under French rule in North Africa, to the British colonies of Kenya, Uganda, and Tanganyika, to Somaliland, and even on occasion to the Portuguese colony of Angola."[6] The tone of these broadcasts is all the more disturbing since the Western powers agree that Egypt is the key country through which to work in improving Arab-Western relations generally.

A new Western policy, when agreed upon, must be impartial between Arabs and Israelis. In general it must be based upon the premise that, although the creation of Israel caused a great injustice to the Arabs of Palestine, the destruction of Israel by the Arabs would create a second historic injustice, this time to the Jews of Israel. Both sides must then be assured that the West intends to support the legitimate aspirations of Arabs and Israelis alike, and that both sides are there to stay.

Once their impartiality is made clear, the Western powers could devote their diplomatic energies to fostering those conditions within which a modus vivendi between Arabs and Israelis might be feasible. A key weapon in this attempt is the Jordan River development plan advanced by the United States, to be described in a later chapter. Another weapon is United States willingness, as expressed by Secretary of State Dulles, to take the initiative in compensating Arab refugees for the property they lost in Palestine, and to ensure that funds are available for the rehabilitation of those refugees in Arab lands. Neither of these weapons, however, can be effective until Arab distrust of the West is removed; until the United States in particular is viewed with something the same trust as the Arabs lavished upon American Protestant missionaries in the early days of the century; and

6 *The New York Times*, February 29, 1956.

until Britain again is looked upon by the Arabs as it was before the mandates. A start toward such trust, though it may never be achieved in full, is to assure the Arabs of Western impartiality.

Since the effectiveness of the Soviet campaign in the Middle East is largely economic, the Western campaign must answer the challenge. Since, however, the Communist bloc welcomes Egyptian cotton and other Arab agricultural products and the West does not, the task is made that much harder for the West. The answer would seem to be a Marshall Plan for the Middle East, a long-range integration and development plan in which the High Dam at Aswan, gigantic though it is scheduled to be, would be only one detail.

In particular the plan must not be made up of hastily contrived defensive moves to combat the Soviet campaign, as Western support for the High Dam to some extent was. Instead, the whole concept must be a daring program designed to take some of the dazzlement out of Arab eyes as they regard the Soviet offers. The goal for which the West would be striving would not be immediate unity so much as stability, in which Arab, Israeli, and Western interests alike might progress.

The stupendous difficulty of formulating such a program and of carrying it through is made obvious by the fact that American, British, and French officials are in almost daily consultation over how to meet the Soviet challenge in the Middle East. Politically, also, the issue is fraught with meaning in the United States. To date, despite the urgent need, no concrete Western program has emerged. In no area of the world, perhaps, have big power disagreements and the rivalries of local peoples combined so effectively to throttle Western diplomacy as in the Middle East.

Yet the stakes are vital. They involve not merely the loss of Western oil and strategic bases, important as these are, nor even merely the aspiration of Arabs and Israelis to work out their own destinies in their part of the world. More is involved, since the loss of the Western position in the Middle East might mean the accretion of Arab oil to the Soviets, and ultimately an open field for Communist penetration leading through the Middle East, to Africa beyond.

CHAPTER 8

Westernization in the Middle East

To understand these confused relationships among the Arabs and their attitudes toward the outside world, the impact of Westernization upon the Middle East must be taken into account. More than any other single thing the process of Westernization, which basically is the penetration of Western methodology into Arab thinking, has launched a revolution in the Middle East. Reduced to its essentials, this revolution is the rebellion of the newer generations against the encrusted feudalism of the past, which has laid its static grip over the political, social, and economic development of the Arab world. The rebellion, ranging from café gossip to street riots in which the urban rabble plays an unwitting role, is given its dynamic force in almost every Arab state by young men generally educated in Western schools, and themselves heirs of the Westernizing process which sent them to those schools in the first place.

The mental climate these young men breathe tends to make them think alike regardless of their national origins or the feuds which their leaders carry on. Thus I have had young Arabs in Damascus, Beirut, Amman, and even in Saudi Arabia tell me that their first duty, as Arabs, was to rid their lands of feudal overlords. Translated into specific terms this would mean the removal of many of the dominant politicians of Lebanon, Syria, and Iraq, and of the royal family of Saudi Arabia. It would not mean the removal of the present Egyptian Government, because that government is made up of "Young Turks" who already have gone through the process of overthrowing a king and his corrupt political following.

These revolutionaries, of whatever country, tend to be pan-Arabists. That is, they favor a unified Arab world in order that the Arabs may most efficiently develop their potential economically, socially, and politically. Because they are patriots, they are anti-Israel. Denied a significant role in their own governments, they tend to congregate in clandestine groups with extremist leanings, such as the Syrian Socialist National Party (PPS) founded by Anton Saadeh. In some cases these frustrated young nationalists, for many of whom the religion of Islam has little meaning, gravitate toward communism.

What is the process which has bred these men, among whom are businessmen (often representing Western firms), junior civil servants, army officers, doctors, dentists, and lawyers, their ranks steadily being reinforced by students coming up from below?

The source of Westernization among the Arabs, according to Raphael Patai, the anthropologist, was the cultural affinity between West and Middle East which afforded a bridge over which the technological aspects of culture could be loaned and borrowed.[1] These similarities of culture (stemming from Greek and Roman domination of the ancient Middle East, and from the religious impulses sent westward in the form of Christianity and later of Islam) diminished sharply when the Industrial Revolution transformed Europe and left the Mideast far behind.

From the vantage point of technology, Europeans now looked down upon the unchanged culture of the Middle East and found it backward. Middle Easterners, for their part, perceived that they had been far outstripped and, realizing this, were willing to grasp at the use of technology, though they could not, and still cannot, emulate its production. Thus was set in train the first trickle, later to swell to a flood, of those alien influences which could not help but upset the old and established order.

First to be affected were the top layers of Middle Eastern society, whose positions of wealth and leadership had caused them to be the sustainers of all that was the best in Islamic culture. Abruptly these people deserted the old for the new "prestige" products of the West and became, in the words of Dr. Patai, "avid consumers in all fields of importations from the countries of the West."[2]

Shorn of their most effective inspiration and support, native arts and crafts declined and, in some cases in order to recapture a market, became tawdry copies of the West. The cultural link between top and bottom classes was destroyed, for the upper classes, instead of demanding and consuming the finest of the local goods, now had moved into a Westernized orbit of their own. Those who could not afford the trappings of the West—the new hallmark of status—inevi-

[1] For a more complete discussion of the process, see Raphael Patai, "The Dynamics of Westernization in the Middle East," *The Middle East Journal*, Vol. 9, No. 1 (Winter, 1955), pp. 1-16.

[2] *Ibid.*, p. 5.

tably were regarded as primitive and backward by those who could. Thus began the uprooting of an established order, and the first rumblings of frustration which later was to manifest itself through such movements as the Moslem Brotherhood, xenophobic, conservative, fanatic, dedicated to the removal of Western influence from the Middle East.

With the development of incipient industrialization in the Middle East came a flow of labor to the cities, creating at once an urban proletariat depressed in status and at the same time a concept that coming to the "town" meant an advance in social ranks. All too often, however, the fellah, or peasant, who left his family and his fields found no sense of belonging in the city slums to cushion the disruption. Gone was the accustomed round of seedtime and harvest, of festivals and family life, even the comfort of devotion in the village mosque, and in their place were bewilderment, loneliness, and economic depression which made the worker fair game for rabble-rousers who would pay to put a mob upon the streets.

Along with the urban proletariat came the growth of a new middle class, composed partly of those members of the old craft guilds and merchants who were able to adapt the products they manufactured or sold to fit the new consumer demands, and partly of the new professional class of white-collar workers and intellectuals, recruited from the ranks of the middle class and from the sons of the rich. The latter in particular, imbued with the notion that Western-type professions connoted prestige, aimed at an education which would allow them to work in the towns, as far removed as possible from hand labor and work in the fields. Few of them by comparison, however, chose the woefully under-staffed professions of medicine, engineering, architecture, and technical fields of all kinds. Instead, by obtaining a surface gloss of Western methodology, they set out to claim clerical, administrative, journalistic, political, and occasionally teaching and religious positions. The result was a glut in the Middle East of white-collar people, abhorring the rural life from which they felt they had escaped, but underemployed or without work because Arab business enterprises and the bureaucracies of their governments already were saturated with "intellectual" help.

All too often the religion of Islam lost its hold over the new urban masses, particularly among the white-collar classes (who, for one thing, watched the casual religious observance of many Westerners whom they admired), because Islamic observance was rooted in the family and the individual's integration in it. In many cases, as has been seen, the shift from the country to the town broke up family groups.

Those who acquired only a tinge of the Westernizing process—who became half-educated, so to speak—often did not find within themselves the capacity for revolutionary zeal, but merely caught hold of the ladder up which they saw the more fortunate advancing, and tried to scramble up. This group, by and large, is included in the great sea of underemployed white-collar workers of the Middle East, who will stay with the status quo or flow with change as it serves them best.

Generally speaking, the dynamism behind the spirit of change abroad in the Middle East comes from the professional class—army officers, doctors, lawyers, and others— men who have gone far enough into the Western educative process to glimpse something beyond self-interest. In these men lies a hope for the Middle East as the area shrugs itself out of the slough of the past. In them also lies a danger, unless their zeal is channeled along constructive lines. Whether or not this will be so depends upon the tenacity of opposition they receive from the traditional leaders of the past.

The process of supplanting the old order with a new is far more complicated in the Middle East than the mere toppling of a regime by force of arms, or even through the ballot box. This the young officers who led Egypt's revolution have discovered. In the four years since they seized power in Cairo they have learned that to plot a *coup d'etat* is one thing; to shoulder the long-term administration of a country with staggering social and economic problems is quite another.

Nowhere are they more handicapped than in the lack of trained technicians of the right sort, Egyptians willing to dedicate themselves to the task of leavening the whole social lump, at the modest salaries which the government can afford to pay. The thin crust of Egyptians who had become technicians long ago was eaten away by those who deserted to the ranks of the old political orders, where the pastures looked greener, and who now are suspect in the eyes of the Revolution Command Council.

Egypt's land reform program is a major case in point. From the beginning of their revolution the "Free Officers" stressed a program of land reform, formally approved September 9, 1952, under which a great social evil was to be corrected by seizing 656,140 acres of arable land from Egypt's big owners and distributing it among the peasants. In 1953, according to Sayed Marei, executive director of the government's Agrarian Reform Committee, 187,000 acres were requisitioned and distributed, followed by an additional 117,000 acres in 1954 and 172,000 acres in 1955. The remaining acreage, about 180,000, is scheduled for seizure and distribution in 1956, at which time the confiscatory portion of the program will have been completed.

Rich cotton fields, orchards, and sugar cane groves belonging to King Farouk were among the lands seized, as well as two-thirds of the estates of the family of the late Prince Mohammed Ali, uncle of Farouk. Other large owners have been reduced to the statutory limit of 200 acres which the government has decreed any one person may own. These lands have been broken up into plots of from two to five acres and handed over to the fellahin of the locality. The dispossessed owners (with the exception of Farouk) have been compensated in state bonds redeemable in 30 years with an annual interest of three per cent. Value of the land was assessed at 70 times its basic annual taxes, which was also the price to be paid by the peasants in installments spread over 30 years.

From the social point of view the need for this land reform program was apparent. Agriculture in Egypt furnishes 96 per cent of the export trade and contributes 60 per cent of the annual national income. Yet the greater part of the land producing this income was owned by a small group of immensely powerful landlords, headed by the king himself. This group, centering the country's economy in its own hands, held a similarly viselike grip over the nation's political life, a grip which was not effectively challenged until 1952 when a segment of the Egyptian officer corps launched its *coup d'etat*.

Then appeared the first hope of attacking a feudal system which so long had contributed to the abuse and decline of Egypt's human resources, and the consequent decline of the land resources upon which Egypt depended. On paper the new land reform program is proceeding well, and in fact a good deal of progress has been made. But problems have arisen which the figures on acres seized do not reflect.

The landlord, it was discovered, in addition to depressing his peasantry through usurious land rents and interest rates, also performed certain essential functions which the peasant could not provide. Thus the landlord bought fertilizer for his holdings, built communal granaries, maintained irrigation ditches, and arranged for the transport and marketing of the matured crop. He served, in effect, as an individual credit institution, from which the peasant "bought" fertilizer and "rented" tools, in return for which the landlord obtained an additional share of the peasant's crop.

Under land reform, however, there were few landlords altruistic enough to continue such services for land which shortly would be taken away from them. Thus more than one landlord privately declared his intention of choosing the best 200 of his acres, lavishing upon them the finest of fertilizing and irrigation care, and letting the rest—to be appropriated by the government at fixed rates—figuratively go to seed. The result in many cases was that the fellah, lacking credit, transport, and marketing facilities, inherited a fragmented holding that had declined in value.

The obvious answer was, and still is, the training of agricultural leaders similar to county agents in the United States, who not only could advise newly-landed farmers on irrigation, transport, and marketing problems, but who also could manage peasants' cooperatives, in which the farmers would pool their resources and from which they would draw their supplies. The cooperatives, in other words, would take over the needed functions of the landlord. To this end the Egyptian Government is attempting to establish in every agricultural village a farmers' cooperative directly under government control. In addition to supplying the landlord's former services, the cooperative goes further and teaches the peasant more modern farming methods, provides a health and community center for himself and his family, and plans a rotation of crops designed to replenish the soil.

A program also is underway to tear down the typical mud and reed hovels of the Egyptian fellahin, in which the gamoosa, or water buffalo, often has the best quarters, and replace them with small brick-and-plaster cottages. Each fellah is to help in the building of his new home, and will pay the partial cost in installments over 20 years.

Initially the Egyptian peasant, rooted in a way of life extending back through centuries, resisted the strange cooperatives and their methods. Gradually, however, according to Egyptian Government sources, this resistance is being broken down and replaced by cooperation, particularly since the peasant saw that in the years since 1953, output from land worked under cooperatives increased by about 30 per cent.

In its program Egypt is hampered by lack of trained technicians to manage the cooperative system. In a land where the ingrained tradition has been control of resources by an elite few, it is difficult to find educated men with a sufficient sense of public service, or to educate illiterate fellahin up to the needed levels. A great percentage of Egypt's white-collar class treasures its own emancipation from the mattock and hoe and refuses to go back to the land, even in the guise of management.

It is here, in the opening and supervising of rural extension schools, designed to train up cadres of agricultural workers, that the United States Point Four program is making one of its most significant contributions to the Middle East. Here it is also that Point Four runs up against some of its most subtle opposition, for vested interests see the seeds of their own destruction in the program which Point Four is helping to introduce. In Egypt, at least, the government and

Point Four are on the same side in the struggle, since the government is dedicated to the removal of the old landholding system. Even in Egypt, however, opposition or apathy toward land reform are widespread enough to cause many individual holdings, and consequently village life, to deteriorate gravely before there is a sufficient trained reserve to put the new program over.

In application, land reform is one aspect of Westernization in the Middle East. In Egypt this aspect of Westernization finds its most favorable climate in which to work, since Colonel Nasser and his cohorts see the success of their revolution in terms of the emancipation of the peasantry, forming the broad base on which Egypt's economy is built.

It is also apparent that, despite dedication and zeal at the top of the governmental structure, the old feudal elements who controlled so much of Egypt's wealth still are deeply enough entrenched through their followers in the government's bureaucracy, and still influential enough in Egypt's finances, to threaten the success of land reform. Given these handicaps, it is by no means certain that Colonel Nasser will be able to do enough for the masses, both urban and rural, to forestall new unrest and prevent the overthrow of his own regime and the possible restoration of the time-honored, but otherwise discredited, status quo.

Elsewhere in the Middle East the situation is less favorable. Egypt today is the only Middle Eastern country with a government in office specifically to eradicate social ills. (Israel is an exception because it is establishing a new society, rather than working with a legacy from the past.) In other governments there are reformist elements, but nowhere are they in a clear majority.

In this context Iran illustrates the difficulties which Point Four as one aspect of Westernization has encountered in the

Middle East. (Iran is not an Arab land. But it is an important Middle Eastern country in which the conditions of land tenure are almost identical to those in Iraq and Syria, and formerly in Egypt. Iran is an example, therefore, of what very likely would occur should Point Four, or some similar agency, begin extensive work in Syria and Iraq. Point Four, it should be added, already is at work in Iraq. Syria so far has refused to accept American technical aid.)

Iran, formerly called Persia, has some 200 landlords who own 10 to 50 villages each, and 7,000 landlords owning one, two, or three villages each. Shah Reza Pahlevi, despite the fact that he has given a number of villages away, still owns in the neighborhood of 2,000 villages. As a result of this system Iranian crops are divided so that one-fifth of each crop goes to a man for each of the five elements which he provides—land, water, seed, equipment, and labor. Since the landlord automatically provides land and water, and generally seed and equipment as well, he often receives four-fifths of the crop, while the peasant who provides the labor gets only one-fifth. The worst evils of the system creep in where wealthy absentee landlords hire overseers for their estates, often "selling" this job to the highest bidder, who then is determined to get back his money with usury.

Point Four officials stress, however, that the majority of landlords are "small" operators who live close to their villages and are just as bound to the land, and almost as poor, as the villagers themselves. As one landlord told an American: "I didn't ask for this land, I inherited it. All my living is tied up in it, and there is no way I can get out. I'm just as tied to the land as the peasants."

A practical way to work, as Point Four officials in the field see it, is to provide those services which directly benefit the peasant and only indirectly the landlord. Among those services are introduction of sanitary facilities into as many villages as possible, and aiding rural schools even in such simple matters as repairing windows and doors and providing blackboards, paper, and pencils.

It is the hope of Point Four experts to build at least one agricultural demonstration school in each province of Iran and to train elementary teachers to take over existing rural schools. The gradual effect of such policies—if given time to mature—would be to prepare the peasant to look after his own interests, should the landlord system one day disappear and the land be sold to him.

The landlords are fully aware of this fact and, according to one American official, over-all relations between landlords and Point Four might be termed "grudging cooperation." (Americans, for their part, are fully aware that they are revolutionaries in the land. So far the bulk of Middle East peasantry is politically inert. The things which Americans are teaching them, however, when contrasted with the land tenure system under which they have been living, could explode in an immense challenge to the area should the peasantry finally become aroused.) Point Four representatives are convinced that should the day arrive when the peasants themselves will be able to administer their village cooperatives, many smaller landlords would be glad to sell their land and free themselves from a system which, in a sense, has victimized them as well.

One of the best examples of the gradual and careful approach to land reform is afforded by the village of Galehnow, a little mud town north of the Iranian capital of Teheran. Galehnow rises like a collection of brown blisters from the stubbly plain which, since there is water for irrigation, grows wheat for the peasants of the village.

Within the strawed mud walls of Galehnow are dirt streets beaten to dust. Elms and sycamore trees, the latter with smooth gray trunks and dust-coated leaves, line the streets, while behind the trees run the mud walls of courtyards. In each courtyard are several dome-shaped mud homes with whitewashed inner walls and ceilings, and each, despite the poverty of the village, with one or two Persian carpets on the floor. Also in each courtyard is a dome-shaped kitchen open at one end shared by the women of the yard, who use dried cattle dung for fuel to cook their families' simple meals. Chickens scratch and peck in the courtyard dirt as the women work, while huge sheep dogs with great square heads and filthy matted hair, growl briefly at every movement and then resume their slumber in the dust.

Outside the walls of Galehnow is a narrow ditch through which the village water runs. The women take their dishes there every morning to wash them with handfuls of mud scraped off the banks; and the village farmers splash water over their oxen until the animals glisten.

All these features might be found in many other villages throughout Iran. There is one thing, however, which sets Galehnow apart from most other villages—the plots outside the village walls, where lima beans, sweet corn, cucumbers, cabbages, and other vegetables grow. From these simple gardens has sprung a better life for the villagers of Galehnow; and in them also lies one of the most successful Westernization efforts in the Middle East. Put another way, what has happened in Galehnow is an American success story in a part of the world where many American programs have failed in recent years.

In 1946, at the invitation of the Iranian Government, a private American organization called the Near East Foundation came to Iran to work at improving the lot of Iran's illiterate peasantry, forming 80 per cent of the country's population. As elsewhere since 1930, when it began its work in the Near and Middle East, the Foundation came only upon invitation, and with the understanding that the Iranian Government would pay the major part of the expenses for the services the Foundation would provide.

The village of Mamazon, about 20 miles southeast of Teheran, was selected as headquarters for the Foundation team. For nearly a year Americans worked in the village, studying the villagers' needs and gaining their confidence. Then, gradually, new seeds and new fertilizers were brought in, new crops were planted, and those that prospered were introduced in other villages, where peasants and landlords would accept them. Deep wells were dug, a public bath was constructed, and simple sanitary facilities were provided for the Mamazon peasants, who never had heard of such things before.

The most revolutionary aspect of the Foundation's work was that the peasants were required to furnish labor, and the landlords and the government were to supply most of the funds and equipment, while the Foundation furnished the technical know-how and supervision. Partly this policy was followed because the Foundation, as a private organization headquartered in New York, has relatively little money with which to work. Even more the policy is the result of the Foundation's conviction that only by furnishing labor and materials themselves will peasants and landlords take the needed lessons to heart and keep up the work in an area when the Foundation's men are gone.

The Foundation soon discovered that the diet of most peasants consisted of bread, tea, and sugar. In spring they could milk their animals and turn the milk into yoghurt. Women also picked a few green weeds and planted beans along the ditches in the spring. But the landlords never had permitted any portion of their wheat and barley lands to be used for truck gardens to feed peasants.

Thus fresh fruits and vegetables, to be seen in profusion in the stalls of Teheran, never were tasted by the vast majority of peasants. The answer, as Foundation men saw it, was to persuade the landlords to allow the Foundation to plant vegetable gardens for villagers, on patches of land within the village used for nothing else. The task was not easy, but when the author first visited Iran in the fall of 1952, the Foundation had won through to planting gardens in five villages, one of which was Galehnow.

Since that time gardens have been planted in many other towns, as the Foundation's work has spread. Ten years after the first team arrived in Iran, a program embracing 350 villages in the Veramin area (which includes Galehnow and Mamazon) is supervised by the 16 American members of the Foundation's staff and their Iranian helpers. The program includes exhaustive agricultural training, livestock and poultry improvement, soil and water management, establishment of rural cooperatives, a home and family welfare program including health and sanitation training, and education for children and adults.

In the field of education the Foundation has achieved some of its most spectacular results. When work was begun in 1946, there was one school with 10 pupils in the area of which Mamazon forms a part. At this writing the Foundation has organized 40 new schools, with an enrollment of 2,500 adults and 5,200 children. Staffing these schools are native village teachers, graduates of the Foundation's Teacher Training School.

Because of its manifest success, the budget of the Foundation in Iran swelled from $35,000 to $400,000 within little more than a year of the program's inception, by far the greater part of those funds being supplied by the Iranian Government and by landlords. Even during the depths of Iran's oil famine, when government and army salaries were running far in arrears, the government of Mohammed Mossadegh kept up its payments to the Near East Foundation. Today the United States Technical Cooperation Administration, or Point Four, supplies funds for Foundation projects, and there is close staff liaison between the Foundation and Point Four. The Ford Foundation also has made grants, and the Near East Foundation itself continues to draw on its own resources.

In February, 1955, at the 25th annual anniversary dinner of the Foundation in New York, Shah Reza Pahlevi personally decorated Cleveland E. Dodge, chairman of the board of directors of the Near East Foundation, with Iran's Order of Homayoun as a token of the esteem in which the Foundation and its people are held in Iran.

None of this means that the Near East Foundation has challenged, except by indirection, the land tenure system as practiced in Iran. There are probably no fewer big landlords in Iran as a result of the Foundation's work. What it does mean, however, is that if and when the landlord system does disappear one day, some villagers at least, trained in irrigation, sanitation, agriculture, and the running of a village cooperative, will be able to take care of themselves.

The process is slow, necessarily so, since to push too fast might mean sabotaging the whole program through the opposition that would be aroused. Thus the 350 villages affected by the Foundation's work do not bulk large when compared to the 47,000 villages of Iran. One thing, however, the Near East Foundation has done, and that is to introduce an aspect of Westernization successfully, on a microcosmic sale.

Significantly, the Foundation has operated in Syria for several years, where the official United States Point Four program never has been admitted. As already mentioned, one reason would appear to be that the Near East Foundation goes in only where invited and requires the host government to bear the major portion of expense. Thus there can be no feeling of an American project being pushed down the Middle Eastern throat. The Foundation works also in Afghanistan, and surveys for a project in Jordan have been completed. Twenty-five years of successful Foundation work in Greece ended in June, 1956.

Apart from agriculture, the impact of Westernization in the Middle East has been most keenly felt in the field of education. Here again the meaning of at least part of the process can be told through the experience of a private American enterprise, the Jubriel Rural Fellowship Center, a tiny school high up in the Akkar hills of north Lebanon. Started in 1944 by an American couple, the Reverend and Mrs. Samuel Neale Alter, under the auspices of the Presbyterian Church mission in Lebanon, the school physically is little more than a cluster of stone buildings. In fact, however, Jubriel is a noteworthy experiment in rural education, mirroring in its own experience many of the problems involved in transplanting a leavening but alien kind of teaching to the Arab world.

Purpose of the school, as Dr. and Mrs. Alter conceived it, was to teach village boys and girls, often illiterate when they came to the Center, how to earn livings and, if possible, live happily in their mountain towns, at a time when the tendency was more and more for villagers to drift down toward the cities. The task of the school has not been easy, for the Akkar is a region where apathy, poverty, and tradition often resist the changes which the Center is trying to bring about. It is an area of rounded hills, with gray rock showing through on the ridges, where the soil has eroded. A narrow road comes out on the lip of a cliff, and the vista drops away to brown fields laced with stone fences, and here and there oxen plowing.

Every few miles the road passes through a stone village, half-hidden among olive trees. Generally the houses are poor affairs, with barefoot children playing in the yard or in the tiny streams which flow down the sides of the road. Often the men and women themselves are barefoot, and they stare, sometimes with hard eyes, at the foreigner in his car, waiting to see whether the stranger will wave and nod. Groups of men cluster all day at the simple open-air cafés, because there is no work for them in the fields.

Corn and wheat are the main crops of the Akkar, and tenant farming is the chief occupation. Here and there the red tile roof of a landlord's house stands out against the hillside. When the sun is shining and the wind ripples through the yellow wheat in the valley, it is an attractive scene; but because of the general poverty—and the new attractions of the cities—the old cohesiveness of village life has gradually crumbled away.

To combat this condition the Alters conceived of a village school which, using only such equipment as a student might find in his own village, would reduce illiteracy and teach a boy or girl new crafts and methods to apply in the home and fields. Jubriel was chosen as a site because all the people were of one religion, Greek Orthodox, thus eliminating the possibility of religious strife, always a factor in Lebanon, and because the village was on the road which other villagers would take on the way down to Tripoli, the city of the region.

A curriculum was formed based on 10 points, including homemaking skills, health and hygiene, infant care and child training, each point designed to meet a specific village need. A girl student learns to sew, to weave on a simple loom, to cook over a charcoal or primus stove, to read and write Arabic, to plan a balanced diet for a baby. A boy, in addition to reading and writing, learns carpentry or stonecutting, how to plant vegetables to supplement wheat and corn (reminiscent of Galehnow in Iran), how to raise a hutch of rabbits, and other homely duties designed to increase his income or improve the family table without upsetting the village way of life.

A chapel service is held each day at Jubriel, including readings from the Bible and a short discussion of the lesson. The purpose is to teach a knowledge of the student's own religion, and tolerance for the other religions of Lebanon, since the country is maintained on a delicate religious balance.

Across the valley from the school the village of Jubriel climbs up the opposite slope, from which the Center moved to its present site in 1949. Relations between the village and the school have not been clear sailing. In the beginning at least 50 per cent of the villagers were opposed to the school, partly because they did not understand its methods and feared an upsetting influence in their lives, and in some cases through disappointment that the school did not bring revenue to the village.

An example was the attempt of Munir Khoury, at that time chief assistant to Dr. Alter at the school, to supply water from a well on his own land across the valley. A group in the village found the original deed on the well, which said that 15 meters of water from that well must be for the common village use. Therefore, the group said, Khoury had no right to give the school unlimited use of the well. The village itself might sell water to the school, it was hinted. The Center refused to buy, and instead hired men to lug water to the school in jars. Finally the altercation was settled in the Center's favor, but not before one villager, worked up by the arguments of village leaders, threatened the people of the Center with a gun. Over the long run, however, Dr. Alter and his associates are less concerned with an episode of this kind than with breaking down the more pervasive barriers of suspicion and resistance to new methods.

"How can we expect the villagers to appreciate ideas which they do not understand?" one teacher, Miss Selwa Khoury, said to me. "When I first came here, I could not understand what the 10 points meant, and I had had a college education."

There are no examinations at Jubriel, and no rigid length of time in which to finish the course. Most students complete their 10 points in three years, but if a student needs four, no obstacle is raised. "The only examination is success in village life," Miss Khoury said. One requirement is that the student must spend his last year as a boarder in order to apply his new skills and crafts in a practical way. All the work at the Center—cooking, house cleaning, simple repairs, and construction—is done as much as possible by the students themselves.

A kindergarten is held for children from three to six years old, from which the children go back to the village and, theoretically at least, to a government school until they are 12. Then, if they desire, they come back to the Center for their 10-point course.

Both Miss Khoury and Miss Hoda Butrous, in general charge of the girls' section of the Center, are village girls, and both came up through the Presbyterian mission schools in Lebanon. Another girl came to the Center illiterate, took her course, and stayed to teach in the kindergarten. One boy, illiterate and almost destitute, came to Dr. Alter in 1948. Since then he has acquired skills which earn him a decent living, and has built himself a comfortable house close to the school, where he teaches and practices stonecutting and carpentry.

Miss Khoury drove me about the valley to see the villages from which the students came. We passed a group of farmers gathered about a threshing floor, a sheltered spot in a field around which stacks of wheat were pitched. On the "floor" itself a little girl stood on a wooden platform, drawn by a horse. Around and around the horse trod, the girl standing on the platform, and the wheat separating from the chaff beneath her weight. I asked Miss Khoury whether I might take their picture, and she hesitated. "They are opposed to us," she said. "It might be better not to."

Here was a glimpse of the difficulties which the teachers and the founder of the school still face in their daily work and living. There have been times, when village feelings were heated over some issue concerning the school, when neither Miss Khoury nor Miss Butrous cared to walk alone in the village at night.

Each year (and this is the only reward the Alters seek), the school graduates from among its students a few like the girl who teaches kindergarten and the boy who cuts stone, and a few more village homes benefit from lessons in cleanliness, hygiene, and child care. Even among these few, however, the tenacity of tradition continues to pick and to cavil.

Some years ago, for example, a young villager named Faris (a real boy, though this is not his name) so grasped the import of the school, and of what its lessons might mean to the poverty-stricken district in which he lived, that he resolved after graduation to become a teacher, just like the Americans who were teaching him. After studying in the United States, he went back to his native Lebanon, full of fire to put into practice the principles he had learned at much sacrifice and cost.

So imbued was he by this time with Western concepts, that it never occurred to Faris to do anything else, when the bus rolled to a stop before the coffeehouse in his village, than to reach up where the bags were stacked and pull down his own. But it occurred differently to the men of his village, gathered in their noonday idleness at the coffeehouse. "So!" they jeered at him now. "This is what you have learned with all your books, to carry your own suitcase!" And the jeering grew while Faris silently shouldered his heavy bags and carried them down the street to his village home.

During the weeks that followed, as Faris persisted in doing work no longer fit for him, the feeling deepened to real hostility in the village. Here was a man violating two tenets of the village code—in the first place, doing work fit for a woman servant or a lackey, and in the second place, doing work with his own hands despite the fact that he had gained a certificate of some sort at a school in the States!

The pressures on Faris grew, pressures which an American in the Arab world seldom feels, because the Arabs long have been convinced that Americans have deluded notions concerning work, and there is nothing the Arabs can do about them. But for a villager of their own to accept such notions was another matter. Gradually, in little ways so subtle and so seemingly unimportant in themselves that Faris himself scarcely noticed them, his resolve, his fire, and his purpose were eroded away.

In the summer of 1954 a significant event occurred in connection with the Center and the village of Jubriel. A building, a goat barn, to put it simply, was erected near the school. Not that all the villagers of Jubriel would agree that the event was significant. Many of them—dwelling in stone houses far more humble and less clean than the new building intended for goats—viewed with deep suspicion the erection of such an imposing edifice merely to house some goats.

Have not the goats of Akkar, they asked, indeed the goats of all Lebanon and of other Arab lands, wandered for centuries unhindered and unchecked upon the hillsides and valleys, eating what they would and spending the nights in whatever caves or rude shelters their poor shepherds could provide? Tradition, linked with apathy and poverty, is heavy in Jubriel, and the building of a goat barn better than the houses of the villagers themselves was misunderstood.

The barn was put up by 29 young campers of five nations, cooperating with the International Work Camp Division of the United Nations Educational, Scientific, and Cultural Organization and with Dr. Alter's mission school. With their own hands the campers put up the building, for a purpose wholly apart from that of impressing the villagers with the poverty of their homes.

These campers knew what agronomists long have taught—that the goat of the Middle East, generally black, scrawny, and voracious, has done as much as any other single factor to denude the Arab world of its sparse cover of green and to prevent the growth of new trees which one day might hold in the soil the region's rainfall and prevent its wasteful running off in swollen streams, dark with the topsoil of the hills.

Reforestation programs in more than one Middle Eastern country have been frustrated by myriads of shepherds stubbornly refusing to understand why their herds should be denied what little forage remains to them. Dr. Alter foresaw the building of a model goat dairy barn by the campers as a project of long-range signficance to the future of the Akkar and of Lebanon as a whole.

The breeding of a species of goats domesticated for stall-feeding exclusively not only would remove by degrees the present black scavengers from the hillsides, but would provide the shepherds of Lebanon with herds giving more abundant supplies of milk. Hence the generous dimensions of the barn at Jubriel, designed not only to stall 50 white Swiss goats, but also to serve as a demonstration project for the district.

The reaction of the villagers—critical, suspicious, scornful, according to their bent—was not surprising. Indeed, it was one more example that the most stubborn obstacle in the path of the rural school has been that of persuading the people of Akkar that the practice of simple farming skills and home crafts might increase the productivity of their lands and lend new purpose to village life.

Only five Swiss goats arrived in 1954, to be followed the next year by a few more animals from Cyprus. At this writing the arrival in Jubriel of 30 more goats is imminent, donated by the Christian Rural Overseas Program (CROP) in the United States. And during 1956 Dr. Alter hopes to complete a second barn, built by similar campers. The Center then will have two barns, one for goats and one for cattle, with facilities for 500 chickens as well.

This growth symbolizes the fact that the Jubriel Center, which clung to the lip of existence for years, now is in the Akkar to stay. Today the "campus" boasts two separate schools, one for boys and the other for girls. In the girls' section stands the Alters' residence and a house for the Edwin Hannas, Dr. Alter's new assistants. There is a main classroom building, two dormitories, a cooking building, and a small house occupied by a Lebanese family whose members do cooking, gardening, and other chores.

For the boys' school there is a shed containing looms and a simple machine shop, a classroom and assembly building with a dormitory on the second floor, and an unfinished building in which the Center's truck, tractor, and other equipment are stored.

This is in addition to the first goat barn, standing as a symbol of the endeavor of Dr. Alter and those who work with him to enrich the lives of villages whose men too often spend their days in clusters around outdoor cafés because there is little work for them in the fields, and whose women toil listlessly in stone huts so dark and unattractive that their ambitions remain unstirred. And almost certainly, as in every other project Dr. Alter has tried, one or more Arab boys or girls, watching the work of their teachers in the goat barn, will catch at least a glimpse of what this change in method might mean to their district. Then the faint stirrings will have spread to one or two more families, dwelling in a poor mountain district which, whether they like it or not, the villagers must call home.

In the development of its personnel the Center has expanded also. Munir Khoury, following study at Cornell, has gone to the Point Four program in Lebanon, where he is a key official in agricultural work. Selwa Khoury came to the United States for study also, and now divides her time between the Jubriel Center and the task of establishing Y.W.C.A. units in the villages of the district. Hoda Butrous has graduated from the Beirut College for Women, another

Presbyterian activity, and is back at the Center, sharing direction of the girls' school with Miss Khoury.

Relations with the village of Jubriel have improved, symbolized by the presence of Abu Farid Ma'mary, a prominent man of the village, who teaches mathematics and agriculture at the Center and serves as unofficial liaison between "town and gown." In other words, in this specific school, in this particular town, in this one section of Lebanon, a part of the battle has been won. Like the Near East Foundation in Iran, the Jubriel Rural Fellowship Center has succeeded in implanting one small application of Westernization.

There are other mission schools in Lebanon, and elsewhere in the Arab world. Some of them have been as successful as Jubriel, others less so. At each one I have visited, the American educator concerned, sooner or later in the conversation, has voiced this thought: What would become of my school, and of the concepts I have tried to impart, should I and every American on my staff be forced to leave?

Each educator points with pride to a few Arabs who have imbibed the gist of his teaching. Yet those Arabs, were they in charge of the schools, would be under far greater pressure to conform than are the American teachers now present. The fact is that the Arab world, somewhat conscious of the value of unversities, has not yet assigned a place —in the home, the farm, the shop, or the small office—to the Arab who is partially educated, whose comparative learning could make the home and the workshop more attractive and productive places than they are today. This fact, to the educator, represents one part of the enormous inertia which must be overcome, as an age-old civilization struggles to adapt itself to Western ways.

Perhaps the most spectacular American institution in the Middle East (apart from oil companies) is the American

University of Beirut, established as the Syrian Protestant College in 1866 and given its present name in 1920. Occupying one of the most beautiful campuses in the world, with the Mediterranean Sea in the foreground and the tall peaks of Mount Lebanon behind, AUB has become the educational mecca to which young Arabs whose parents can afford it come, from throughout the Arab world—from Yemen and the Sudan, Syria, Iraq, Kuwait, and elsewhere—and go back to their homelands with the equipment to become, as some of them do, the reformist leaders in their lands, or, as many others do, the shrewd politicians and businessmen whose first concern appears to be their own careers.

No other school in the Middle East has furnished so high a percentage of cabinet ministers and deputies in various Arab lands. No other school has given such direction, by its spirit of free inquiry and liberalism, to the Arab nationalist movement, since the latter years of the nineteenth century, when the Arabs began to shake themselves awake under the yoke of the Ottoman Turks. No other school, therefore, as nationalism has sharpened through the days of Western colonialism and even to the present, has become such a center of agitation as has AUB.

These pressures were tolerable to university authorities so long as Lebanon was an Ottoman sanjak (district) and also when the country was under the French. In neither case did the government concerned consistently blame the university for the nationalist sentiment on its campus. After World War II, however, when the foreign rulers were gone, nationalist agitation turned in many cases into demonstrations against the Lebanese Government itself for failure to progress as quickly toward Arab goals—pan-Arabism and freedom from corruption and nepotism—as the students had imagined would happen when the mandate power was gone. In such cases the university found itself squarely in the middle between its host government and its students, and increasingly blamed by both sides for allegedly siding with the other.

Though instances of this are legion, a striking case occurred before the author's gaze on the morning of March 27, 1954, when the iron gate of AUB clanged shut between a band of angry Arab students on the campus and a phalanx of armed Lebanese gendarmery on the streets outside. Suddenly the students, brandishing the black, white, green, and red "Arab National Flag," broke howling through the gate and flooded out against the armed police.

Fire hoses leveled at the students' heads drove them back. Once more they broke through, and this time they hurled bricks and paving stones at the men lined up against them. An order cracked out and the police began to fire, at first in the air, then point blank at the charging youths. A wounded student was carried out by two of his fellows. Police charged the bearers, who dropped their comrade and fought with the police over the body of the fallen youth. When the fighting at the university gate was done, one student had been killed, others severely wounded, and a number of policemen and demonstrators hospitalized. The Arab national ensigns lay torn on the pavement, to be swept up by the street cleaners who followed.

The tragedy was twofold; first, because of what had happened, and second, because the whole thing so easily could have been prevented. Though Lebanon at the time was less than 10 years old as an independent state, the event was a repetition of what already was an old story in Lebanese politics and in the relations of the university with the government of the country.

A few days earlier, in this case, a group of Arab students at AUB had announced their intention of demonstrating against Iraq, on the grounds that the latter nation was thinking of joining the Baghdad Pact. (Almost a year later Iraq did join the alliance.) Many of these students were Arab nationalists, embittered against the West for its colonial past and for its support of Israel. For Iraq to join the Baghdad Pact, it was argued, would give comfort to the United States and Britain, seeking to bolster Middle East defense. Hence, these students said, Iraq as an Arab nation should not join the pact lest the Western "enemies" be satisfied. Another element was the desire of some students, mainly Syrians and Egyptians, to oppose any strengthening of Iraq.

Immediately the Lebanese Government forbade the students to parade through the streets of Beirut, declaring that any Lebanese student who did so would be arrested and any non-Lebanese deported. At this point Arab politics entered the scene. Opposition leaders, eager to embarrass the government, floated a report among the students that any student arrested would be freed as soon as the Lebanese premier had fallen. One powerful politician, with ability to command religious as well as political support, sent the students an open telegram praising their patriotism, urging them on.

Had the Lebanese Government, with similar past examples to profit from, declared in the beginning that the students might demonstrate peaceably under police protection, it is likely that the parade soon would have dissipated and few persons would have been more than amused by the whole thing. Backed into a corner by its original decision, however, the government stuck to its guns, despite the alarming tendency of opposition leaders to enter the fray. Thus the stage was set for the tragic drama to unfold.

The whole episode was one more in a long line of examples of what happens when Arab politicians descend to the streets to whip up popular support. In this instance, however, the riot illustrated something else, and that was the willingness of Arab governments to use the Western institutions in their midst as whipping boys whenever the occasion permits. As soon as the Lebanese Government had banned the demonstration in advance, the American University of Beirut—which perforce obeys the laws of the land—declared that any student who defied the government would be defying the university as well, and would be subject to punishment including expulsion.

When the smoke of battle had cleared, however, and the government discovered that its heavy handed tactics had gotten it into trouble, the premier declared that the first shots had come from university buildings and that the police merely were returning fire. This allegation the university forcefully denied, a denial supported by every independent observer on the scene.

Next the government closed the university for one week, implying that the school itself was responsible for the outbreak. The government further implied, in a complete reversal of role, that any student dismissed by the university would be reinstated by government fiat. Thus the premier, who had banned the demonstration, sought to pose as the friend of students who now were held to have been "handled" by extraneous political elements who had climbed the university walls and mingled with the demonstrators.

Two years earlier the university had been forced by the same premier to take back several students who had been expelled for complicity in a similar kind of riot. This time the university chose the better part of wisdom, ignored its earlier edict, and did little but prohibit future political ac-

Tent of woven black goat hair, used by the Bedouin nomads of Arabia.

Bedouins are shown within their tent. Man in foreground carries prominently his silver dagger and his Moslem prayer beads.

In the Arabian desert the chief building material is mud, with logs
of wood across the ceilings and roofs. This is a large Arab house,
suitable for several families, on the outskirts of an oasis. As in the
Bedouin tent, the living quarters of the family are separated from
the public section in which visitors are received.

Stark contrast between desert and oasis. Mud wall keeps blowing
sand from engulfing palm trees of the oasis.

Donkeys haul water from the depths of an ancient hand-dug
well outside the oasis of Hofuf, in eastern Arabia.

Closeup of the wheel of such a well. Over the wheel runs a
rope, one end of which is fastened to a goatskin water bag.
The other end is tied to the animal which hauls the bag up
and down.

Arab women of the oasis of Qatif, on the shores of the Persian Gulf
in northeastern Arabia, sell vegetables grown in oasis gardens.

Busy market corner in the oasis of Qatif.

Sheikh, or leader, of a tribal section.

Bedouin of the desert, with his long uncut hair curling down below his shoulders. Almost no Bedouin cuts his hair.

King Saud ibn Abdul Aziz, ruler of Saudi Arabia.

To catch the welcome evening breeze the family moves to the roof (divided, as is the house beneath, into private and public sections). A section of the roof of a royal palace in Riyadh, capital of Saudi Arabia.

In Egypt, as in Arabia, the continuity of living conditions from ancient times to the present is marked. Here two Egyptian fellahin, or peasants, carry an Archimedean screw, which they use to lift water from a Nile canal to their fields.

Attributed to Archimedes (287?-212 B.C.), the screw is here literally "screwing" water up into irrigation channels.

An Egyptian boy leads his gamoosa, or water buffalo, along a Nile canal near Cairo, with the great pyramids of Giza in the background.

Fellahin flail wheat in the threshing floor of an Egyptian village.

Typical fellahin of
Egypt.

Typical fellahin of Egypt.

Old Jerusalem, held by the Arabs of Jordan, seen from the road leading south toward Bethlehem.

A market street within the walls of Old Jerusalem, showing baskets and pottery water jugs for sale.

Overlooking the Mediterranean, the St. George Hotel in Beirut is the most noted hostelry of a city which has become a great trading center of the world.

North of Beirut along the Lebanese coast, the stone house of an Arab fisherman is built on the cliff which fronts the shore.

In the fall of the year, when forage is exhausted in the desert, Bedouins from Syria bring their camels to the rich pasturage of Lebanon's Bekaa valley. In the background loom the Anti-Lebanon Mountains, beyond which lies Damascus.

Symbolizing the plight of Arab refugees from Palestine, this child stands before the tent which is her family's home at Nahr el-Bared refugee camp in north Lebanon.

Grandfather and child in the Arabian oasis of Qatif.

tivity on the part of student clubs. An open clash between government and university thus was averted. The control of school authorities over their student body, however, and in particular over the vocal Arab nationalist fringe, had suffered one more notch of decline.

Paradoxically enough, almost every one of the Lebanese politicians involved, though not the premier, was a graduate of the American University of Beirut. Almost any one of them would have declared, and meant it, that the training he had received at this American school had been a major influence in fitting him for a career of eminence among his fellows. Few such politicians, however, would have had the courage openly to defend the university against political pressures which might have jeopardized the individual politician's position, or even safety.

Thus the process of Westernization in the Middle East rolls on; inevitably, inexorably, since the first mission school opened its doors in an Arab town, since the first manufactured goods of the industrialized West found their way into Arab souks, or markets, and since the Western powers first cast covetous eyes on Middle Eastern lands. Ultimately the Westernizing process would seem destined to benefit the great mass of population, though not without the sacrifice of those traditional elements at the society's top.

Revolution in many forms is involved in the process, so deeply entrenched are the forces of opposition. Indeed, even now the Middle East is in the turmoil of revolt, evidenced certainly by street riots and *coups d'etat*, but also in such things as the operation of an oil well near an Arab town, the teaching of political science at a university, the building of a goat barn in a mountain town, and the planting of a vegetable garden in a village of the plains.

Standing in the way of Westernization is the great obstacle of feudalism, which more than anything else threatens revolution of a violent kind. Apart from feudalism, however, is the enormous drag of inertia and apathy on the part of a peasantry ground down by centuries of poverty and serfdom. There is also the danger, as evidenced by the political implications of the university riot, that some Arabs trained up under the Westernizing process will pervert that training to ends which become a new form of feudalism and mass control.

The stresses and strains of the process result from the sudden impingement of a twentieth-century technology and culture upon a society which, isolated within a largely barren geographic environment, had been left hundreds of years behind when industrialization transformed the West. In the case of oil, some of the most complex aspects of Western technology are being thrust upon those areas of the Middle East least prepared to receive them. Hence the growing tension within Saudi Arabia, and the harrowing experience of Iran in the nationalization of her oil.

Other aspects of Westernization—political, social, agricultural, commercial—are mirrored forth in varying degrees of tension and strain, as well as achievement, as the old society struggles to adapt to the ways of the new and as, within this process, those who wish to "catch up" contend with those who cling to the past.

Iraq is an Arab land in which the promise of Westernization is great, because of the country's agricultural potential and income from oil, and also because Iraqi leaders, generally speaking, are among the most pro-Western of all Arabs. This was evidenced in Iraq's conviction that her own security was best served by joining the West in the Baghdad Pact. At the same time the success of the Westernizing process in Iraq is threatened by the grip which feudalism still holds on the thinking of the country.

From its inception as a state after World War I, Iraq was closely associated with Britain. This association, as elsewhere in the Arab world, had two aspects. On the one hand Iraqi nationalism sought to oust the British mandatory government from Iraq. On the other hand the educative and administrative system established by the British permitted Iraq's rapid assimilation of the Westernizing process. Nationalist agitation led the British to exercise their Iraqi mandate, assigned them by the Allied Supreme Council in San Remo, through a treaty rather than a formal mandate, though the degree of British control was scarcely lessened. This treaty, concluded on October 10, 1922, gave Britain the right: (1) to appoint advisers to the Iraqi Government; (2) to assist the Iraqi army; (3) to protect foreigners; (4) to advise Iraq on fiscal matters, and (5) to advise Iraq on foreign relations.

From that time almost until the present Iraqi nationalist pressure, erupting in sporadic violence, forced the gradual reduction of British control, the stages of which were marked by successively more moderate treaties. These treaties culminated on June 30, 1930, when the British high commissioner and Nuri es-Said, then Iraqi foreign minister, signed an Anglo-Iraqi accord which led to Iraq's admission to the League of Nations as a fully sovereign state, though Britain was granted, among other rights, two major Royal Air Force bases at Habbaniya, near Baghdad, and at Shaiba, in southern Iraq. Only in May, 1955, did Britain relinquish control of those air bases, in return for Iraq's adherence to the Baghdad Pact.

The Iraqi throne was strongest under Feisal himself, who became King of Iraq on August 23, 1921, after his deposition in Damascus by the French. Feisal was a brave soldier, as evidenced by his leadership of the Arab Revolt during World War I, and a forceful politician, who centered power in his own hands as far as Iraq's internal policies were concerned. His premature death in 1933 brought his ineffective son, Ghazi, to the throne, and ushered in a period of political instability in which members of a tight political oligarchy, dominated by Nuri es-Said, handed cabinets back and forth among themselves.

On April 4, 1939, King Ghazi was killed in an automobile accident and a regency was set up under pro-British Prince Abdul Ilah, maternal uncle of the new king, infant Feisal II, who ascended the throne in his own right on May 2, 1954. It is too early to predict the relative influence in Iraq of Feisal II, now 20 years old.

Only in relations with Israel has Iraq proven uncooperative with the West. Iraq has been the most adamant of all Arab lands in refusing to settle refugees of the Arab-Jewish war. From the first Iraq opposed the Zionist settlement of Palestine, and many Iraqis enlisted in the "National Liberation Army" of Arab irregulars which infiltrated into Palestine during the last days of the British mandate. When fighting broke out between Arabs and Jews, Iraqi regular detachments were at the front, though Iraq itself lay hundreds of miles away. Even today Iraq has refused to conclude an armistice with Israel.

On July 15, 1948, the Iraqi chamber of deputies passed a bill making Zionist activity in Iraq a criminal offense, and so intolerable did conditions become for Iraqi Jews that, by June 1951, 160,000 of them had emigrated to Israel. Their going left gaps in the shopkeeper and artisan class which could be filled, partially at least, by Arabs from Palestine.

To date, however, Iraq has accepted a scant 4,000 refugees in all.

Underpinning this political and diplomatic background are Iraq's enormous natural resources. Land of the Twin Rivers, occupying the same fertile ground which bred the Sumerian, Babylonian, and Assyrian civilizations of antiquity, and the great Abbasid dynasty of the Middle Ages, Iraq has the most striking potential of any Middle Eastern land. The Tigris and Euphrates Rivers provide fertile soil and water in abundance. Relatively little of this soil is cultivated, for Iraqi agriculture never has recovered from the Mongol invasions of the thirteenth century, which destroyed the complex of irrigation works built up through the ages. Yet Iraq today possesses the income from oil—$204,000,000 in 1955 —to develop all and more land than the ancients did. And finally, Iraq needs people. Potentially, Iraq could accept every one of the 900,000 Palestine Arab refugees, absorb their skills as farmers and townsmen, and still need more people. (Egypt, whose chief problem is overpopulation, has less than one-third of Iraq's cultivable land, and a population more than four times as large as Iraq's 5,000,000 persons.)

Geographically Iraq, which is about twice the size of England, Scotland, and Wales combined, is divided into three distinct sections: the Mesopotamian plain, the Uplands, and the Folded Mountain Belt. Historically the Mesopotamian plain is the most important of the three, for here it was that the great civilizations of the past were nurtured. Here it is also that the flood control and irrigation projects of modern Iraq will have the most effect.

Through this plain flow the Tigris and Euphrates, which, in their annual floods, deposit silt and provide water for irrigation. It is these floods (in late March or early April for the Tigris, a few weeks later for the Euphrates), which

Iraq plans to control and put to more efficient use. Cultivation in the plain depends almost entirely on irrigation, rainfall being insufficient generally to mature even a winter crop. North of the city of Basra the two rivers unite in a single broad channel, the Shatt el-Arab. Also above Basra lie the marshlands where the Muntafiq Arabs dwell, living on hummocks of watery ground and tending their water buffalo from shallow-draft canoes.

North of the alluvial plain rise the Uplands, undulating gravel plain and rich plowland, also the source of Iraq's oil. In an average year Upland rainfall, about 13 inches, is sufficient to produce a single crop without irrigation, though in the Kirkuk and Erbil sections rainfall is supplemented by the "linked well" system of irrigation practiced widely in Iran. Between the Tigris and Euphrates in the Upland area is a region of uncultivable gypsum desert called El Jezira (the island).

Northeastern Iraq comprises the Folded Mountain Belt, including the basins of the rivers Dyala, Lesser Zab, Greater Zab, and Khabur. Here dwell the Kurds, a hardy mountain race wholly different in outlook and habits from the plain-dwelling Arabs. Sympathies of the Kurds lie more with their brethren in neighboring Turkey and Iran than with the Arabs of Iraq. These people live in stone villages, cut into the hillsides, which are terraced for cultivation, including vineyards and tobacco.

Development of Iraq's potential is hindered by an internecine scramble for power, predating the British mandate in many cases, among the Shiite and Sunni clergy, the landed families, the army officers, and the tribes. The net result of this struggle has been government by and for a close oligarchy, which, though it shifts kaleidoscopically within itself, has neglected the people at large.

Part of the conflict stems from the religious composition of the country. Iraq is at least 96 per cent Moslem, but within this Moslem community Shiites outnumber Sunnis eight to five, and the two sects are mutually intolerant. Nor is this all, for the Sunnis themselves are divided about equally between Arabs and Kurds, between whom lies racial antagonism. In the past the situation was thrown further off balance by the fact that a Sunni elite, comprising the educated few, held the reins of government over the Kurds and the Shiite majority. This trend has been somewhat halted by the spread of education, but the tendency still is toward rivalry rather than cooperation.

Personality instead of principle has been the keynote of Iraqi politics. In the first 22 years after the establishment of the Iraq Government following World War I, there were 33 changes of cabinet and 85 different individuals held ministerial posts, according to the Royal Institute of International Affairs in London. Some of these men still figure in Iraqi politics, and have been in and out of office like jack-in-the-boxes.

Generally speaking they have been members of King Feisal's Hejazi officer corps (most notably Nuri es-Said, present premier of Iraq), or Turkish-educated members of prominent families. Their principal supporters were the Shia or Sunni clergy (principally the latter), tribal sheikhs, and other feudal proprietors. Taken as a whole the governing oligarchy owned, and still owns, most of the real estate in Iraq. Their method of government, based largely on nepotism and the building up of personal followings, reinforced an already entrenched feudal system.

Feudalism, more than anything else, has depressed the state of Iraqi agriculture and frustrated efforts toward reform. Little enough of Iraq's land is farmed at all, a late

estimate being about 5,700,000 acres out of a total of 30,-
000,000 acres of cultivable land.[3] Yet of this 5,700,000
acres, almost none is worked by the people who own it.
Tenant sharecroppers, whose share often is as low as 30-40
per cent of the crop, do the actual farming, and they have
little incentive to improve the holdings of their absentee
landlords. Thus Iraqi agriculture remains primitive, and vast
lands lie fallow.

Efforts at reform are being made, as pressure on the government increases from young Western-educated Iraqis,
some of whom have begun to work their way into government posts. Most notable achievement of reformist elements
in Iraq has been the setting up of a Resources Development
Board, whose task over a five-year period ending in 1960 is
to spend $1,165,000,000 in oil revenues for the economic
betterment of the country.

Approximately thirty-six per cent of this spending
(though the percentages are subject to change) is allocated
for irrigation and flood control projects; 19 per cent for road
building; 15 per cent for public works and building; mining
and electricity, 14 per cent; railroad development, 5 per cent;
and housing, 3 per cent.

The Resources Development Board includes full-time
voting British and American members, and is backed by the
United States Technical Assistance Program (Point Four).
In 1955, for example, $2,300,000 of American money went
into surveys, education, and supplying of technicians and
advice on programing the Board's expenditures.

A major problem facing the Board, and hence the Iraq
Government, is how to meet popular demands for immediate
economic improvement without dissipating funds needed

[3] Doreen Warriner, *Land and Poverty in the Middle East* (London:
Royal Institute of International Affairs, 1948), p. 101.

for long-term development. This problem becomes acute as calls for reform grow stronger, and opponents of the Resources Development Board charge that oil money is being spent on projects designed to benefit the rich.

This charge is difficult to refute, since a good deal of the Board's efforts necessarily are aimed at improving agricultural land already owned by the rich, though the intent also is to reclaim additional land and give it to landless peasants. Furthermore, these projects will not begin to bear fruit for several years. Hence the Board is forced to invest in some short-range programs with immediate visible appeal. These include the building of health and educational facilities, and the creation of employment in areas where the population is most restive. Thus nearly $50,000,000 has been allocated for a program of public building, including 100 schools, 12 hospitals, and more than 400 homes for workers, the last being a sore point in a land where the lower classes traditionally are poorly housed. Also, more than 150 artesian wells have been drilled to improve the quality of rural drinking water.

On the long-range side, the Wadi Tharthar flood control project was finished in 1956, as was a similar plan to control Euphrates River flood water. Construction has started on the gigantic Dokan Dam on the Lesser Zab River, largest project yet undertaken by the Development Board. Contract for this dam has been awarded to a French firm.

The first of long-term dividends on these and similar projects will soon appear. Given efficiency and the best of intent on the part of government leaders, Iraq should approach its goal of a rich agricultural and industrial land within 25 years. Whether this development will benefit the population as a whole, however, or will serve merely to widen the gulf between privileged and poor, remains to be seen.

Bolstered by its expanding income from oil, Iraq could become the granary of the Middle East, and an example among the Arabs of orderly development from a feudal past to democratic government. A first step has been taken in allowing Western technicians to participate in the country's planning. It still is too early to tell whether the really big step will be taken, more difficult by far than the technical development itself. That step is reform, implying a revolution within the thinking of Iraq's governing class, enabling them to accept a scaling down of their own wealth and power, in return for a wider spread of prosperity. On their willingness to accept such change depends the future stability of Iraq. On their willingness to do so also depends the success of Westernization in Iraq, where the Westernizing process is at its most advanced in the Middle East.

CHAPTER 9

Communism in the Middle East

The other side to the coin of Westernization is the influence of communism in the Middle East. Generally of subdued import since World War II, this question has been ballooned to new importance by the recent attitude of the Soviet Union toward the Arab world, and toward colonial lands within Africa as well. Not since 1946, when a Soviet-created puppet state in Azerbaijan collapsed, has the U.S.S.R. paid such concentrated attention to the Middle East as it has since 1955.

One apparent reason is the difficulty which the Soviets are experiencing in expanding further in Europe, where Western defenses are strongest, and also in the Far East, where Communist initiative has devolved upon China. A second reason is the gradual shift of the Cold War from reliance on military power blocs to the plane of economic competition between East and West. In the realm of technical and economic assistance to backward areas, or at least in the promise of such aid, the Soviets see a vast and fertile field for penetration among the underdeveloped nations of the Middle East.

In the promotion of this campaign the Soviet leaders are taking the place of the czars in seeking to extend Russian influence down to the warm water world of the Mediterranean, opening up on Africa and Asia to the south. Nearly 200 years ago the czars, claiming to be the spiritual heirs of the Orthodox Byzantine Empire, posed as "protectors" of Eastern Orthodox Christian communities in the Middle East, then under Ottoman Turkish rule. In so doing Russia was emulating the example of France, which so successfully claimed guardianship of Catholic communities in the area that France gained formal mandates over Lebanon and Syria after World War I.

Following the Bolshevik Revolution, however, the Communists renounced the church, and Russia temporarily lost its weapon, or excuse, for intervention in Middle Eastern affairs. Later, during World War II, the Soviets revived the Orthodox Patriarchate in Moscow and began to reclaim church property in Lebanon, Syria, and Palestine which had belonged to the czars. This device was made effective by Soviet financial support of poverty-stricken bishoprics in the area, which brought an increasing number of Orthodox bishops into sympathy with Soviet aims.

In late 1955, however, it became clear that in the area of the Middle East the Soviets were breaking over into direct political competition with the West. The most striking Communist move was the conclusion of an arms deal between Egypt and Czechoslovakia whereby Egypt contracted to buy, at cut-rate terms, arms believed to include 200 Soviet MIG jet fighters, an unspecified number of jet bombers, 100 tanks, several submarines, and considerable artillery. The decision to buy Communist arms was made after Egypt unsuccessfully had sought large quantities of arms from Britain and the United States.

Though the arms deal, introducing as it did a number of Communist technicians into Egypt, was the most spectacular Soviet move, it was followed by other offers of even greater possible significance. Daniel A. Solod, at that time Soviet ambassador to Egypt, announced in October, 1955, that his government would offer industrial and agricultural equipment and technical assistance to all underdeveloped Arab and Asian countries that desired it. Specifically Mr. Solod pledged Soviet assistance in building the High Dam at Aswan, an offer which was repeated by East Germany and Hungary. It was these Communist offers which galvanized the United States and Britain into pledging a $70,000,-000 grant-in-aid for the Aswan Dam and brought Eugene Black, president of the World Bank, to Cairo for consultations leading to a projected $200,000,000 Bank loan for the all-important dam.

In November, 1955, Egypt and Communist East Germany signed a new trade payments agreement, extending a 1953 trade pact which provided for exchanges of Egyptian cotton, rice, and other products, against East German machinery, electrical equipment, precision instruments, chemical products, and fertilizers. Dr. Gottfried Lessing, president of the East German Chamber of Foreign Trade, declared that his country was "prepared to advise the Egyptian Government on drawing up plans and blueprints for new plants or extensions of existing industries."[1]

A few days later Poland offered to take "large" quantities of Egyptian cotton in return for Polish industrial equip-

[1] Reuters dispatch, Cairo, November 10, 1955.

ment, and offered also to send Egypt complete factory installations and technicians. During the flurry of Communist commercial activity in Cairo, Egypt and Czechoslovakia raised their diplomatic missions to embassies, while Egypt and Hungary replaced their chargé d'affaires with minister plenipotentiaries.

Egypt was not alone in receiving Communist overtures. Syria exchanged ambassadors with the Soviet Union and concluded trade and payments agreements with the U.S.S.R., Poland, and Czechoslovakia. Ahmed Shukairy, Syrian delegate to the United Nations and also assistant secretary-general of the Arab League, declared in New York that Soviet Foreign Minister V. M. Molotov had left him convinced of "the possibility of wide cooperation between the Soviet Union and the Arab world in all fields," including the supply of arms.[2] When Syrian settlements east of the Sea of Galilee were attacked by the Israeli Army in December, 1955, it was the Soviet Union which championed Syria's cause in the UN Security Council.

The tiny Kingdom of Yemen in southwestern Arabia, which has opened its doors only a crack to the West, on October 17, 1955, renewed a 1927 treaty of friendship with the U.S.S.R., exchanged diplomatic representatives, and agreed to strengthen trade and economic relations. In this respect the Soviet Union offered to erect factories in Yemen, to supply agricultural machinery, roadbuilding equipment, and arms, in return for Yemenite coffee, tobacco, and other agricultural products.

Afghanistan, which late in 1955 received a showy visit from Soviet leaders Nikita S. Khrushchev and Premier Nikolai A. Bulganin, accepted a $100,000,000 Soviet loan for road, airfield, pipeline, and other construction. Afghanistan

[2] Associated Press dispatch, United Nations, N.Y., October 11, 1955

will draw equal amounts of the loan each year for 22 years, the whole to be repaid during the following eight years at three per cent interest. In addition the Afghans are dickering for Communist arms along the lines of the Czechoslovak-Egyptian deal.

Many of these and other Soviet offers in the Middle East, when it comes to brass tacks figuring, are likely to be rejected by the peoples concerned or will amount to much less in practice than they seem on paper. Nevertheless, they add up to a determined Soviet effort to convince the Arabs that the Communists are ready to offer attractive economic terms with no strings attached. In particular the Soviets are stressing their readiness to take all the cotton Egypt wishes to provide in return for Russian industrial equipment and technical aid. This is of cardinal importance to Egypt, which must sell her cotton to live, and which perennially fears that her exports of long staple cotton to the United States will be reduced. Currently Egypt sells about 40,000,-000 pounds of long staple cotton in the United States yearly. Of special concern to Egyptian growers is the development in the southwest United States of a new extra-long staple whose growers are conducting a vigorous marketing campaign.

Soviet leaders also are informing their own people of the new importance attached to the Middle East. In a dispatch from Moscow, January 12, 1956, Welles Hangen reported to *The New York Times* that *Pravda* and *Izvestia*, leading Moscow papers, each published that day about 10 articles and editorials devoted to Middle Eastern affairs. Five themes were cited by Mr. Hangen as particularly stressed by the Soviet press: that the Baghdad Pact is an aggressive alliance forged by the United States and Britain to preserve a colonial empire in the Middle East; that most Arab states are successfully resisting Western efforts to force them into the Baghdad Pact; that popular dissatisfaction with this alliance is rising in Pakistan, Turkey, and Iran, states "inveigled" into joining the pact; that the Baghdad Pact is doomed to dissolution due to increasing British-American rivalry in the Middle East, and to the determination of Middle Eastern peoples to follow a neutral course; and that Israel is pursuing an aggressive "positions of strength" policy toward the Arabs similar to that practiced by the United States against the Soviet Union.

What do the Soviets expect to gain from this determined campaign? Many observers believe that the Soviets, by arming the Arabs disproportionately vis-à-vis Israel, hope to precipitate a second round of Arab-Israeli fighting. In such a war the disunited Arabs, though strengthened individually by Communist arms, almost certainly would lose, in the view of Western strategists, a view shared presumably by the Soviets as well.

This result would topple at least the Syrian and Egyptian governments, and the Soviets would hope that in the vacuum which followed, popular-front-type governments might rise, in which Arab Communists would play important roles. This theory gains additional credence when the situation in Syria is recalled. Of all Arab lands Syria is the one most deeply infiltrated by Communists. In part this is the result of the welter of confused politics which has dominated Syria almost since the country achieved independence in 1945. And special impetus was given to Communist efforts in Syria following the overthrow of Army dictator Adib Shishakly in February, 1954, which ushered in a period of near political anarchy in the Syrian state.

Since that time a wide variety of conflicting political elements, none with a clear majority or popular mandate, has occupied the Syrian Parliament, and the Syrian Army, as in the past, has grown increasingly restive at the inability of Syrian politicians to chart a definite path. This time, however, these Army circles include officers of left-wing tendency, some of them in sympathy with the fellow-traveling Arab Socialist Resurrection Party of Akram Hourani. An Army *coup* today, by no means ruled out by diplomatic observers, might result in a left-wing junta rule of Syria quite different from the conservative anti-Communist regime of the fallen Shishakly.

On other fronts Syrian Communists have been active. Khaled Bekdash, a forceful and prominent Communist of Kurdish descent, was elected to the Syrian Parliament in September, 1954, making him the only admitted Communist to hold a parliamentary seat in the Arab world. In addition Bekdash sits on several parliamentary committees, including that on foreign affairs. Bekdash is believed to head both Syrian and Lebanese Communists, operating as a single unit, and to head up as well underground Communist activities throughout the Arab world. In other words Syria, in the diplomatic view, is believed to be the center of Communist espionage in the area.

In the 1954 election Syrian Communists polled 45,000 votes in a total population of 3,100,000, many of whom were ineligible to, or did not, vote. In particular Communists operate a lever on Syrian affairs through their association with the Arab Socialist Resurrection Party in a "popular-front" type of alliance. Through this alliance Communist influence extends, directly and indirectly, into the Syrian Army which in practice holds the balance of political power in the country.

An Associated Press report some time ago noted the estimate of an American Embassy official in Damascus that one-third of Damascus newspapers follow the Communist line, another third frequently support the Communists, and the remaining third are neutral. Even among these last, the report said, almost every paper has at least one known Leftist in a key position.

Syrian trade unions and a variety of cultural organizations are other fields in which Communists are known to operate. In some rural areas, according to the Associated Press report, Communists have set up "private" primary schools, and urban bookshops feature large displays of Communist literature, attractively bound and cheaply priced. Forty-eight hours after the fall of Dienbienphu in Indochina, two Communist books on the surrender of the French garrison, printed in Arabic, were on sale in Damascus.

To counteract this trend, the United States Information Service in Damascus has started a "book club," the first in the Middle East, which offers Syrian subscribers 13 books a year for about $1.50. Primarily the book club offers familiar American reading—Mark Twain, for example—in an effort to crowd Communist publications out of Syrian hands. Once every six months openly anti-Communist literature is offered.

In an effort to frustrate the Baghdad Pact, Egypt has engaged Syria, Saudi Arabia, and Yemen in military pacts under which the armed forces of the four countries have been merged under over-all Egyptian command. Given the known infiltration of communism in Syria, it is conceivable that military information given to Syria by these other Arab states might find its way clandestinely to Israeli and Soviet Communists. This is especially true in the present atmosphere, when Communist-bloc overtures are being warmly welcomed by Arabs in general. It is noteworthy in this respect that Arab Communists openly have urged that Israel be considered a permanent entity in the Middle East, and that Israeli Communists did not join in a Knesset (parliament) resolution October 24, 1955, condemning the sale of Communist arms to Egypt.

To trace Syria's political history since World War II is to understand why this country has become the spearhead of Communist activities in the Arab world. In the first place, Syria is the most anti-Western of all the Arab states. Reasons for this are complex, but they had their beginnings in the fact that Damascus, late in the nineteenth century, became the center of Arab nationalism, dedicated to the expulsion of the Ottomans, and later of the British and French. With the emergence of the Palestine problem, Syrian xenophobia extended to include the United States, because of the latter's role in the creation of Israel.

No Jew is allowed to enter Syria, even as a tourist. At one period Syria refused to grant a visa to any traveler who had a Cyprus visa in his passport, on the assumption that anyone who had visited Cyprus had done so en route to Israel. (A clandestine way to enter Israel from the Arab world was to fly to Cyprus, obtain an Israeli visa on a separate piece of paper, and destroy the paper when the visit was done. Thus the passport showed only a Cyprus visa. The great bulk of visitors to Cyprus, of course, sought a vacation in a garden spot that was quiet until Cypriote feeling against the British broke out.)

Since World War II, when Syria gained her independence from France, Syrian politics have been violent, almost chaotic, reflecting the inability of any one group to govern long with the support of the people. In 1949 alone there were three military *coups d'etat*, followed by a fourth in February, 1954, when the dictatorship of Colonel Adib Shishakly was overthrown. The present political situation in Syria is a weak mixture of party alignments, into which Arab Communists have penetrated deeply.

For more than three years after World War II Syrian politics were dominated by leaders of the National Bloc, notably Shukri el-Kuwatly, Jamil Mardam Bey, Saadullah el-Jabr, and others. These men, who had spent their lives fighting for the independence of their country, proved singularly inept at evolving a forward-looking policy for Syria as a whole, once freedom had been achieved. Indeed, their critics charged that leaders of the National Bloc sought chiefly to perpetuate their own rule.

A tenet of these men was republicanism, and hence the National Bloc opposed any larger unification of the Arab world, in which the identity of Syria would be submerged. In particular this meant opposition to the Greater Syria scheme advanced by the Hashemite kingdoms of Iraq and Jordan, under which one vast Arab state was to be created, comprising Syria, Lebanon, Jordan, Palestine, and Iraq. In the Hashemite view this new state was to be a kingdom, under a Hashemite crown.

Some Syrian groups also favored a Greater Syria, though not under Hashemite rule. These groups included the Syrian Socialist National Party of Anton Saadeh, with a following in Lebanon as well as Syria, and the People's Party, founded by a group of Aleppo men who were semi-Socialist, pan-Arabist, and who believed in democratic principles, as opposed to the leadership cult of Saadeh's party.

Gradually the National Bloc—feudal in nature and dominated by wealthy landed interests—and the antifeudal People's Party became the main poles of Syrian politics, around which lesser interests revolved. Then came the Palestine War in 1948, whose bungling by the National Bloc exposed the regime's weakness and caused a near-revolution in the country, quelled only through the utmost efforts of Colonel Husni Zaim, Syrian Army chief of staff. When the Kuwatly group tried to shift blame for the Palestine debacle to the army, Colonel Zaim overthrew the government in the first of 1949's three military *coups d'etat*.

The Zaim regime professed to aim at a "New Order" of reforms, including the extension of suffrage to literate women, curbs on the Moslem clergy, separation of church and state, a new civil code based on European models, and inauguration of large-scale public works. Externally, Colonel Zaim leaned first toward cooperation with Iraq and Jordan, who were Syria's best customers for grain, and then switched radically to a policy of alignment with Egypt and Saudi Arabia, chief opponents of the Hashemite kings and the Greater Syria scheme. Saudi gold and Egyptian diplomatic backing of Zaim were factors in the shift.

This about-face on the Greater Syria plan lost for Zaim the support of many young pan-Arabists, who had seen in the colonel a champion of reform. Their loss, together with Zaim's gradual assumption of almost royal trappings, his ban on all political parties and suspension of the Constitution, and, above all, his lack of momentum toward real reform, caused with stunning swiftness his seizure and execution by Colonel Sami Hinnawi, leader of the second *coup* of the year.

This *coup*, according to Hinnawi, was undertaken to fulfill the aims of the first *coup*, betrayed by Zaim. To this end the new leader pledged the election of a Constituent Assembly, which would draw up a new constitution to replace that suspended by Zaim. In the November, 1949, elections to this Constituent Assembly, boycotted by the National Bloc, the People's Party emerged with the largest number of seats. Not unnaturally, therefore, Colonel Hinnawi turned away from the Egyptian-Saudi Arabian axis and opened negotiations with Iraq and Jordan, a move in which he was backed by the People's Party, a consistent supporter of Greater Syria.

To forestall any move toward union with Iraq, an army clique led by Lieutenant Colonel Adib Shishakly deposed Hinnawi in the final *coup* of the year. Declaring himself opposed to union with Iraq, Colonel Shishakly set about implementing the aims of the first *coup*, working through a parliamentary regime in which the army's chief civilian spokesman was Akram Hourani, leader of a Socialist-minded group which later was organized as the Arab Socialist Resurrection Party.

Prominent during the years of the Shishakly regime was the virulently anti-American tone of the Syrian press, taking its cue from the government, a tone deriving from the Truman administration's support of Israel. Also apparent during these years was a persistent campaign on the part of National Bloc and People's Party leaders to sabotage the program of Shishakly. This clandestine campaign, conducted by men whose authority had been rudely diminished by the successive military *coups*, had a good deal to do with slowing down the reforms which Shishakly had hoped to introduce.

So effectively did old-time political leaders hamper his efforts during the period when Shishakly tried to govern through a parliamentary regime, that in 1951 the Syrian leader dissolved Parliament, suspended the Constitution of 1950, and thrust the army into the forefront as the country's visible governing force. Increasingly from that time on Shishakly was forced to devote his efforts toward combating the negativism of the now-underground politicians and toward consolidating his position within the army itself, which on more than one occasion provided groups of officers intent on removing him from power.

One result of this preoccupation with security was that his program of reforms in the fields of education, social legislation, and land reform never began rolling as he had hoped. Furthermore, his early popular support began to slacken to apathy toward a leader who was not delivering at a pace which the public had been led to expect.

In a dramatic effort to increase his popular appeal and to attract to his government some responsible civilian support, Shishakly promulgated a new Constitution in June, 1953, had himself elected President, and announced that parliamentary elections would be held in October. Almost immediately the leaders of the dissolved political parties—whose only basis of unity was opposition to Shishakly—banded together in the so-called National Pact, demanded a return to the Constitution of 1950, and announced they would not participate in elections. The result was that in October Shishakly's regime gained a parliamentary façade, but it was a Parliament comprised almost entirely of members of his own "party," the Arab Liberation Movement, and which in no way represented an accretion of political support to him.

Emboldened by the fact that they had not been arrested after the National Pact was formed, leaders of this coalition —spearheaded by the National Bloc and People's Party—then met in open defiance of Shishakly's "parties and societies law" and let it be known that they had decided on a program of action "in case something happened to President Shishakly." It was this chain of events, culminating in violent antigovernment student demonstrations in Aleppo, Damascus, and elsewhere, that led Shishakly on January 27, 1954, to arrest 13 of Syria's most prominent politicians, invoke martial law, and thus expose himself as a military leader bereft of important civilian support and dependent upon his army for continuing tenure in office.

Less than a month later the blow fell. Colonel Shishakly, who had seized power at the head of a *coup*, was deposed in the same manner, and the Syrian strong man fled his native land. This time the army *coup* was backed by the National Pact, which, after an interim period, brought Shukri el-Kuwatly, the old National Bloc leader and fighter for independence, back from exile in Egypt and made him President of Syria, a post he still holds.

Apart from politics, Syria is rich in economic and agricultural potential, though plagued by the same brand of feudalism which marks Iraq. Syria is medium-sized as Arab countries go, containing 66,000 square miles (a little larger than Illinois), of which roughly one-third is cultivable. East of the Anti-Lebanon range which forms the Lebanese-Syrian frontier lies the oasis of Damascus, where many fruits are grown. North of Damascus a plateau slopes eastward to the Euphrates valley, while even farther to the east, comprising the northeast corner of Syria, lies the Jezira, a region of hills, fertile valleys, and some desert. South of Damascus the plateau of Hauran rises toward the east to the somber heights of the Jebel Druze, 6,000 feet above sea level. The northern plateau, the Jezira, and the Hauran are suitable for cereals. East and south of the plateau stretches the barren Syrian desert, good only for nomadic pasturage.

Total population of Syria is about 3,100,000, of which perhaps 500,000 are nomads or seminomads, the former breeding camels and sheep, the latter cultivating the land as well as raising sheep and cattle. Sixty per cent of Syria's population is agricultural, much of it in a depressed state of tenantry. Almost 70 per cent of Syrians are Sunni Moslems, with Moslems of various schismatic sects comprising another 15 per cent. Ninety thousand Druzes, or roughly three per cent of the total population, inhabit the fastnesses of the Jebel Druze, ultimately responsible to the government at Damascus, but almost autonomous in local affairs. Something less than 15 per cent of Syrians are Christians of various sects, chiefly Catholic and Orthodox.

As indicated in preceding pages, Syria's postwar political history provides a key to understanding why the Communists, presenting a definite program in a country wracked by indecision, have been able to penetrate so deeply into Syrian life. Because of a vitiating struggle for power among rival political groups, Syria is possibly the least stable politically of all Arab lands. And the struggle is far from ended. Under President El Kuwatly the issue of union with Iraq has been shelved. But popular pressure for such a move still is as strong as ever among certain groups, and the tendency of this inner conflict is toward the kind of immobility of government which bred the former *coups*.

Notable in this respect is the growth of Akram Hourani's Arab Socialist Resurrection Party and its increased fellow-traveler tinge. Marked also is the ability of Syrian Communists, given the political vacuum existing in the country, to influence Syrian cultural, journalistic, and political life to a degree that makes Syria the most likely Arab land to produce the kind of popular-front government which the Soviets desire.

With Syria particularly in mind, it is possible that the Soviet Union, despite her arms aid and economic offers to the Arabs, is aiming at the very condition which would do Arab leaders the most harm; namely, a second round of Arab-Israeli fighting in which the Arabs would be defeated.

The aftermath of such a situation might well be the direct intrusion of the Soviets into Middle Eastern affairs.

On February 13, 1956, Moscow made it clear that it considers the Middle East within its own orbit of interest by warning the West against sending troops to that area without a prior agreement and United Nations approval. This warning followed the so-called Declaration of Washington, in which President Eisenhower and British Prime Minister Sir Anthony Eden referred obliquely to an international army to guard the frontiers between Israel and the Arab states. Though the Western leaders spoke specifically only of willingness to support any UN action to preserve Middle Eastern peace, both British paratroopers on Cyprus and the United States Mediterranean Sixth Fleet have been cited by observers as elements already on hand to maintain peace. The Moscow warning said in part:

> Any act such as the entry of foreign troops on the territory of nations of the Middle and Near East, without the prior agreement of interested governments and without the sanction of the Security Council of the United Nations, would be a rude disruption of the principles of the United Nations and the sovereignty of a number of nations.
>
> The Foreign Ministry considered it necessary to state again that any activities aimed at complicating and increasing tension in the region of the Middle and Near East cannot but be a matter of legal jurisdiction and interest for the Soviet Union.

In particular the Soviet statement aimed at invalidating the 1950 Tripartite Declaration of the United States, Britain, and France, by which the three nations pledged themselves to preserve the territorial integrity of Israel and the Arab states. By forcing any Western action into the Security Council, the Soviets, through their veto, would hope to forestall Western punitive action in the Middle East, or make such action appear to be a flaunting of the UN's will.

The Soviet aim would be to permit any Arab-Jewish fighting to take its natural course, with the likely result of an Arab defeat.

The Soviet offensive in the Arab world has a second prong, however, and that is economic penetration. Should Arab-Israeli fighting not develop, the Soviets still hope, by offering technical assistance and economic aid, to shift Arab trade and economic dependence from West to East. In this campaign the Soviets are aided by the fact that they appear to be preaching, not political revolution, but beneficial trade, and second by the fact that they are offering to buy the agricultural products which the Arabs must sell and which the Western powers now largely reject.

Though large-scale Communist technical assistance inevitably would bring Soviet technicians into the Middle East, the Arabs appear to feel no great concern. When Colonel Nasser was asked about this very thing by J. B. Slade-Baker, special representative of *The Sunday Times*, the Egyptian leader replied:

> Czechoslovakia and Russia naturally wish to establish and maintain good relations with us. To attempt to spread Communist propaganda would create a bad impression and worsen relations. The news of the arms deal is of far more value to them than any amount of propaganda. To equal it they would have to spend 100,000,000 pounds. Its effect has been felt throughout the Arab world and beyond.[3]

This enthusiasm for external Communist aid stands in marked contrast to the attitude of Arab governments toward their own internal Communists. The Communist party is outlawed in every Arab state (including Syria, despite the presence of Khaled Bekdash in Parliament). Colonel Nasser himself frequently has called Egyptian Communists "trai-

[3] Copyrighted article in *The Sunday Times*, November 6, 1955.

tors to Egypt, financed by a foreign power." Long ago the
Revolution Command Council launched a campaign to
crush communism in Egypt. In part this drive partook of
raids by Interior Ministry security officials on underground
cells and the arrest of subversive agents. In other part the
campaign consisted of the military junta's attempt to dis-
credit Communists in the eyes of the masses and to pose as
the true friend of the working class.

In its land distribution program and in the setting up of
village cooperatives, the Revolution Command Council is
hoping to steal a march on the Communists by accomplish-
ing the very things which the Communists promise they
would do. The regime is working also among urban laborers by organizing social service units in the cities and by
forming progovernment unions for factory workers.

Iraq also has been stern in repressing communism. Only
200 miles south of the Soviet Union, and possessing rich
oil fields which the Soviets covet, Iraq feels directly Communist pressure from the north. This is one reason Iraq entered the Western-sponsored Baghdad Pact when no other
Arab state would join. Iraqi Premier Nuri es-Said, through
an emergency decree, has dissolved and outlawed all organizations suspected of being Communist fronts, and has
made Iraqi Communists liable to loss of citizenship and de-
portation.

Apart from Egypt and Iraq, however, other Arab states
have been less than systematic in opposing the Communists
in their midst. Saudi Arabia and Yemen claim they have no
Communists. Jordan intermittently has cracked down on
Communists, when it has been clear that they had a hand
in fomenting riots or antigovernment demonstrations.
Though Lebanon, like other Arab states, has outlawed the
Communist party, the Lebanese Government permits Com-

munists to operate in comparative freedom. Communists in Lebanon have their own newspaper, *As-Sarkha*, plus a number of fellow-traveling dailies. Syria, as noted above, has been the most lax of all in combating communism; or, to put it another way, in the confused Syrian scene the Communists have found their greatest opportunity for advancement.

Despite this generally anti-Communist stand by Arab governments internally, the Soviet Union has been able to pose in recent months as a true friend of the Arabs. To achieve this, the Soviets have lavished enormous care upon their campaign, directed toward penetration of an area which always has glittered as a Russian foreign policy prize. Since the West has dominated the Middle East so long and has become unpopular in the process, it became necessary for the Soviets to stress the similarities between the Arab countries and themselves, and the sharp differences between the Soviet Union and the West, and between the Arab countries and the West. In this the Soviets were aided by their general absence from the area since World War II, when the Arabs became most politically conscious. The Arabs, in other words, were less aware of the Soviet Union and her methods than they were of the Western powers.

Knowing that the Arabs, bitter over the experience of the mandates, considered colonialism an enemy second only to Zionism, the Soviets stressed the anticolonial nature of the socialist creed which they profess. Here again the Soviets were aided by the fact that vast numbers of Middle Easterners had little knowledge of the ruthless colonial system operated by the Soviet Union in her own satellites. Instead, as concerned the immediate experience of the Arabs, the Soviets came to the Middle East with clean hands.

Also welcome to Arab ears was the Soviet stress on "neutralism," or coexistence, as opposed to the military blocs which the West was urging on them and which, to the Arabs, smacked of a new form of colonialism because of the source from which they came. Seeking a new national identity in the midst of the pressures of Westernization, the Arabs found a retreat to neutralism far more attractive than a new proximity to the powerful West in the form of junior partnerships in military alliances.

Above all, the Soviets sought to make it clear that they were coming, not to communize, but to extend a neighborly hand toward the improvement of economic relations. Confronted by a West which sought to ally them militarily, but often rejected them economically, many Arabs saw in the Soviet offers a straw at which to grasp. "The West prods the Arabs into alliances," Mario Rossi wrote in *The Christian Science Monitor*, "which the Arabs fear would cause them to lose whatever identity they have acquired so far. The Soviets prefer to insert themselves in the present evolutionary process of Arab nationalism. Their aims are not immediate, like those of the West, but fraught with consequences. For the Soviets have realized that in order to penetrate the Middle East (and Asia as well) they must proclaim loudly their resolve not to interfere."[4]

The Soviet campaign to achieve an Arab climate in which the Russians could work predated by far the conclusion of the Czechoslovak-Egyptian arms deal, which was the overt act bringing Soviet aims forcibly to the attention of the West. In particular the Soviets saw in the ulemas, or Moslem religious councils, a vocal opponent of communism in the Middle East. To mollify this important group the Soviets developed a campaign to persuade Mos-

[4] *The Christian Science Monitor*, February 6, 1956.

lem leaders that freedom of worship for Moslems had been restored in the U.S.S.R.

In this campaign the Soviets were joined by the Chinese Communists, who were at pains to convince the Arabs that freedom of religion for Moslems never had been abrogated in Communist China. Thus an Egyptian religious leader was invited to visit China after the Bandung conference (at which Colonel Nasser was studiously lionized by the Communists) and came back favorably impressed with the religious freedom which he believed he had seen. Similarly carefully conducted tours of the Soviet Union have been made by Moslem leaders from the Arab world. (At least one such tour backfired for the Communists when an important Egyptian journalist toured methodically what he was allowed to see, and reported back to his readers that the Soviet Union was, in effect, a police state.)

As part of their campaign the Soviets increasingly posed as the friends of the Arabs in the Palestine issue, seeking to stand in contrast to what the Arabs regarded as the pro-Israeli position of the Western powers. A notable instance was the Soviet championing of the Syrian case after the Israeli Galilean attack in December, 1955. So effective were Russian tactics that the United States, Britain, and France were forced to sponsor a sterner condemnation of Israel than they had intended, to avoid being completely outmaneuvered by the Soviets.

Apart from whatever policies the Soviets themselves may attempt, there are, according to Arab scholars, certain factors deep within the Arab character which make it easier for many Moslems to listen to the Communists than to cooperate with the Christian West. These scholars point out that the basic outlook of Islam itself, plus the long history of Islamic-Christian warfare, has given many Moslems a deep-seated prejudice against Christianity which influences their general attitude toward the West. Though far anterior to the mandates, this prejudice was buttressed by the colonial activities of the Western powers. No such historic prejudice exists against communism, however, and the relative decline of Islam as an intellectual force motivating the upper classes often removes another barrier against Communist doctrine.

This is borne out by the fact that historically the appeal of communism in the Arab world has been primarily to the intelligentsia, partly because of the decay of Islamic society and many of its values, and partly because there have been in the Middle East no liberal or social-democratic forces (as in western Europe) to challenge the revolutionary appeal of communism, an appeal which found ready ears among Arab intellectuals eager to overthrow the feudal, conservative, and vested interests of the past. Gradual reforms such as those introduced by Point Four and the Near East Foundation, though gradual for a necessary purpose, failed to excite the imagination of the impatient intelligentsia.

"Communism in the Middle East," wrote Walter Z. Laqueur, "has functioned widely as a movement of a middle class revolt against feudal rule."[5] New in its political emancipation, and ignorant of actual conditions within Communist lands, the Arab middle class in many cases found no ready channel for its reformatory zeal save through the "easy" way of communism. For all except those with real stamina and conviction, it would have seemed too hard a path to try to build up social consciousness in the land through legal and parliamentary means, particularly in view of the powerful opposition of the vested interests.

[5] Walter Z. Laqueur, "The Appeal of Communism in the Middle East," *The Middle East Journal*, Vol. 9, No. 1 (Winter 1955), pp. 17-27.

Thus, communism found its widest appeal among those men who are the most promising in the Middle East when their gravitation is in the direction of moderate reform and who are the most dangerous when they slide off into extremism of the left or right. In Iran, for example, at a time when the Iranian Air Force was rife with sabotage, Iranian officials told me that if they were to remove all known Communists from the Air Force, some of their best training officers would be gone and the training program started by American military advisers would fall apart. In Cairo Colonel Nasser had still another reason to be soft on Communists in the first days of his movement. Leftists occupied key posts in the military junta which overthrew King Farouk, and the first public struggle within the regime was over the ouster of its pro-Communist members.

It is upon Arab Communists of the middle class, including army officers, together with what rabble they could rouse, that the Soviets would depend should their campaign of arms aid and technical assistance lead to a situation which the Communists might exploit. In no one thing have the Soviets been more successful so far in the Middle East than in separating their own apparent interests from the interests of those Arab Communists who are, directly or indirectly, agents of Moscow.

A United States Government study, quoted in *The New York Times*, gave a total of 50,000 members of the Communist party in Syria, Lebanon, Jordan, Egypt, Iraq, Iran, and Israel. The bulk of this membership, according to the study, was drawn from the middle class and minority groups. Little following has been gained among the peasants and urban working class, and there has been surprisingly little gain, as noted by other observers, among the Palestine

Arab refugees who still stagnate in tent camps throughout the Arab world.

Communist membership in the various countries was broken down by the study as follows: Syria and Lebanon, 18,000 (in elections the Communists poll far more votes than their membership figures); Iraq, 1,000; Jordan, 250, plus 4,000 active supporters; Egypt, fewer than 3,000; Sudan, 200 to 300; Iran, estimated at 20,000; and Israel, 3,700.[6] Since the time the report was written, early in 1954, it is probable that the number of Communists in Syria has increased, perhaps markedly, and that the number of Tudeh (Communist) supporters in Iran has declined as the renewed output of Iranian oil begins to make itself felt in Iran's internal economy.

The position of the Israeli Communist party is unique in the Middle East, in that the party is a legal entity in Israel, holding six seats in the current Knesset. Prior to the establishment of the state of Israel, the Communists had 16 local branches in Palestine, and had increased that number to 69 by the end of 1952. Similarly, Communist voting strength rose from 15,000 in the general elections of 1947 to 27,000 two years later, due mainly to the votes of Arabs and new immigrants.

Sharp reverses were suffered by Israeli Communists, however, following the 1952-1953 anti-Jewish purges of Czechoslovakia and the Soviet Union, causing not only the disaffection of Communist sympathizers within Israel but the resignation of some cardholding members as well. Since that time the Soviets' anti-Israel policy has remained generally constant, to the point that today, in statements to the Arabs, Moscow brands Israel as an "aggressive" state harboring designs upon her neighbors. Under these circumstances it is

[6] See *The New York Times*, May 10, 1954.

doubtful that Israeli Communists would hold all their six Knesset seats in a new general election.

The sheer number of new Soviet moves in the Middle East, made all the more impressive because there were so few of them before, should not obscure the fact that in no case, with the possible exception of Syria, does Arab trade with the Communists come close to the volume of business conducted between the Arab states and the Western world. Egypt, Syria, and Lebanon in particular have increased their trade with the Soviet bloc. Western goods still predominate, however, in Lebanon's free port of Beirut, while the United States, Britain, and West Germany are closely bunched as the three nations with which Egypt has the most trade. West Germany, in particular, has made recent rapid strides in the Egyptian market, as elsewhere in the Arab world.

Even Yemen, where the Soviets made impressive flourishes when renewing a 1927 treaty of friendship, still weights what little external trade it has toward the Western world. And Yemen, like Saudi Arabia to the north, granted its first petroleum and minerals concession to an American, rather than to a Communist, firm (the Yemen Development Corporation, of Washington, D. C.). Saudi Arabia, chiefly supplied by the United States and Western Europe, and the traditional British markets, Iraq and Jordan, still have little or no trade with the Communist world.

In the context of Communist penetration of the area, however, the point is not so much the volume of Arab trade with the Communists as the increased willingness of Arab states to consider such trade. In short, because Soviet influence was almost at zero before, whatever successes Moscow is able to chalk up stand as gains for the Soviets. In this their chances are enhanced by the manifest suspicion with which Westerners are regarded in the Arab world. Only the most imaginative policy on the part of the United States and Britain, it would appear, can prevent some eroding away of Western influence in the area and its consequent accretion to the Soviets.

In this whole matter Western stakes are high. Middle Eastern oil is deeply important to the United States. To Britain, however, it is vital. Britain must trade to exist, and the industrial machine which provides British goods for trade is fueled by oil from Iraq, Kuwait, and elsewhere in the Persian Gulf. Without this oil, British industry would come to a halt, and the trading empire which Britain controls would be threatened with bankruptcy by the staving in of its financial base. This in turn would diminish the value of Britain as a NATO base, vital to the United States in the alliance system of the West.[7]

In this context must be viewed British opposition to the efforts of Saudi Arabia to expand toward the Persian Gulf at the expense of the Trucial Coast sheikhdoms whose defense and foreign relations are controlled by Britain. Over the past few years the Anglo-Saudi dispute has centered on the Buraimi oasis, an oil-rich district as yet undeveloped and lying in the ill-defined desert region between Saudi Arabia and the Trucial states. In the contest over Buraimi, which British levies have occupied in the name of the Sheikh of Abu Dhabi and the Sultan of Muscat, Britain sees a Saudi expansionist threat aimed not only at the Trucial area but toward Kuwait as well, currently the largest single producer of crude oil in the Middle East. In this respect Saudi Arabia unwittingly is the ally of the Soviet Union, since the whole

[7] For a more complete discussion of this aspect of the problem, see Joseph C. Harsch, "State of the Nations," in *The Christian Science Monitor* of February 1, 1956.

trend of Saudi activities in the Persian Gulf tends toward the potential weakening of Britain, and hence the NATO alliance.

No avenue is considered too small to be followed by the Soviets in the development of their aims. The number of Armenians in the Arab world, for example, is not large, and their influence is minuscule. Yet early in 1956, when the election of a new Armenian Patriarch of Cilicia was due, the Soviet Government "allowed" Vazken Baldjian, Catholicos (Patriarch) of Eshmiazine in Soviet Armenia, to fly to Lebanon to urge the election of a patriarch friendly to Eshmiazine, i.e., the Soviets. While in Lebanon (the Cilician patriarchate is located in the town of Antelias, just outside Beirut), Catholicos Vazken called for a general conference of Armenians to reconcile the split between the patriarchates of Eshmiazine and Cilicia.

While the efforts of Vazken may have little over-all effect, they typified the thoroughness with which the Soviets are preparing the ground in their penetration of the Middle East. In his keynote address before the Twentieth Congress of the Soviet Communist Party on February 14, 1956, Nikita S. Khrushchev singled out five countries with which the Soviet Union desired a "strengthening of bonds." Three of them were Syria, Egypt, and Afghanistan. Only the success of Arab Communists within Syria, and the meaning of that success to the developing Soviet campaign, would cause the foremost spokesman of world communism to single out a country so relatively unimportant in the scheme of things.

Until a fresh Western policy is promulgated, free from the tincture of colonialism and any pro-Israel bias, the United States and Britain are largely barren of resources with which to regain the loyalties of the Arabs and undermine the Soviet campaign. Economically the Western powers are not likely to lose the field, unless the dumping of surplus American cotton drives Egyptian cotton out of the free world market. The persistence of Cairo in seeking a World Bank loan and Western aid for the High Dam at Aswan shows the basic good sense of Colonel Nasser and his advisers in this respect. Even in Afghanistan, where the Soviets have achieved their greatest economic success, Communist projects still are outmatched dollar for dollar by American commercial and technical works.

Thus, Communist economic gains in the Middle East will be relative, rather than absolute. In the more important realm of men's thinking, however, the West is at its most vulnerable, because of its record in the past. The Soviet Union will do all it can to agitate the Palestine dispute, and to fan the Arabs' already aroused suspicions against colonialism from the West. For these reasons the United States and Britain regard with gravity the Soviet campaign among the Arabs. For these reasons, also, the Middle East has moved to the center of the stage in the Cold War.

CHAPTER 10

Sunnis and the Census

Iraq's problem of feudalism can be solved, given good will on the part of the country's leaders. The same is true of Syria and its political indecisiveness. At the core of Lebanon's national life, however, is a problem almost beyond the ability of the Lebanese to solve alone. This is the confessional system, bequeathed to Lebanon by the French.

Lebanon is a small land, 120 miles from north to south and 40 miles wide, in area less than Connecticut. Within Lebanon's 3,900 square miles is a great variety of climate and scenery, giving to Lebanon the title "Switzerland of the East." A narrow coastal plain, varying in width from a few yards to several miles, fronts the Mediterranean Sea and is lush with semitropical growth. Directly to the east of the coastal plain rise the majestic Lebanons, towering to 10,000 feet in places, with peaks snow-capped from November to April.

Crossing these mountains by road, one leaves the damp heat of the coast behind and ascends by hairpin turns to a world above timberline, lost in the clouds. Then, breaking from the fog and beginning the downward trek on the other side, the traveler sees the green and pleasant valley called Bekaa, while to the east, across the valley, rise the bare red slopes of the Anti-Lebanons and Mount Hermon, beyond which lies Damascus and the Syrian hinterland. This, in brief, is Lebanon—the coastal plain, the green and folded Lebanons, the valley called Bekaa, and the foothills of Anti-Lebanon to the east. To these mountains during the Middle East's parched summer come those Arabs who can afford to from Egypt, Jordan, Iraq, and Saudi Arabia.

This tiny land is the stepchild of the French. To understand this fact, and to comprehend the country itself, it must be recalled that during the centuries of the Ottoman Empire, from 1516 to the end of World War I, the district of Lebanon meant chiefly the high mountain range called Mount Lebanon, where dwelt the Maronite Roman Catholics, virtually unconquered and independent of the Ottoman power.

To this mountain stronghold, during these centuries, fled other minorities persecuted by the Sunni Moslems of the Middle East, chief among them Shiite Moslems, Druze religionists, adherents of the Greek Orthodox Church, and finally, after World War I, the Armenians. Thus was fostered over the years the concept of Lebanon as a refuge from persecution, and gradually there was built up also the concept of French "protection" over the Maronite Roman Catholics, largest by far of the Christian groups which had sought refuge in the mountains of Lebanon.

So successfully did France press its claim of "protection" that, following World War I, France was granted a mandate over Syria and Lebanon which lasted to the close of World War II. During the mandate period France sought

to ensure for Lebanon a place unique in the Arab world—
a republic founded largely on French political and cultural
traditions, dominated by the Maronite Roman Catholic
faith, and a refuge for minorities in a predominantly Sunni
Moslem world.

To this end France carved out Lebanon as an independent
state, and, to make the new state politically and economically viable, added to Mount Lebanon four predominantly
Moslem districts of Syria, thus achieving the 55 to 45 per
cent Christian-Moslem relationship which was noted in the
official French census of 1932.

To govern such a multisided citizenry, France established
in the Lebanese Constitution a delicate and complex governmental structure which calls for the President of the
Republic to be a Christian (in practice always a Maronite),
the Premier to be a Sunni Moslem, and the Speaker of the
House to be a Shiite Moslem. The same sectarian division ob-
tains in all governmental departments, including Parliament.
Within this structure the Druzes, Armenians, Protestants,
Jews, Baha'ists, and Jehovah's Witnesses are represented
according to their percentage of the population.

This is the setup which so far has provided a system of
checks and balances on antagonisms within the community,
though at the same time it has tended to fragment political
life within the nation, thus making it difficult, if not impossible, for any government to weed out the frequent
corruption and inefficiency which has sprung up as a result
of the system. Some cabinet ministries have become by tradition the property of specific sects. The defense minister,
for example, almost always is a Druze, while the foreign
minister usually is a Maronite. Even in the civil service the
same system prevails. If the number of Sunnis in one gov-

ernment department is large, compensation must be made by increasing the number of Maronites in another department, and so on.

The cumbersome system worked fairly well during Lebanon's first years of independence, from 1943 to 1947 (Lebanon had some of the trappings of independence prior to the departure of the French in 1945), when two strong leaders, President Bishara el-Khoury and Premier Riad Solh, exercised firm paternal control over their respective Christian and Moslem communities. With the assassination of Riad Solh, however, and the enforced resignation of El Khoury in 1952, the Lebanese political scene degenerated largely into attempts by various political leaders to protect and promote the positions of those religious and feudal groups they had been elected to represent.

The Moslems of Lebanon have become increasingly restive under the system. The first open move (of insubordination, the Christians would call it) came early in 1953 when the orthodox Sunni Moslems of Lebanon, following a "general congress" in Beirut, demanded a new census in the country to determine whether or not the Moslems now were in a majority and thus entitled to take over leadership of the country. This demand, and others, were framed in a memorandum presented first to President Camille Chamoun, who, as a Maronite Christian, had been elected to replace El Khoury. Then the memorandum was distributed to Christian and Moslem organizations throughout the land, and was widely published in the Lebanese press.

Immediate reaction of the Christian sects was to convene a conference of their own, where a counterresolution was drawn up expressing "shock" over the memorandum of the Moslem congress, and seeing in it "the destruction of the basic principles on which the existence of Lebanon is founded, and a strange departure from the history and tradition of Lebanon." Of equal significance, perhaps, was the calling of a second conference by Al-Kataeb, a Christian youth movement, at which leaders of "all sects"—Christian and Moslem—set up a "watchdog" committee to defeat, if possible, the aims of the Moslem memorandum, in which the conference claimed to see a danger to the republic.

Other demands put forth in their memorandum by the Moslems included the stripping of Lebanese citizenship from all Lebanese emigrants—the majority of whom are Christian—and the granting of Lebanese citizenship to all Palestinian refugees now within the country, the great majority of whom are Moslem. There is little doubt that the granting of these last two demands would find the Moslems in a clear majority in Lebanon. Some objective Lebanese, in fact, are convinced that the higher Moslem birth rate, plus the emigration of Christian Lebanese, already have placed the Moslems in this position, though the truth of the matter is obscured by the fact that there has been no accurate population count since the French-controlled census of 1932, which found the Christians in a 55 to 45 per cent majority over Moslems. That census merely confirmed and formalized a situation which the French had built up arduously over a long period of difficult and sometimes bloodstained years.

Almost as soon as the Moslem memorandum was published, however, certain other factors made it clear that the Sunnis would not press their claims as vigorously as their circular first had made it appear. It developed, for example, that the Sunnis appeared to be speaking primarily for themselves and not for Shiite Moslems, and that their memorandum apparently was not even speaking for some of the most responsible members of their own community.

Such figures as Abdullah Yafi, Saeb Salam, and Sami Solh, all former Lebanese premiers, had been present at the Moslem general conference, yet none of them would admit to authorship of the memorandum, nor go beyond saying that such ideas had been "discussed" at the conference. The memorandum, it appeared, had been drafted by less prominent members of the congress, some of whom allegedly were influenced by such organizations as the Communist Partisans of Peace, more interested in stirring up trouble for their own ends than in attaining Sunni Moslem objectives. This lack of avowal of the memorandum by the most responsible Sunni leaders, plus the strength and determination of Christian opposition, as well as the realization that the pressing of their aims might bring on bloodshed which would be condemned strongly not only by the Western world but possibly by other Arab states, caused the Lebanese Sunnis to abandon plans for a second general conference. As a consequence, the "watchdog" committee established by the Al-Kataeb conference also slipped into abeyance.

A few months later, however, in January, 1954, the scene once again was stirred by the publication of a booklet called *Moslem Lebanon Today*, which called for the scrapping of the Lebanese Constitution and of the country's unique form of government. Charging that the Christian-dominated government deliberately discriminated against Lebanese Moslems, the booklet went on to allege that powerful Christian groups in the country were "collaborating" with Israel "to pave the way for the elimination of Moslem Lebanon" and for the formation of a totally Christian state on the northern borders of Israel.

Since no more serious charge could be brought against any Arab than that of collaboration with Israel, the booklet clearly was a major step in the Moslem campaign to undercut Christian dominance in Lebanon and replace it with Moslem rule. The booklet, whose unnamed authors claimed to represent the "Permanent Conference of Moslem Organizations of Lebanon," was viewed as a sequel to the Moslem general congress of the year before.

The booklet reinforced the claim of the earlier conference that the French mandate power deliberately wrote a Lebanese Constitution designed to perpetuate the privileged position of Lebanese Christians, and that the present government was using that Constitution to discriminate against Lebanese Moslems, who now, according to the Moslems, formed a majority of the population. (Lebanon's total population now is estimated at 1,200,000.) Not until the publication of *Moslem Lebanon Today*, however, had Moslem groups gone so far as to accuse Lebanese Christians of collaborating with Israel, and to demand that the Moslems of Lebanon, with the support of "the Arab peoples around Lebanon," organize themselves for "resistance," using "every legal means" to avoid "the same fate as the Arabs of Palestine."

Publication of the pamphlet shook responsible Lebanese of both faiths, for it is generally recognized that the present sectarian form of government—guaranteeing proportional representation to Lebanon's many sects—is all that holds in check religious frictions which otherwise might become intolerable. It is a fact that riots in Syria or Egypt, for example, take place at least within a predominantly Sunni Moslem atmosphere. In Lebanon, however, the least disturbance runs the risk of degenerating into internecine religious fighting.

Complicating the picture is the fact (as seen by observers free of the stresses of Lebanese politics) that the Moslems of Lebanon—taking together Sunnis, Shiites, and Druzes—do indeed outnumber the Christians of the land, and that the Christian-dominated government holds on to the fiction of Christian numerical superiority only by various subterfuges, which the Moslems easily expose.

It also is a fact that some of the claims of the Moslem memorandum, when viewed strictly in a "democratic" light, apart from the peculiar context of politics, contain elements of justice. The case appears particularly strong for the granting of citizenship to Palestinian refugees, not only because the Hashemite Kingdom of Jordan has set a precedent with its far larger number of refugees, but also because the Palestinians now in Lebanon would appear to be refugees in much the same sense that the ancestors of most Lebanese citizens once were.

The government's refusal to grant this citizenship is based on the claim that, with 60,000 unemployed in Lebanon already, the assimilation of 100,000 new citizens would cause economic havoc. It also is based, of course, on the claim that almost 100,000 additional Moslems would upset the sectarian balance so carefully maintained over the years.

Whether or not Lebanese emigrants should lose their citizenship is a moot point in Lebanon today, with the government claiming, as all Lebanese admit, that at least one-third of its revenue comes from those same emigrants, located chiefly in North and South America, and in Australia. (Many "Syrians" in the United States actually are Lebanese.) This financial support, the government argues, precludes the emigrants' loss of political rights.

In the last analysis, the most potent argument against governmental reform is the fact that Lebanese Christians, who achieved their privileged position in the mountains of Lebanon only after centuries of intermittent persecution in the Moslem world, almost certainly would fight against any change in the status quo. And many observers foresee actual civil war in Lebanon should the Moslems press their claims to the point of open revolt.

The situation has bred ill-feeling between Lebanon and neighboring Syria. Many Lebanese Moslems live in those districts which were geographically, ethnically, economically—indeed, in every way—parts of Syria until the French arbitrarily took them away. These Lebanese irredentists make no secret of their longing to return to the homeland. Lebanese suspicions are not wholly unfounded that some elements in Syria, even within the government, would like to seize the Moslem sections of Lebanon and incorporate them within Syria, if only it could be done without antagonizing the West and other Arab powers.

The problem lends itself to no easy solution. On the one hand, the higher Moslem birth rate will increase the pressure for a new census. The increasing fragmentation and impotence of Lebanese parliamentary life adds weight to the Moslem call for a general review. On the other hand, changes such as the Moslems advocate would destroy the very basis of Lebanon as it was established by the French.

This is the political framework within which the peoples of Lebanon—Arabs, Druzes, Armenians, and others—live, work, and play. The situation is of primary concern to them, since their daily living is involved in it. It is of lesser, but still sharp, concern to the Arabs of other lands, many of whom see in the desire of some Syrians to amalgamate Moslem Lebanon with Syria an attempt to upset the larger balance of power existing in the Arab world.

Ultimately, if the present tendency within Lebanon continues, it may involve the Western powers as well. Should civil war erupt in Lebanon, or even a disconnected series of Christian-Moslem clashes, the United States, Britain, and France in particular would have to define a concrete policy toward the largest Christian enclave in the Arab world, which, though it enjoys a privileged position within Lebanon itself, is overwhelmingly outnumbered by Moslems in the surrounding lands.

CHAPTER *11*

Plumaged Birds
Slightly Soiled

Southeast of Lebanon lies another Arab land with a problem equally grave, though of a different nature. This land is Jordan; its problem is economic. Merely to drive through Jordan is enough for the traveler to grasp this fact, for most of Jordan is either desert, fit only for the grazing of camels and sheep, or wilderness highlands, on which nothing can grow.

Indeed, except for the clothing of the village women, almost all the colors of Jordan are pale, the muted colors of a desert land. The roads are the color of dust, and the hillsides, except in springtime, are faded by the sun to a scorched tan, overlain by a faint white tracery of lines, cut by generations of hoofs and camels' feet. Yet through this pallid landscape, like plumaged birds, stride the women of Jordan, wearing, as though in rebellion against the pale coloring of their land, costumes almost breath-taking against the dun stone of the village walls.

Their feet, splayed from the burden of enormous head-borne loads, are broad and flat, hardened by years of walking on Jordan's terrain, and their skin, dark to Western eyes, is tattooed often in triangle designs of blue. Yet each but the very poorest, bearing home her load of faggots on her head, is an individual, not beautiful of face, perhaps (though sometimes even that), but lovely of line, supple and graceful as a willow as she sways beneath her head-borne load.

A sense of color, of dignity and gravity, as she strides the undulating paths of her village fields—these qualities the Arab peasant woman possesses to an astonishing degree, when one considers the barrenness of her background and surroundings. The sash about her waist, and the shawl flowing from her head (not as a veil, for village women are seldom veiled), range from vermilion to blue, while the gold embroidery of her vest stands out above a robe of black or dark green velvet.

On the road to Bethlehem, in the cool morning hours, I have seen such women returning from the market place at Bethlehem, toward which in the dark hours of night they had set out from their villages, laden with the grapes of the family vineyard or the fruits of the village trees. Along one side of the road these women would be streaming back, some in the splendid finery of their particular villages (for the dress of each village differs slightly), others in the humblest of rags, but each with a round flat basket now empty on her head, gay and tossing if the girl were young and fresh and this game of marketing still new to her, or less jaunty and more determined if the morning walk were merely one of thousands already taken by an older village Ruth.

To watch these women—to see them against the background of the meager terraced groves of figs and olives on the stony hillsides; to see one stoop, perhaps, through the door of a tiny house of worn cut stone, or pass before a great cave cut in the hillside, where a shepherd would shelter his flock that night—to see them thus, is to catch the real favor of the Bethlehem countryside, both as it is today, and as it must have been 2,000 years ago.

What a contrast between these village women and their men! At the Pool of Siloam one day, just south of Jerusalem, I saw a man labor up the stone steps from the pool, bearing two heavy cans of water. One of these a young woman took, and with a swift movement lifted it to her head and made off, the line of her back unstrained, straight as an arrow. Behind her toiled the man, the water from the second can splashing about his knees, as he lugged it with both hands. A little girl hailed him and he set down the can so that the child might drink. By this time the young woman had disappeared into a stone house far up on the hillside.

As in this case, so generally, the village man comes off second best in comparison with the village girl. A part of this, a great part, is due to the fact that the poor land of Jordan will not support the full-bodied labor of every man, and the result of lack of opportunity too often is apathy and indolence. But beyond indolence is custom, decreeing what an Arab man may and may not do; and to many villagers, housework, marketing, and even much of the field work as well, fall within the forbidden list.

The result, though there are exceptions in every place, is that the village girl seldom is idle and her menfolk often are, frequently sitting dully in groups about the thresholds. One wonders at first that this is not an Amazonian society, since the women are so much more active than their men. Yet such is not the case. Indeed, within the village the man is unquestioned master, so much so that, to many village girls, the walk to the market place is a lark and an outing, the only freedom of their day, when they can laugh and chat, one woman to another, across the dusty roads.

Change comes slowly in rural Jordan, and it is difficult to draw a moral in this pale and famous land. Western dress, as adopted by the girls in Jordan's larger towns, may imply a certain kind of freedom or escape, but it will be years before the freedom thus symbolized penetrates the villages of stone and mud. And it will be just as many years, for better or for worse, before the village girls, graceful symbols of their strictured life, cease their barefoot morning walks to the markets miles away.

A part of the land in which they live once was called Palestine, before the political entity of that name disappeared after the Arab-Israeli war of 1948. Today east and west banks of the Jordan River have been joined in the Hashemite Kingdom of Jordan. To reach this land of Jordan from Lebanon (the accustomed route) the traveler may either fly, crossing the Lebanons, the valley of the Bekaa, and the Anti-Lebanons, then swinging south through the sky down the valley of the Jordan River to Jerusalem, which crowns the Judean Hills; or he may drive across the Bekaa, through the passes of the Anti-Lebanons to Damascus, capital of Syria.

From Damascus the road strikes south through a light tan landscape, past mud villages whose walls, baked hard by the sun, are marked by the small dark holes of windows above the dusty streets, from which the houses rise like great square bubbles of mud. An occasional patch of dark green evergreens marks an oasis, with a village clustered about it. Dull water glints in a stream as the traveler passes. Now and then a rider on horseback, his clothing ragged but his dark face haughty, stares down at the passing car. Long swaths of yellow wheat and brighter clover climb up gentle slopes as though stroked on with a brush. Mile after mile the fields of wheat and yellow clover stretch, with the mountains of the Jebel Druze misty in the distance to the east.

Now and then a somber village looms on a small hill to one side or the other, somber because its buildings are made, not of mud, but of the black lava through which the road now runs. Here and there a threshing floor in such a village is set off by a stone fence, and inside lies the golden wheat, with men tossing it high in the air with pitchforks to let the chaff spin away in the wind, and the wheat fall in a golden rain back to the ground.

Suddenly the lava is gone, and once again the land on either side is alternately tan and light gold beneath the burning sun. Over the slopes of the land wander herds of camels, sometimes in long single lines, their great necks thrust forward, their bodies almost the color of the sand, with here and there a white camel in the herd. Always the landscape is the same, beneath a sky milky with haze at the horizon, ranging to deeper blue at the zenith, with white puffballs of cloud drifting high.

Flocks of black goats move over the tan of the earth, and an occasional Bedouin's black tent is pitched on a slope. This is nomad country, and the Bedouins file past on their way to a new location, a girl stretched out on a camel's back, sleeping, as it undulates along. The hair of some of the men is long and curly, falling in dirty ringlets down to their shoulders, framing their sun-darkened faces. These are lean people, always on the move, always searching, wandering as their forbears for millennia before them over the same barren plains and slopes. It is a landscape of pleasing desert colors, in which the human actors and the camels parade slowly and soundlessly by. And through this ageless scene the ribbon of road cuts, and the modern cars and busses speed.

This is the Hashemite Kingdom of Jordan, which, like Lebanon, lives with a grave problem to be solved. Lebanon's problem of confessionalism in government, however sharp it is, in a sense is easier to solve than is Jordan's, for Lebanese leaders, theoretically at least, have it within their power to subjugate their differences. Jordan, however, cannot even exist without outside support. A glance at a map explains why this is so. One look is enough to show that the angular borders of this strange desert land were drawn not for economic reasons but for compulsions of an entirely different sort. Indeed, here is a land which is three-fifths desert and whose remaining territory is too underdeveloped to feed and support the 1,400,000 persons now dwelling within the realm.

Yet out of the history which brought this barren state into being have sprung four factors which make Jordan of compelling interest: the existence of many of Christendom's holy places within her borders, her possession of the best-trained army in the Arab world, her joint 350 miles of border with the Jewish state of Israel, and Jordan's pivotal place in the relations between Iraq and Egypt. Such are the legacies of history which began April 1, 1921, when the British called an Arabian prince named Abdullah, second son of King Hussein of the Hejaz, to be Amir of Transjordan under a British mandate. For generations the desert tribesmen of the area which Abdullah took over had known little interference from the Ottoman Turks who nominally ruled them, a situation which had been rudely interrupted by World War I battles between the German-supported

Turks and the British-supported Arab army which had come up from Hejaz under Prince Feisal and Lawrence of Arabia.

The outcome of these desert battles was the short-lived establishment of Feisal in Damascus as monarch of the Arab kingdom of Syria, and his subsequent deposition by the French. It was then that Abdullah, at the head of a large tribal force, appeared in Transjordan with the avowed aim of marching north to Damascus and restoring the Syrian kingdom to his younger brother, Feisal. Unwilling to see an outbreak of fighting between their chief allies in the Middle East—the Hashemite princes of Hejaz and the French—the British persuaded Abdullah to give up his foray in return for the Amirate of Transjordan.

Thus there was carved out of the desert the economically artificial state of "across" Jordan—whose frontiers, however geographically odd they might appear to outsiders, were perfectly logical from the points of view of the British and Abdullah. At the same time Britain had given an important job to an ambitious Hashimi prince through whom the British could guarantee stability in the area, and had also secured the final link in the British-controlled land route from the Mediterranean to the Persian Gulf—the so-called imperial lifeline to India. Across those land links was soon to be built the magnificent "imperial highway" called the Haifa-Baghdad road, now potholed from constant use.

From the standpoint of the outside world the Bedouin Amirate of Transjordan, utterly dependent economically upon British subsidy, slumbered peacefully between World Wars I and II, its chief "foreign" problem being halting tribal raiding between Jordanian Bedouins and fierce Wahhabi tribesmen of Arabia's Ibn Saud, who in 1924 had driven Abdullah's father, Hussein, from the Hejaz.

To the end of pacifying the Jordanian-Saudi border, the British built the nucleus of that famous desert force known as the Arab Legion, soon to mushroom into the most effective fighting force in the Arab world and the only Arab army to give a markedly good account of itself during the Palestine War. A familiar sight to every traveler in Jordan today are the Arab legionnaires, trim and hard in British-type uniforms surmounted by red and white kaffiyahs and black agals (head bands), with silver daggers in their belts—including sons of the desert not only from Jordan but from Hejaz, Syria, Iraq, and elsewhere. For the Arab Legion and for stability in the area Britain paid a price—the price of an increasing subsidy to help keep this state afloat.

In 1946 Britain granted political independence to Jordan (economic independence being beyond her power to grant). Elevating his own title to that of king, Abdullah now dreamed of ruling a Greater Syria. Following the Arab-Israeli war of 1948, he took a first step in that direction by unilaterally annexing to Transjordan all of Palestine not occupied by Israel.

Though this move angered the other Arabs, there was little they could do but accept it. Abdullah, for his part, renamed his enlarged state the Hashemite Kingdom of Jordan. Abdullah's new accretions, however, brought troubles as well as added influence to the king. Jordan's population had been more than doubled by those Palestinians who lived in the annexed portion of the land. In addition, Abdullah had to feed and shelter more than 400,000 refugees from other parts of Palestine, who had been displaced by the Arab-Israeli war. To these homeless people Abdullah offered Jordanian citizenship, an example which remains to this day the sole instance of an Arab state giving citizenship to those refugees who fled to it during the Palestine War.

Before the annexation, Transjordan had been a Bedouin kingdom, with a largely nomadic or seminomadic population, illiterate and unversed in Western ways. Following the annexation, however, the new Jordan gained a body of citizens many of whom had been educated and trained by the British. This changed the political complexion of the land. Indeed, it was not long before the new Jordanians—"west bankers," they were called, because they came from the west bank of the Jordan River—occupied half the seats in parliament and held several ministerial posts.

These newcomers tended to scorn the patriarchal outlook of those deputies and ministers from east Jordan, "Bedouin land," and differences of opinion grew sharp. A grave example of this were the riots which shook Jordan during the winter of 1955-56, when former Palestinians, "west bankers," urged on by Egypt and Saudi Arabia, demonstrated against reports that Jordan might join the Baghdad Pact. In the eyes of these former Palestinians, the Baghdad Pact was a gigantic swindle on the part of the West, designed to make the Arabs forget Palestine by creating a Soviet scare in the north. To many "old" Jordanians, on the other hand, membership in the Baghdad Pact looked like an opportunity to acquire additional economic and military help. This divergence of outlook, which on that occasion threatened the very foundations of the kingdom, still is a central fact of Jordan's political life, though Abdullah himself is gone, victim of an assassin's bullet in 1951, and his 20-year-old grandson, Hussein, reigns in his stead.

Another central fact of Jordanian life is the Arab Legion, Jordan's army. This first-class formation, estimated at 20,000 men (Jordan keeps exact figures secret), was founded by the British and, until March 1, 1956, was commanded by them. On that date King Hussein, to mollify anti-Western sentiment still running high in his country after the Baghdad Pact riots, dismissed Lieutenant General John Bagot Glubb as commander of the Arab Legion and announced that no British officer from that time on would exercise command function within the Legion. Despite Glubb Pasha's dismissal, Britain continues to pay $22,500,-000 yearly to support the Arab Legion. Jordan herself, as poor a land as ever, cannot pay for such a luxury.

Military subsidy to Jordan is only part of the story. In economic aid during 1956 Britain gave Jordan an additional $10,000,000, a subsidy which has risen steadily over the years since Britain first drew lines in the desert and called them Jordan. The harsh fact is that Jordan is dependent upon whatever country gives her the financial means to live. This fact is apparent not only to Jordanians, but to other Arabs as well. To this end Egypt, Syria, and Saudi Arabia, determined to keep Jordan in their camp of the Arab world, have proposed giving Jordan $280,000,000 over a 10-year period, to enable the kingdom to "escape" from British influence. So far King Hussein has rejected the terms of the Arab offer, which would require him to jettison his subsidy from Britain. Any substitution of Arab for British subsidy would appear to put Jordan under new control, primarily that of Egypt, a situation which the Egyptians are anxious to achieve.

The eastern part of Jordan is largely desert, but in the western portion of the country exists the Great Rift, one of the most striking geographic features on earth. This great fold in the earth's crust first is discernible in the north in the course of the Orontes River of Syria, which flows southward until the Great Rift assumes the form of the Bekaa valley of Lebanon. South of the Bekaa, like a snow-capped sentinel above the plain, rises Mount Hermon, source of the

Jordan River. This famous stream drops southward along the Great Rift, through the Sea of Galilee, the level of the land sinking lower and lower, until, where the Jordan empties into the Dead Sea, the lowest known point on the globe's surface is reached, 1,292 feet below sea level. South of the Dead Sea the Great Rift rises gradually toward sea level, temporarily above it, then sinks to ocean level again at the Gulf of Aqaba, which itself is part of the Great Rift.

From a point south of the Sea of Galilee to the Gulf of Aqaba the Great Rift runs through Jordan. East of the Jordan valley in the Dead Sea region rise the tumbled Mountains of Moab, from which Moses looked down at the oasis of Jericho, while to the west of the Jordan rears the wilderness of Judea, crowned on its highest hills by Jerusalem, half in Arab and half in Israeli hands.

Many of Christendom's holy spots are in Jordan, including the Jordan River itself, Jericho, the Mount of Temptation, Garden of Gethsemane, Bethlehem, and the Via Dolorosa in Jerusalem. Nazareth is in Israel, across the armistice line from Jordan. Twice each year, at Christmas time and Easter, the barriers are lifted for Christians in Israel to visit the holy spots in Jordan. Then the Arab Legion and Israeli Army, instead of facing each other as potential enemies, become policemen to direct the flow of traffic.

Jordan's area, including Arab Palestine, is estimated at 36,340 square miles, somewhat smaller than New York state. Its population is 1,400,000, of which more than 400,-000 are refugees, many of whom still live in tent camps maintained by the United Nations. The bulk of east Jordan's indigenous population is in various stages of transition from nomadism to settled life. Jordan's population is overwhelmingly Sunni Moslem, though there is a Caucasian minority of about 10,000 persons—fair-haired, clannish, and distinctive in dress—who are Shiite Moslems. About 30,000 Christian Arabs, mostly of the Greek Orthodox community, lived in Jordan before the annexation of Arab Palestine. The latter event somewhat swelled the total of Christians, through the introduction of Christian Arab townsmen, though the bulk of Jordan's new citizens, including the refugees, were Sunni Moslems.

Jordan's recent political history has only reinforced the fundamental fact that the kingdom, as a poor and under-developed state with no economic reason for existing, has become a pawn in the designs of stronger neighbors. King Hussein's hasty dismissal of Glubb Pasha as commander of the Arab Legion did not change the economic aspects of the case. The fact that Glubb's dismissal was a blow to the British, and that relations between Jordan and the great power which created it have become more tenuous than in the past, does not alter Jordan's absolute dependence upon outside support.

The fact is that there are few natural resources in this largely desert land, and none of them is well developed. There is potash in the Dead Sea, fish in the Gulf of Aqaba, deposits of phosphates and manganese, and some wheat-growing land in the western highlands. It is now the policy of British, Jordanian, and American experts, working in concert, to develop these resources and at the same time to build up the port of Aqaba, thus hoping to evade the heavy transportation charges on goods which now must be hauled in and out of Jordan through the Lebanese port of Beirut and the way station of Damascus.

Ambitious plans exist for utilizing the waters of the Yarmuk and Jordan rivers in the creation of an estimated 11,570 new farm holdings in the Jordan valley, a plan which might be greatly facilitated should Israel and the Arabs agree jointly on distribution and storage of Jordan River water. All these projects are vital. Yet if all of them so far envisioned by British, Jordanian, and Point Four economists should be realized, it is highly doubtful that Jordan could support more than two-thirds its present population without outside subsidy.

Few things could be more deceptive, then, than the brave appearance of prosperity put up by the new cut-stone buildings rising all over Jordan's capital city of Amman. Up and down the slopes of the dusty river valley along which Amman is built, handsome villas and apartment houses of native white stone are springing up and renting at prices which in some cases return the total investment of their owners within five to eight years.

Supporting such a pattern in most countries would be an industrial or agricultural boom of similar proportions. In Jordan, however, there is almost no industry, only 10 per cent of the land is arable, and the nation bends beneath a yearly trade deficit in the neighborhood of $39,000,000. The answer to Amman's strange boom, which has transformed a sleepy desert town into a minor metropolis, lies elsewhere.

It began with the $56,000,000 brought in by some of the refugees who flooded into the country after the Palestine War, money which found few investment channels except in new homes for those Jordanians and Palestinians who could afford them, for the foreigners of the diplomatic colony, and in municipal and state buildings for the government. Already, however, this artificial injection of capital has begun to dry up, and many Jordanians foresee the day when the boom will slacken, rents will tumble, and Amman will provide one more evidence that this country is basically as poor as when the British carved it out of the Syrian desert more than 30 years ago.

In other words, whether Jordan's subsidy continues to come from Britain, or is paid by Saudi Arabia and Egypt, does not remove Jordan's basic need for aid of some sort in order to exist. It can be argued that the hegemony of Britain allows Jordan more freedom of action, more of political independence, than would control by Egypt and Saudi Arabia, seeking to build their own power bloc in the Middle East. In either case, however, Jordan's underlying problem of economic insufficiency has not been solved.

Only in union with Iraq, her sisterly Hashemite kingdom, could Jordan, at the expense of losing her national entity, gain economic well-being as part of a wealthier nation. On this issue, however, Jordan is basically split, with "west bank" Jordanians generally favoring such a move, and elements surrounding the royal family opposed to a merger. That is why a solution to Jordan's problem almost certainly will not come about short of significant, and possibly violent, social change. Until that time, though Jordanians may not like it, their country will continue to be a pawn in the rivalries of other powers, since Jordan must depend upon outside help to live.

CHAPTER 12

Arabian Nights 1956

Saudi Arabia is the largest of Arab lands, with an area estimated roughly at 800,000 square miles, or about 12 times the size of New England. It is also the most unrelievedly barren of Arab states, being largely sandstone desert and naked limestone steppe, intruded by basaltic lava rock, the whole thinly inhabited by wandering Bedouin tribes. Here and there a date palm oasis is made possible by permanent springs bubbling up through the desert floor.

The Arabian peninsula, nine-tenths of which is controlled by Saudi Arabia, forms part of the vast desert belt beginning with the Sahara of Africa on the west and moving through the Middle East to the desert regions of Central Asia. Thus the Arabian desert is at one with the Syrian desert to the north. Arabia is one of the most rainless lands on earth, what little ocean-borne moisture there is in the area being almost entirely dissipated before reaching the peninsula's superheated sands.

Topographically the Arabian peninsula is a vast plateau sloping gently from the mountains of the southwest toward the north and east, where the peninsula shelves into the Persian Gulf. On the western side of the country, bordering the Red Sea, a narrow coastal plain terminates abruptly at the foot of the massive Hejaz range, a bare and gloomy wall of igneous and metamorphic rocks 1,000 miles long from north to south, rising to 9,000 feet above sea level in Saudi Arabia and to a maximum of 11,000 feet in the Yemen. Eastward of this mountain wall the great Najd plateau slopes downward, broken in the center of the peninsula by a secondary range, the Tuwaik Mountains. East of Tuwaik the plateau, interrupted only by minor scarps, continues its slope toward sea level until it reaches the Persian Gulf.

This vast eastward-sloping plateau is sedimentary, much of it being hard gravel pan or naked limestone steppe. It is marked in the north by a huge moving desert of shifting sand called the Great Nafud, running, as it were, into the Dahna, a twisting "river" of moving sand leading down the eastern side of the peninsula to the immense desert of the south, the Rub al-Khali, or Empty Quarter. These three areas—the Great Nafud in the north, the Rub al-Khali in the south, joined together by the Dahna—are, together with a band of dunes along the east coast, the real sand deserts of Arabia.

The Empty Quarter in particular still is a name of terror throughout Arabia. The author has been in the northern fringes of this great desert, where the dunes towered 70 feet high. Farther south, in places where no man is known to have been except in an airplane, dunes rise as high as 500 feet. Until the Arabian American Oil Company began exploring this desert, the Rub al-Khali had been crossed by only three westerners, all British—Bertram Thomas in 1931, H. St. John B. Philby the following year, and Wilfred Thesiger, 1946-48. These intrepid men traveled by camel, equipped only as the Bedouins who accompanied them. American oil men of Aramco, systematically and with purpose, are exploring and mapping the Empty Quarter in desert-equipped vehicles operating out of air-conditioned base camps.

Throughout the centuries Semitic nomads have wandered the deserts of Arabia in tribal groups, each tribe within its own dirah, or grazing range, warring often with the tribes around it. To this patternless and shifting scene a semblance of unity was given in 1902, when Abdul Aziz ibn Saud, scion of the Najdi House of Saud, captured the oasis city of Riyadh and began the establishment of a new kingdom in Arabia. Gradually over the years, and often through bitter tribal warfare fought on camels, Ibn Saud subdued the tribes and brought more and more of the peninsula beneath his sway.

In 1921 he was proclaimed Sultan of Najd and its dependencies, including the Sultanate of Hail. On January 8, 1926, after deposing King Hussein, friend of the British in World War I and father of Abdullah and Feisal, Ibn Saud became King of the Hejaz, including its holy cities of Mecca and Medina. On September 22, 1932, the great "Lion of the Desert," as he was known by now among the Arabs, united the two areas he ruled and proclaimed himself King of Saudi Arabia, comprising nine-tenths of the Arabian peninsula. Ibn Saud was undisputed master of the desert world.

Until the discovery of oil in the 1930's, possession of the holy cities of Islam, centering on the annual pilgrimage to Mecca of Moslems from all over the world, was the chief economic asset of the barren desert kingdom. Today, though protection of the pilgrims remains a duty of the king, the pilgrimage itself has faded into economic insignificance, except to the merchants of Hejaz. It has been replaced by oil, which has ballooned the economy of Arabia beyond recognition and in other ways is changing the land.

On May 29, 1933, the Standard Oil Company of California obtained a 60-year concession covering a vast area of eastern Arabia, and an operating company called the California Arabian Standard Oil Company was formed. In 1944 this name was changed to the Arabian American Oil Company (Aramco). The Texas Company joined the venture in 1936. Later additions were the Standard Oil Company (New Jersey) and the Socony Mobil Oil Company, completing the roster of companies now owning Aramco.

Though the first strikes were made in the late 1930's, in the so-called Dammam dome near the Persian Gulf, development was largely halted by World War II. Not until 1945 did commercial production begin in earnest. Since that time production has swelled to the 1955 figure of just under 47,000,000 tons (nearly 1,000,000 barrels a day), affording the present King of Saudi Arabia an income estimated at $250,000,000 a year.

The discovery of oil in the peninsula and the rise of the House of Saud combined to cast the shadow of Arabia large across the future of the Middle East. What was there in the character of the giant Abdul Aziz ibn Saud which enabled this sheikh to weld the tribes of Arabia into a nation when so many desert leaders before him had failed? What caused some of the most individualistic warriors on earth to flock to his standard until every tribal coalition raised against him was crushed? Who was this Ibn Saud, that even his enemies dubbed him "Lion of the Desert" and "Lord of Arabia"?

Above all, Ibn Saud owed his greatness to his superb understanding of the desert and its way of life, and to his ability to build a kingdom within a pattern which his countrymen understood and would accept. Though Bedouin life seems colorful to the Western sense, it is, within the peninsula itself, a stern and spartan existence, limited by the harshness of the desert climate and bounded by rules of conduct and loyalty which every sheikh must obey if he would remain in power.

Ibn Saud, despite a personality whose vitality impressed Arab and Westerner alike, was no exception to the general rule. Only through supreme exemplification within himself of what are deemed desert virtues was he able to bring the tribes beneath his sway. Seldom did he violate desert rules and it was, in fact, his introduction of an alien people and culture—the Americans of the Arabian American Oil Company—into his simple Islamic land that brought him his gravest challenge from conservative tribal and religious elements to whom innovation was anathema.

First among desert virtues embodied in Ibn Saud was the ability to wage war in the time-honored Bedouin fashion, requiring that a man ride both camel and horse, shoot well, exhibit courage and ruthlessness in combat, and, last but far from least, practice magnanimity toward a defeated foe. It was young Ibn Saud's capture of well-armed Riyadh with a small band of 20 men in January, 1902, that first endeared him to desert hearts. The tale of this feat has been told and retold around campfires in Arabia, and has grown no doubt in the telling. The following version is the one which Saud ibn Abdul Aziz, the old King's eldest living son and present ruler of Saudi Arabia, allows to be recounted in his majlis as the accurate account of his father's deed.

It is known that in 1891 Abdul-Rahman ibn Feisal Al Saud, head of the Saudi clan, was driven from his ancestral seat at Riyadh into exile in Kuwait by Mohammed ibn Rashid, ruler of Najd, or north central Arabia. Across the back of one of Abdul-Rahman's baggage camels, as he fled the gates of Riyadh, two saddle bags were slung. In these rode his children; a girl named Nura in one, and in the other Abdul Aziz, her 11-year-old brother.

The boy grew up in Kuwait, under the patronage of the ruler of that northern sheikhdom, Mubarak ibn Sabah. Even in his late teens Abdul Aziz had shot head and shoulders above most desert Arabs, and his strength was immense, equaled only by the zeal which burned within him, according to legend, to recapture his family's home.

By the time he was 21 the restlessness had grown too great to contain, and, gathering about him a small band of men, he struck south through the desert toward the Rub al-Khali, garnering Bedouin allies as he went. It was now January, 1902. Selecting 60 of his closest friends, including his trusted cousin, Abdullah ibn Jiluwi, Abdul Aziz whipped his camels toward the outskirts of Riyadh, arriving there one dark night.

Here, at an oasis two hours' walking distance from the city, 40 men were left with the animals, with instructions that if they did not hear from Ibn Saud within one hour after the next dawn, they were to return to their homes with a report of failure. The other 20 men, on foot, proceeded to the city walls, arriving some hours before dawn. They uprooted palm trees, and, using them as ladders, six men scaled the wall. The other 14 were left outside, on the alert for whatever might transpire.

The six, under the leadership of Abdul Aziz, made their way through the dark streets to the home of the Rashidi governor of Riyadh, a man named Ajlan. They found first a servant, and then Ajlan's wife, from whom they learned that the governor would come to her at dawn for morning coffee and breakfast. Ajlan himself was then sleeping in the fort, under the protection of his troops.

Ibn Saud and his men waited for the sun, setting up their positions outside the great door of the fort. Their plan was that when the small door of the fort first should move, one of the six would race for the outer wall, there to call for the 14 men outside. The door opened and the governor came out, surrounded by eight soldiers. Additional troops were on the wall above, watching his progress. One of the soldiers on the wall saw the man of Ibn Saud running and gave the alarm. The governor and his eight guards turned back, but too late. Two men of Ibn Saud's stood between them and the door of the fort. A battle began. The two supporters of Abdul Aziz were killed and the governor gained the door.

Ibn Saud threw himself upon Ajlan, catching him about the legs, his hands slipping to Ajlan's feet. The governor pointed his gun at the future king, when Abdullah ibn Jiluwi hurled his spear. The spear missed and stuck in the door of the fort, where the head of it still remains (shown to me with pride on my first visit to Riyadh).

As Ajlan moved to avoid the spear, Ibn Jiluwi threw himself forward and slashed the governor across the stomach with his knife. Ajlan staggered through the gate to a prayer ground, and here Ibn Jiluwi finished him with a rifle. When Ajlan's troops saw that their governor was dead, they threw down their arms. By this time the 14 men from outside had arrived, the soldiers were imprisoned, and Riyadh again was a Saudi town.

Thus began the Kingdom of Saudi Arabia, and the career of a man who became so powerful that President Roosevelt welcomed him—together with a retinue of Arabs and droves of live sheep—aboard an American warship in the Great Bitter Lake in Egypt in 1945. The capture of Riyadh was the first act in years of warfare which led Abdul Aziz ibn Saud east, north, south, and west throughout Arabia until the

Turks were removed from Hofuf and Al Hasa, King Hussein was driven from the Hejaz, the old enemy Rashid was overthrown in Hail, and, finally, the Imam of Yemen was taught that Ibn Saud was the master of Arabia.

As Mohammed the Prophet before him, Ibn Saud shrewdly invested his fighting with a religious motive—the restoration of Wahhabi Islam in a land grown lax and careless in religious observance. (Wahhabism was a school of Islamic interpretation founded in central Arabia by a religious reformer named Mohammed ibn Abdul Wahhab in the early eighteenth century. A political-religious alliance had been formed between the House of Saud and Wahhab, who preached a return to the strictest obedience to Koranic precepts.) To this end young Ibn Saud raised an army of fanatic desert warriors called the Ikhwan (Brotherhood), who soon became both famed and feared throughout Arabia for their savagery and fanaticism in the face of the severest odds.

As many autocrats, Ibn Saud soon discovered that an army fed on religious zeal seldom understands the subtleties and compromises of diplomacy and statecraft. After crushing a revolt by the very Ikhwan troops who had gained him his kingdom, the young monarch played down the Ikhwan and began a policy of settling them in agricultural units on the land. Today, in traveling throughout Arabia, it is possible to find Ikhwan settlements still flourishing, but more often one comes upon abandoned settlements, half-drifted over by the desert sands, deserted by men whose hearts were too untamed for a sedentary life.

No law of the desert is more demanding than that of hospitality, requiring that the Bedouin kill his last sheep if necessary for a guest, that he never turn away a suppliant from his tent, and that he protect with his life the stranger who throws himself upon his mercy, even though that stranger may be an enemy of his host's tribe. Nothing "whitened the face" of Ibn Saud among his people more than the monarch's strict observance of the laws of hospitality, including his generous treatment of conquered sheikhs and even his assumption of responsibility for the families of those leaders whom his men had slain.

Even during the years of fighting, while the kingdom still was being built, Ibn Saud consolidated his position both among friendly and conquered tribes through shrewd "political" marriages, designed to bind the tribes to the House of Saud by ties of blood, strongest tie of all in desert Arabia. These marriages—more than 300 by the King's own words—gave Ibn Saud an enormous number of sons (as well as daughters who mattered less), each one of whom was styled a royal prince and each one of whom became an additional drain on the royal exchequer of a generous father.

It was indeed finances—the need for subsidies to the tribes, salaries to the army, the running of the government of an expanded kingdom, and maintenance of the royal house—that finally led Ibn Saud to declare to H. St. John B. Philby: "I tell you, Philby, that if anyone were to offer me a million pounds now he would be welcome to all the concessions he wants in my country."[1] And which finally led, in 1933, to the granting of an oil concession to the Standard Oil Company of California.

It was then that Ibn Saud's kingdom began gradually to change, a process greatly accelerated by the huge postwar expansion of Aramco which brought enormous wealth to a barren desert land. This wealth the royal family was quite

[1] H. St. John B. Philby, *Arabian Days* (London: Robert Hale, Ltd., 1948), p. 291.

unprepared through experience to handle, and the result was a proliferation of royal luxury.

The King proved a shrewd bargainer with Aramco, but perhaps the truest test of Ibn Saud's ability to lead a new kind of Arabia would have come only had the King remained in full control of affairs through 1953, his last year on earth, when his government faced labor and technological problems inconceivable to the monarch in his younger days. As it happened, however, the King's physical condition forced his gradual relinquishment of royal duties, until, during the last two years of his life, the *de facto* ruler of Saudi Arabia was the King's eldest living son, Saud (now King), and a group of advisers, many of whom were not Saudi Arabians but Arabs from other lands.

In November, 1953, there passed from the Arabian scene a towering personality, one of the great Semites of history. He brought into being a kingdom of tribesmen, and he allowed into his land an industry which has challenged and changed his kingdom in many ways. He left many sons behind him, and to the eldest fell the task of ruling in his father's stead, over a kingdom in which indigenous problems were little changed from his father's day, but in which strange new problems had been added by the advent of oil. In the new ruler's favor are the facts that through him is channeled the tremendous wealth which Arabia's oil provides, that he has a more or less modern army which so far has proved loyal to the House of Saud, and that he was hand-picked by his famous father—though the latter may have little bearing in the eyes of many desert sheikhs to whom the law of primogeniture is less valid than that of leadership through proved ability.

Militating against the stability of the present King's reign are labor unrest among Aramco's 15,000 Saudi oil workers,

growing restiveness among Saudi merchants and businessmen at what is considered unfair distribution of the country's wealth, and possible jealousy among the royal princes
on the score that Saud earned the throne chiefly because he
was the old King's eldest surviving son, and not because he
was necessarily the most capable among them. Less tangible
but possibly overshadowing in importance the other nega-
tive factors listed above, is the fact that desert tribes, which
traditionally have been at each other's throats throughout
Arabian history, gave up their feuding because Ibn Saud's
sword proved stronger than theirs, and because his personality sparked a fanatic loyalty in many desert hearts. The
burden of proof now is on King Saud in the task of persuading tribal sheikhs that he is a worthy successor to one of the
greatest desert leaders of all time.

My own acquaintance with the House of Saud, its splendors and its problems, began on a bright February morning
in 1953, when Saud, then Crown Prince, was swept in a dark
green Cadillac past a Dhahran railroad siding to a waiting
Diesel train, gleaming like silver in the sunshine. This was Al
Hasa, oil province of Arabia on the eastern fringes of
the country, and the event was the day on which the Crown
Prince was to return to Riyadh after a month-long visit to
Al Hasa, where—through a series of shrewd promotions and
banquets—Amir Saud had sought to improve his position
among the sheikhs who one day would call him king.

A trip 30 years ago through the eastern province would
have been a more cumbersome affair, conducted by camel
train and forced to follow the long and tortuous route of the
water holes which, through centuries, have determined the
caravan trails of the desert. But the royal family, and those
who can afford it, now may glide at 70 miles an hour in a
Diesel coach through the rolling dunes over a roadbed fi-

nanced by revenue from oil and completed by American engineers in 1951, at the special request of the late Ibn Saud.

This was the way the Crown Prince had chosen to return to Riyadh, and there was a scramble of white kaffiyahs and flowing robes as the tall figure of the heir apparent, clad in a brown robe of camel hair trimmed with gold, stepped from the Cadillac and made his way toward the train. Bands played, Saudi soldiers jumped to attention, green flags bearing the crossed swords of Islam snapped in the air, and sheikhs, both minor and important, crowded forward to kiss the Prince's hand.

In the royal car itself were three American guests including myself. Otherwise the car was filled with Saudis, some elderly, with trimmed white beards, others young, with merry impudent faces and a mixture of Arab-Western dress, some of them princes, others sheikhs, and still others soldiers, heavily armed and with their uniforms criss-crossed by ammunition belts, into which were thrust gold-encrusted daggers. Slipping in among the throng now and then were two young Americans, one an ex-marine and the other an ex-sailor, dressed in white Tuxedo coats with red flowers in their lapels, in charge of the dining car which would furnish meals and soft drinks (liquor is forbidden in Saudi Arabia) for the Crown Prince and party during the day-long trip to Riyadh.

A corner seat was reserved for the future king himself, who now folded his long frame into the seat and stared out the window through dark glasses, rising now and then to receive the greetings of those who came forward to kiss his hand. The Prince was heavily built, even in proportion to his height, wearing a tailored gray robe beneath the outer robe of brown, a snow-white kaffiyah on his head and flowing about his shoulders, the kaffiyah crowned by a golden agal, or head band. Beneath the sun glasses the Crown Prince wore a black moustache and small trimmed beard of black.

Across the aisle sat Saud ibn Jiluwi, governor of Al Hasa Province, his great dark visage dominated by fiercely rolling eyes and heavy black beard, his feet shod in simple sandals rather than the Western shoes which the Crown Prince wore. I asked the two to sit for a picture, and Amir Saud patted the seat beside him. Instead, however, Ibn Jiluwi fell kneeling to the floor of the car, grasping the other's hand, and there he remained until the picture was taken.

Here was a meeting, surely! Eldest sons of the two men who had led the tiny and fateful expedition against Riyadh 50 years before! One of those men had become king, and the other his strong right arm in battle and in peace. Indeed, it had been old Abdullah ibn Jiluwi who had slain Ajlan, governor of Riyadh, even as the latter grappled with Ibn Saud, and in return the Ibn Jiluwi family had received the governorship of Al Hasa in perpetuity. Now the governorship was vested in the man who knelt before me at the feet of the Crown Prince, in symbolic devotion even as his father undoubtedly had knelt many times before Ibn Saud.

At one point in the journey toward Riyadh the Crown Prince called one of his sons, Mohammed, to come forth. This young man, smiling broadly, a blue tweed sport jacket contrasting strangely with the white robe beneath it, settled down at his father's direction and began sketching people in the car. The Crown Prince leaned back at this, enjoying himself hugely, chewing on a miswak stick, branch of an aromatic tree used as a toothbrush by the desert Arab. Across the aisle Saud ibn Jiluwi, gazing somberly behind his beard at the work of the artist, sported a pocket full of miswak.

Then the train was at Abqaiq, oil station stop one hour south of Dhahran, and the local amir, Hamid ibn Sa'id, a Negro with a crisp black beard, son of a former slave, came aboard to greet his royal master. Hamid had moved his majlis to the railroad station, covering its floor with rich Persian carpets, in the unlikely event the Crown Prince should wish to descend. In that majlis, for my own journey ended there, I saw pourers spill left-over tea on those rich rugs, in the manner of simple men who have lived all their lives outdoors.

Within one month after that initial meeting came the invitation to visit the Crown Prince in his palace at Riyadh. The invitation reached me at Beirut, Lebanon, and immediately I flew across the desert to Dhahran in Al Hasa, to meet the Saudi Government plane which would carry me to Riyadh. There were two others in our party which assembled at Dhahran—Dr. George Rentz, an American Arabist of Aramco, long trusted by the royal family, and Hafez Baroudi, a university-trained Saudi citizen (originally from the Sudan) who would act as interpreter.

At the air strip outside Riyadh, following the two-hour flight west across the desert from Dhahran, we were met by Colonel Mohammed al-Dibh—Mohammed the Wolf—commander of the King's bodyguard, a soldier with lean dark face and black beard. Swiftly the colonel led us to the airport building, where, over the buffet door, there was a sign in Arabic: "There is no God but Allah, and Mohammed is His Prophet. Kingdom of Saudi Arabia." Behind the airport building a new white mosque gleamed on the sands.

Then a long black limousine carried us over the tarred road leading to the square mud towers of the King's Murabba Palace, looming above the sands, and the enormous Murabba Guest House, where we would stay. Through the great gate, guarded by soldiers, we drove, and up to the door of the guest house. We were led down a long carpeted hall, with mirrors at the other end, up carpeted stairs, down another hall, until a servant threw open a door and ushered us into the majlis, perhaps 100 feet long and half as wide. Four immense Persian carpets covered the floor, while all around the walls were ranged thronelike chairs, gilded in gold paint and upholstered in floral prints, dazzling to the eye. Hafez Baroudi called the secretary of the Crown Prince to announce our presence. The message came back that we were to meet with the Prince's counselor, Khalid Bey Abu al-Walid, later in the afternoon, and until then we were free to sightsee.

Around us lay the old city of Riyadh. Dust, sun, and dried mud walls. Narrow twisting lanes, built for camels and donkeys, with the mud walls of courtyards rising abruptly on either side. In the old souk (market) gleamed the bright brass of long-spouted coffee pots, such as the Bedouin treasures, the deep reds and blues of quilts and blankets, the mottled enamel of cheap pots and pans.

In one covered street a camel saddler sold in a tiny shop the wooden frames of saddles, lashed together with thongs, and the brightly tasseled bags which I had seen adorning the great beasts all over the Arabian desert. In the tiny cubbyhole next to him squatted an Arab tailor, busy fashioning gold-trimmed robes from black goat hair. Across the way, in the dim light of his little shop, a barber scraped industriously at the neck of a squatting townsman. Women, in their black shrouds and veils above bare feet, moved through the souk, long gold-embroidered tassels dangling from the front of their black abbi, or outer cloaks, an occasional swirl of calico peeping forth from beneath.

Great wooden doors, studded with iron nubs and painted in deep blue designs, hung ajar on their hinges in the dried mud walls, leading to the courtyards within. There loomed the square towers of the same fort captured by the king 50 years before, when he founded his kingdom, and there was the gate itself, with its bit of iron said to be the spearhead cast by Abdullah ibn Jiluwi in the attack upon Riyadh.

The city, however, is changing. A part of the old wall has been torn down to widen the roads, a part of the old souk demolished to make way for a new mosque, its twin minarets looming white and high over the brown mud of the buildings below. American cars throng the market place, push and honk through the narrow lanes, their horns blatant and petulant, while men, women, children, and donkeys move slowly and resentfully from their paths. Along one street a row of new concrete shops is rising, each with its corrugated metal shutter, as seen in Cairo, Damascus, or Beirut.

The old wall, and all that it symbolized, was indigenous, a reflection of Arab culture and of the Arabian way of life. And the way of living of most of the people within that city has changed but little today, while outside the walls are the unchanged Bedouins and their black tents, come to live off the bounty of their King. Now the pattern about them is being broken, distorted by the outward symbols of alien ways, and, where the pattern is gone, too often ugliness takes its place, as seen in the shattered hulks of scarcely used cars resting outside the city walls. Those cars were bought with royalties from oil and brought into Riyadh over the railroad built with royalties from oil. It is the Saudis' right to spend their money as they choose. But the sights and sounds of a traffic jam in congested Riyadh is an odd and disturbing thing when it is remembered that on every side of Riyadh, for hundreds of miles, stretches the empty desert, and that there is little place those cars can drive except within the city itself and through the oasis just outside.

All that we had seen in Riyadh, with its many contrasts of old and new, was soon to be eclipsed by wonders even more dazzling to the eye—Nasiriyah Palace and its gardens in the desert, where we had been invited to lunch. Such an invitation was not to be taken lightly, for this was the first time in several years that the Saudi royal family had invited an American writer to its capital. I had scarcely hoped to see the venerable old gentleman, Abdul Aziz ibn Saud, whose sword and religious fervor had founded this kingdom 50 years before. By now the "Lion of the Desert" was living in seclusion in Riyadh, and many of the reins of government had been taken over by Crown Prince Saud.

The next day at noon we were met at the great gate of the palace by a Saudi captain in olive-green uniform and white kaffiyah, who led us into the gardens within. On every side, interspersed with fountains and concrete pools painted blue, grew beds of flowers of every color and description, while beyond, longer than a city block by far, rose Nasiriyah itself, reached through paths of tile and crushed stone. Off to the right was a grassy plot, where the bright colors of modern hammocks and lawn chairs vied with the flowers in brilliance. Before one hammock, upholstered in bright red, was spread a magnificent Persian carpet, obviously reserved for the Crown Prince himself.

At this spot we were ushered to seats beside other guests, in time to see a cortege of officers winding through the garden paths, while behind them, in robe and white headdress, strode the tall figure of the Prince, deep in conversation with a counselor. Behind, at a discreet distance, walked other notables and princes, all in their Arab robes.

We stood as the Crown Prince reached the circle of grass, and I was led forward to shake hands with His Royal Highness, a giant of a man, wearing the same dark glasses I had remembered from my first meeting with him, aboard his royal train. He asked me to sit in the seat next to his outdoor "throne" that he might talk with me, and an interpreter knelt hastily at his feet on the Persian rug.

Our conversation was stiff and formal, mainly because Arab etiquette forbids business talk at the beginning of a social visit. Social chitchat between a Crown Prince who speaks no English and a Western visitor who speaks no Arabic is necessarily somewhat limited. The Prince talked with me politely about my health, about my travels in his land, about the weather, while I, in return, admired the beauty of his gardens. Saud did inject one business note, asking me whether his advisers had supplied me with information concerning the Saudi Arabian claim to the oasis of Buraimi.

Then it was lunchtime, and the procession formed again. Through a hall we passed, and into the dining room, a room such as I scarcely had dreamed existed in this world. It was at least 100 feet long, with a great table stretching down most of its length, and behind almost every chair, a Negro waiter wearing white gloves, maroon bow tie, and immaculate white jacket edged with red. Behind the chair of the Crown Prince, stood the head waiter, an Italian.

The Prince sat at the head of the table, with the Palestinian Jamal Bey Husseini, a relative of the Grand Mufti of Jerusalem and one of the Prince's most trusted counselors, at his right. As the apparent guest of honor I was placed next to Jamal Bey, who acted as interpreter between the Crown Prince and me. Dr. Rentz was at my right, and down the table on either side were ranged the other guests and members of the royal household.

This was no Bedouin meal, for the Crown Prince seldom dines in desert fashion from a common platter placed on a rug upon the floor. Indeed, the Prince's chief chef is an American, formerly with Aramco, and now, at this luncheon, course after course of Western food followed in profusion—soup, fowl, meats, rice, vegetables, salads.

But it was the room itself, and the decor, that struck one with awe. The walls were green, the floor an intricate mosaic of tile. From the ceiling hung crystal chandeliers, interspersed with the ubiquitous fluorescent fixtures which seemed to have caught the fancy of the Saudis. And along those green walls were ranged some of the treasures of one of the wealthiest men in the world. Here and there stood a silver vase, four feet high—solid silver, Dr. Rentz and I guessed—and next to such a vase, perhaps, an electric water cooler with a foot pedal, such as might be found in a theater in the States. Then a golden candelabra in the shape of a veiled female figure, with branches sprouting from the top, and a tiny light bulb at the tip of each branch. In each corner of the room behind the Crown Prince stood something like a butcher's showcase, with crystalware arranged within, the whole lighted from behind in pale green.

And on the wall behind me was placed a Wurlitzer juke box selector, with its red plastic buttons to be pushed, and its coin slots for nickels, dimes, and quarters. The juke box itself was not in evidence, though Arabic music burst forth from somewhere every now and then. Behind the Crown Prince, frowning down upon him like a ventilator on a ship, was a vast air conditioner, painted green to match the walls, with the swords of Islam overlain in gold leaf.

And all about me desert Arabs in their robes ate gravely of this Western meal, served in this extraordinary room, a meal capped with ice cream and strawberry sauce, and two kinds of milk, camel and cow. Then the Crown Prince rose, and immediately, whether finished or not, every guest rose also, for one could not remain seated while his royal host stood. He strode down the length of the room and into a hall. There a servant poured tiny cups of cardamom coffee, after which Amir Saud walked out into the flaming brilliance of his garden to bid me farewell.

A few miles outside Riyadh, along the banks of Wadi Hanifah, rises another palace belonging to the Crown Prince, called Badiah, the New One. From the whitewashed towers of this palace I looked down another day upon an ancient well, where, half-hidden in a grove of date palms, two tiny donkeys trudged back and forth along a worn path. Each drew by rope a goat-skin water bag up from the depths of the well, and then, when the bag had splashed its contents into a ditch that ran among the palms, each turned and lowered its bag again to the bottom to be refilled. How many decades, perhaps centuries, had that oasis well been used! And how many generations of patient little beasts had raised the precious fluid for their Arab masters!

This well was in context, both with the centuries and with Arabian life as it is lived today, as was the mud Wahhabi mosque standing nearby, a rounded bulge in one of its walls pointing the way to Mecca. Yet just a few yards from this oasis scene, behind Badiah Palace, rose a structure almost literally from another world—a new palace, called Mahattah, the Station, used by the Crown Prince to house royal and presidential visitors to Saudi Arabia. From its gate of wrought iron trimmed with chrome, to its portico of blue around a flower-filled courtyard, to its giant kitchen of stainless steel, Mahattah was a vision of wonder.

Green broadloom carpeting covered the floor of the immense majlis, while above rose walls of light blue. Hundreds of thronelike chairs stood about the walls, glittering in gilt paint and upholstered in imitation leopard skin. From a ceiling of cream hung crystal chandeliers and fluorescent fixtures.

Yet this palace, and Badiah, and Nasiriyah Palace were far from alone in Riyadh, for all about the city the great homes of the princely sons of the House of Saud dotted the sands. When it is recalled that the late King had more than 30 sons styled royal princes, many of whom have princely sons of their own, each requiring a great house and establishment, it is not surprising that an estimated half of each year's $250,000,000 in oil royalties is spent on the royal family itself.

What is the opposite side of this Saudi coin? Every day Bedouin men, women, and children, copper pots upon their heads or in their arms, file through a gate into a government compound in Riyadh and draw rations of rice, and occasionally meat, from the bounty of their King. Every Bedouin who has a need will be fed by his King, reflecting the age-old desert responsibility of a sheikh for his people.

At luncheon a few days before, Jamal Bey Husseini, Saud's counselor, had told me that at least 500,000 Bedouins —stricken by the drought years of late—were living off the government throughout the land. What he did not mention, however, was that Riyadh's water table—barometer of a city's existence in Arabia—was falling steadily, as more water was being consumed by men, animals, and gardens than could be replaced by the region's scanty rains.

It would be wrong to assume, perhaps, that the Bedouin who carries his rations out to a tent within the very shadow of a great palace looks up resentfully at the wall above him and at the desert prince who lives within. There is a quality in Oriental thought which makes the Bedouin glory by reflection in the wealth and splendor of his rulers. Yet many of these princelings, without the advent of oil, still would be living in tents themselves, little more splendid than the goat-hair dwellings of their fellows.

Thus, in the judgment of an increasing number of Saudis, there is a fine line to be drawn between what is proper to spend on a king, a crown prince, and certain other notables, and what is mere prodigality on the part of princelings who are nonproductive in an economic sense. Were Saudi Arabia still almost entirely a Bedouin land, this question might not sharpen. But there is growing up within the country a middle class of Saudis trained by the very oil company which brings his royalties to the King. (Saud's formal accession to the throne came in November, 1953, following the death of his father, Ibn Saud.) At the base of Aramco's policy—a policy endorsed by the King—is a program of training designed to bring the Saudis as much as possible into the actual operation and administration of the company which extracts their oil.

This program divides into two parts: the education of Saudi youth in schools and Western universities up to their capacity to absorb, and the training of other Saudis as truckers, contractors, shopkeepers, garage men, to perform the auxiliary services which an oil company, and an expanding nation, require. No attempt is made to influence the Saudi away from Islam, or from the form of government under which he lives. But to isolate him completely from

Western political and social concepts—at the same time he is learning Western industrial techniques—is impossible.

More and more Saudis, therefore, are beginning to take a closer look at a government which essentially is a much-magnified version of the kind of patriarchal tribal rule so familiar in Arabia, with most of their country's income going to hereditary rulers. Little or no dissatisfaction was expressed against the late Ibn Saud, who possessed an immense and apparently unshakable hold over the loyalties of his people; nor so far against the personal conduct of the new King; nor against such princes as Feisal, now Crown Prince and the second figure in the land. But there are literally dozens of other princes who neither perform services to their country nor adhere to the strict religious standards of Wahhabi Islam, and it is a question whether dissatisfaction against such men is not spreading to the system which breeds them.

One young Saudi sent by his government to college in the United States tried, upon his return to Arabia, to introduce what he considered more efficient practices in the ministry to which he was assigned. When these changes were rejected, he applied for further education in the States, confiding to an American friend that he would never return to his native land.

There are few Saudis who have reached university level, but there are some who are approaching that goal, and there are many others who are shrewd and successful businessmen, largely trained and launched by Aramco. These are the men who are becoming the vocal part of the Saudi state, far more so than the Bedouins who still form a large part of the population. It is the future attitude of these men toward their government which is important—not only to Saudi Arabia herself, but potentially to other Arab states as well. And last but not least, their attitude is important also to American officials of Aramco, who, by the very act of introducing technology to Arabia, became responsible partners in the future of the land.

Early on my last morning in Riyadh I went up to the guest palace roof to look down at the lights of the city, glimmering in the distance across the sands. It was still before dawn, with a half-moon riding in the dark sky, and somewhere off in the desert a dog barked and another answered faintly.

I thought of the silent streets below, and of their square mud-walled houses, with the Arab inhabitants now sleeping within—some, the poor or the more conservative, lying on rugs spread on the floor; others, the royal and the newly-wealthy, sleeping in Western beds. Soon another day would begin for this desert city. The horns of the cars bought by oil would begin their cacophony and wheels would squeal beneath palace walls, while inside, in great rooms more garishly splendid than the eye can readily imagine, princes in their flowing robes would hold morning majlis.

Outside the city, and creeping within its limits wherever space afforded (though I could not see them now), were pitched the tents of Bedouins. In the dust of the streets, close beneath the mud walls of palaces and mud hovels alike, the children of Riyadh soon would begin their play, as oblivious in their games to the wheels flashing past them as the children of 30 years ago had been to the more familiar hoofs and pads of donkeys and camels.

What do these changes portend for Arabia? Is a pattern already established of the gradual disintegration of a society which has maintained its integrity against all the onslaughts of history, but which never before has been called upon to bridge the wide gulf of separation between rulers and ruled which the discovery of oil has brought?

I recall one man, Ibrahim, whom I met on the train which crosses the Arabian desert from Riyadh to Dammam. He was a well-dressed Arab who spoke some English. Noting his fine black robe trimmed with gold, I ventured to ask if he worked for the Saudi Arabian Government. Ibrahim snorted at this, declaring he was a merchant of Riyadh, operating a small fleet of trucks which hauled cement and other materials across the desert.

"Do you know why I am on this train?" he demanded. "Yesterday I bought a ticket to fly from Riyadh to Dhahran on the Saudi Government Airline. Today I went to the airport and was told 'Sorry, Prince So-and-So has taken the plane for himself today.' " He subsided for a moment, glancing out the window at the desert rolling by.

"It's happened before," he added bitterly, "and sometimes, if I'm going to Dammam or Al Khobar to bid on a contract, I miss the bidding."

"What do these people think of their government?" I asked him, nodding about the car.

"The Bedouins?" he replied, glancing in astonishment at the barefoot forms squatting, walking, eating, and arguing, all with equal gusto, in the car. "They think of nothing. They know nothing except the desert, not even their religion. . . . But there are others. Look at myself. For seven years I worked for Aramco, learned English and mechanics, then set myself up in business. There are hundreds, maybe thousands, like me in Arabia today."

"It's all a matter of education," my friend said later, going back to the subject of the Saudi Government. "The religious leaders and some of the people in the government are frustrating the desire for education which is sweeping the country, because they know that with the spread of knowledge will come dissatisfaction with the old."

Then Ibrahim spoke to me proudly of his four sons and one daughter, all of whom he had sent to school in Damascus. It was his desire, he said, to educate them so that they might be free of the desert, and live what he termed a good life, away from these never-ending sands.

It was a sacrifice to him, he said, to live without his family, but it was his duty to see that his sons received an education. He would educate them, he continued, in whatever lines they chose and as far as they wished to go, because that was his duty as a father. But he would never impose his will on them, as his own father had imposed his will on Ibrahim. They would be free to choose their own wives, as he had chosen his own wife freely, and to choose their careers. Then it would become their duty to live good lives, and that was all he asked.

"What about your daughter?" I asked. Would she receive an education also?

Ibrahim answered that he would educate her to be a good wife, to learn to cook and sew well, and such other things as would make her a good wife to a good man. Beyond that he had no duty to educate her. She would, however, be free to choose her own husband.

"How will she have the opportunity to choose, or find, a man in Riyadh?"

Ibrahim looked at me sharply.

" In Riyadh she would not," he said. "But she will never live in Riyadh. That is why I have sent my family away."

Another time I talked with a Saudi merchant of Al Khobar, an oil town on the Persian Gulf, who told me that a few years ago no one expected his wife to go to a hospital at childbirth. "Now we see that the King and the princes have built hospitals for their wives," he said, "and we have learned that a woman need not suffer so. But the King," he added bitterly, "is not building us the hospitals he promised us."

I recall the Saudi who told me that more and more fathers resented the way in which soldiers, policemen, and hangers-on of the King's retinue, when the monarch was out on a trip, "borrowed" Arab daughters for a night and returned them to their families the next day.

And the sleek merchant who told me that the Saudi Government was deeply in his debt. "A prince comes to me and says he wants this and that. He signs a chit and tells me to draw on the treasury at Riyadh or Jidda. What can I do? He is a prince . . . If I try hard, I may get paid a part. The rest is a form of investment." (Independent observers estimate that the Saudi Arabian Government is in debt to Saudi merchants to the extent of about one year's revenue from oil.)

Nowhere in Saudi Arabia is the impact of oil, in all its implications, more marked than in the Arab boom towns of Dammam and Al Khobar, the new commercial centers of Al Hasa Province on the shores of the Persian Gulf. Ten years ago each town was little more than a collection of palm frond huts, housing the Arab divers who eked out a scanty and difficult existence aboard the pearling vessels of Kuwait and other Arabian ports.

Today both Dammam and Al Khobar are headquarters for the Arab merchants and contractors—a brand-new class in eastern Arabia—who have sprung up to serve the needs of the 8,000 Americans of Aramco who live in Al Hasa Province. Naked desert still pushes in from three sides on Dammam and Al Khobar, as it did in the days when only an occasional Bedouin and his flocks were seen in the vicinity of the tiny clusters of pearl fishers' huts.

Today, however, tarred roads have been pushed out through that desert, leading from Dhahran to the two towns, and north from Dammam to the Qatif oasis and the oil refinery town of Ras Tanura. Along those roads flows a heavy stream of red Aramco vehicles and the private cars, taxis, and trucks of enterprising Arab businessmen.

Both Dammam and Al Khobar boast modern shops which sell—primarily to Americans, but also to those Saudi Arabs who can afford them—the latest in washing machines, cooking appliances, cameras, massage and reducing machines, clothing, outboard motors, cosmetics, and other products of Western civilization. Both Dammam and Al Khobar contain such facilities as electricity, ice plants, bottled natural gas for cooking, and garages and service stations to maintain the vehicles and machinery of Arabs and Americans alike.

Already some Aramco offices have been moved from the fenced American city of Dhahran to Dammam to be in closer touch with the people in whose land Aramco works, while an increasing number of American families, temporarily unable to obtain family housing in Dhahran, are snapping up the modern Western-style apartments being offered by Arab landlords at Park Avenue rents.

Deep-water pier and loading facilities at Dammam, built originally by Aramco, now bring in not only vast amounts of oil company equipment, but also a considerable tonnage of goods from all over the world, consigned either to the Arab merchants of Al Hasa, or destined for travel along the railroad from Dammam to Riyadh.

Indeed, so astonishing has been the growth of these two seaport towns, that Amir Saud ibn Jiluwi, governor of Al Hasa Province, has shifted his headquarters from Hofuf to a white palace in Dammam, clear admission that the sleepy oasis town of Hofuf, though storied in Arabian history, no longer is the real capital of this richest province of an oil-rich land.

Behind the development of Dammam and Al Khobar lies the attempt of Aramco officials to train up over the years a class of Saudi contractors and merchants who might provide at least the beginnings of a middle class base on which the fantastic oil boom of Al Hasa might be built. To this end Aramco established in 1945 its Arab Industrial Development Department, designed to make it as easy as possible for potential Saudi businessmen with at least a modicum of technical training to establish their own plants or shops.

Thus, a Saudi who wished to establish a laundry and dry cleaning plant in Al Khobar might come to Aramco's AIDD and receive, free of charge, expert technical assistance at every stage of his project, from the blueprinting of his plans to the ordering of equipment and the negotiation of a bank loan, if needed, to the supervision by American engineers of every detail of the construction of his plant until the day it was ready to open. The number of Saudi contractors, with businesses ranging from construction firms to trucking companies, who have been aided by AIDD over the past 11 years now reaches into the hundreds.

By themselves, the figures of the number of contractors tell only a part of the story, for the wages paid by these new entrepreneurs to their thousands of Saudi employees spread benefit not only to the families of the laborers, but also to the Arab craftsmen and merchants of the oasis towns where the majority of the workers live and spend their money. The system is not without its stresses, as both Aramco and Saudi Government officials are aware, for many of the new class of Arab contractors find themselves better educated, at least in a business and technical way, than most members of the royal family or even of the government ministries themselves.

The result, as has been seen, is an increasing tendency on the part of the growing middle class of Al Hasa to criticize what is termed the government's failure to plan for community development and "middle class" prosperity by budgeting for schools, hospitals, roads, and sewage and irrigation systems throughout the country. These critics know that at least half of Saudi Arabia's annual oil royalties of $250,000,-000 goes to the royal family, with relatively little trickling down to the community level in the shape of improved living standards for urban Arabs.

King Saud, on the other hand, pledged almost immediately after he came to the throne in November, 1953, that his government would concern itself with the raising of education and health standards in the country, and with the increase of public utilities for the benefit of all. The public prominence which the new King has given to such matters indicates that the monarch and his advisers are aware of the need for establishing bonds between the government and the new "sophisticated" class of citizens which never before has existed in Arabia. It is the slowness with which these proposals are being translated from paper into facts, and the consequent doubt that the government's intentions are sincere, which causes grumbling in Al Hasa.

There are signs that the influence of the Saudi merchant class is growing. One example was the successful attempt of Al Hasa entrepreneurs to gain from the government an employees' compensation fund. Under traditional Saudi law, an employer whose laborer was injured or killed on the job was fined so heavily as to bankrupt all but the most affluent businessman. The employers of Al Hasa, studying the example of Western business firms, conceived the idea of a pooled fund to which they might all contribute, and from which compensation might be drawn when needed.

Little success was met in interesting the government in the plan until a delegation from Al Hasa traveled to Riyadh and laid the matter before the late Ibn Saud, who referred the merchants to his minister of finance. For a matter of weeks members of the delegation took turns "camping" in the finance minister's majlis, pressing for their plan and patiently explaining its merits. It was several months before they attained their goal, but now every reputable Saudi businessman in Al Hasa has the opportunity to protect himself from sudden financial disaster by subscribing to the fund.

In essence, the establishment of AIDD was an attempt by Aramco officials, in a situation constantly changing and expanding, to spread the benefits from oil as widely as possible, and thus to prevent the establishment of dangerous classes in Arabia, based on wealth alone. Secondarily, the hope was to train up Saudis capable of performing the ancillary functions, both for Americans and Arabs, from which the company desired to be released.

Observers believe it is still too early to foretell the kind of future relationship which may work itself out between the government and the contractors and merchants of Al Hasa. Aramco officials also admit that, at this stage, at least, the prosperity of Dammam and Al Khobar is almost entirely dependent upon the oil company and its American employees, and that the removal of this influence would bring the encroachment of desert sands upon many ambitious projects of the two towns. (It is also a fact that some of the wealthier contractors are adopting buying habits similar to those of the more extravagant princes.)

However, the very evident prosperity and increasing technical and industrial know-how of many Al Hasa residents indicate that the problems which have arisen in the province in the last 10 years are possibly less grave than those which might have arisen had the largess of oil been allowed to be distributed wholly in the traditional manner of old, or had no effort been made to teach Saudis how to create capital enterprises of their own.

Simply expressed, the basic problem in Saudi Arabia today is the impact of a dynamic technological society upon a stable, conservative, and technically less-developed society. Historically, such impingement almost invariably has manifested itself in social and political turmoil and unrest. In Saudi Arabia the case is exaggerated by the fact that the average Saudi 20 years ago, bred in the isolation of his desert, held himself definitely superior to all other peoples. Thus he looked upon the first American oil men as benighted individuals, bereft of the enlightenment of Islam and whose possession of some technical superiority was of no consequence. Gradually, however, the Saudi learned that the American's knowledge was able to buy him goods and services which he, the Saudi, could not have. Moreover, the Saudi Bedouin or poor townsman saw the upper classes of his own society deserting old ways and emulating the American.

The result was a crumbling of the Saudi's faith in his traditional values, and a growing hunger for the goods of the West. His technical inferiority, however, shut him out from these things, and almost overnight there was imposed upon him a social inferiority new to Arabia. The most capable Saudis, losing confidence in their own culture, perforce tried to replace that culture with something else—the material standard of living of the foreigner. This tended to widen the gulf between the base of the population and the elite few, until, today, the biggest Saudi contractors are equated by the average townsman with that group which has grown enormously wealthy through government.

Aramco officials repeatedly stress the desire of Saudis to imitate the American. Responsible Saudis have said that if Americans lived in tents and rode bicycles, then the Saudis would be glad to live in tents and ride bicycles. Since Americans do not live in tents, but in a manner bewilderingly complex and unattainable, the average Saudi resents the foreign intrusion. Cast adrift from his moorings, he blames his new and debased status, not on his own technical shortcomings, but on the Americans, who must, he reasons, be conspiring to deny him equality. The same sentiments go out to his royal family, whose glaring irresponsibility (in the subject's eyes) is shown by its way of life. To such a Saudi, Aramco and the royal family is one, united in his depression.

The Saudi Government sees it otherwise. Disturbed by the growing restlessness in the country—climaxed in October, 1953, by the strike of 12,000 of Aramco's Saudi workers for improved working conditions—the King tends to blame Aramco for "unsettling" the workers with Western ideas. At the same time the monarch demands that Aramco continue with its education and training program in order that, one day, Saudis may take over the complete management of the industry.

Thus, Aramco finds itself in the middle, with the Saudi people and the royal family going off on separate and opposing tangents, but both suspicious of Aramco as the "cause" of the trouble. In the meantime the King finds it next to impossible to curb the wild spending of his many brothers and their sons, and to weed out those officials—Syrians, Palestinians, Lebanese, and others—whose fingers have been into the pie since the old, relaxed days of Ibn Saud.

Nor does the King appear fully alive to the situation. He put down the labor strike of 1953 by force, which so far has prevented its recurrence. Yet he has taken few visible steps to remove the root cause of the trouble by diverting royal income to public works on any large scale, and to give an example by "house cleaning" at Riyadh.

His advice in this respect appears poor. Insulated largely from his people throughout his life, he is surrounded by a circle of advisers whose own positions might be threatened should the King become "socially conscious." One of his key advisers told an Aramco executive that the King was opposed to the "democratic" ideas being disseminated throughout the world, and being introduced by Aramco into Arabia. When asked what he would substitute for those ideas, the adviser replied that he did not know. Nevertheless, he continued, when he was a boy, it was unthinkable that a nation would engage in war without a formal declaration. Now, with the growth of democracies, this was an accepted practice.

When the American pointed out that it was not the democracies which engaged in this practice, the adviser replied that it was difficult to judge since the "people to the north of us" (the Soviets) claim they have the greatest democracy in the world.

A good deal of the King's attention is diverted to external affairs. Bemused, apparently, by the possibility of becoming leader of all the Arabs, or, at the very least, by the desire to humiliate Iraq, Saud is meddling in Arab relations. Egypt has found him a willing ally against the aspirations of Iraq. Saud's purse is open to those Arabs willing to work against the Hashemites and for the Sauds in Arab councils.

To this end Saud is willing to castigate the United States Government and Americans in general when the occasion arises, apparently hoping thereby to curry favor among the Arabs. This leads sometimes to biting the hand which feeds him. At one time, for example, the King asked the United States to mediate Saudi Arabia's dispute with Britain over the Buraimi oasis. The State Department replied that it could not intervene unless Britain also requested it to do so. King Saud replied in effect that if the United States refused to help him on this issue, he could get along without American aid. The King then canceled the Point Four program in Saudi Arabia, despite the fact that Point Four experts were doing just the things the King wished—surveying a new route for the Hejaz Railway and routing water pipelines, among other projects.

His pressure on Aramco for better concession terms has been no less extreme. From a background of generosity (Aramco early established the principle of a 50-50 royalty split) the company is in a poor position to resist. Today Aramco has conceded to the extent that it now divides its income with King Saud before, instead of after, taxes, and pays fringe benefits as well. The point is visible, however, at which the Saudis' demands might decide the company to shut down operations, at least temporarily. Observers believe that if Saud's income from oil were to stop, his throne would topple, so widespread is unrest in Arabia today.

In such an event, the Bedouin tribes, which still remain the solid base of the population, would merely split up into factions and carry on as they always have, with a recrudescence of the tribal raiding which the Saudis have stopped. But the Saudis whose living now depends upon Aramco, directly or indirectly, would suffer. Dammam and Al

Khobar likely would succumb to the sands. So would the palaces in Riyadh, whose owners would be scattered to the winds. The income from oil, which could do so much to strengthen not only Arabia itself, but the Arab world at large, would be gone. The strategic American air base at Dhahran would be threatened. Nearly 1,000,000 barrels of crude oil daily would have to be supplied from wells elsewhere, principally in North and South America.

Few observers believe that Aramco intends to shut down, or that a shutdown, if it came, would be more than temporary. But the fact remains that the company is in a ticklish position today. It must work with the established government; yet, aware of the forces at work in the country, it must consolidate its relations with the Saudi people in general.

Then, should conflict come, the company would hope that it might sit it out on the sidelines, so to speak, with the struggle solely between the government and its people. This would not be as simple as it sounds, since Aramco is used as a weapon by both sides. (One of the demands voiced by a strike leader in October, 1953, was that Aramco should keep a portion of the King's royalties and spend this portion directly on public works in Al Hasa. The implication, not lost on the King, presumably, was that Aramco would help the citizens and the royal family would not.)

Who would replace the House of Saud if it fell? Possibly another Saudi prince, notably Feisal, might escape the general opprobrium sufficiently to fill the vacuum. Even so, he would not be likely to maintain the loyalty of all desert tribes, and a shrinking of the kingdom would take place, marked by growing insecurity in the farther desert reaches. Should the House of Saud disappear completely, there is no visible group sufficiently organized (including the Army) to take its place. Thus any removal of the Sauds almost certainly would bring about turmoil for an indefinite time, with the Sauds trying to regain, possibly with a segment of their Army, what they considered to be their rightful position of dominance in Arabia.

In the meantime the social structure, already undergoing fundamental changes, would be further disrupted. This in a country which, until the oil boom of the twentieth century, had remained unchanged through the centuries and which, in the uncharted tracts of its deserts, still mirrors the civilization of the patriarchs.

CHAPTER 13

Life Along the Nile

One can learn more about Egypt in a day's drive along the banks of the Nile, or along one of its canals, than in 10 days spent in Cairo. In Cairo are the palaces and the mosques, the mansions and gardens of the rich, the treasures of the moussky, the old market place. Here dwell the former pashas, the old rulers of Egypt, and the generals and colonels, new rulers of the land.

But along the Nile and its canals lives the one unchanging symbol of Egyptian life—the fellah, or Egyptian peasant. Together with his great partner, the Nile, it is the fellah, and he almost alone, who creates the wealth of Egypt. On his back the rulers of the land, whether pharaohs, khedives, kings, or army officers, have ridden, often with the harshest kind of spurs, and from the fruit of his labors they have built their fortunes and their careers.

Setting out south from Cairo along the Nile toward Upper Egypt, or northward through the delta, the traveler comes immediately upon the fellah. Indeed, he can scarcely avoid him. Some 17,000,000 fellahin, in one of the densest concentrations on earth, dwell in the narrow valley of the Nile and throughout the delta, the only habitable parts of this mostly desert land. Two-fifths of the entire population of the Arab world, crowded into one-hundredth of its area!

Truly, "Mother Nile" is Egypt, for without this great river, second longest in the world, all of Egypt would be barren. Indeed, though Egypt contains 363,000 square miles, almost as much area as Texas and California combined, only 13,000 square miles—less than five per cent—presently are cultivable. Into the long green finger of the Nile valley, plus the delta north of Cairo and a strip of land along the Suez Canal, are packed 22,000,000 Egyptians, about 1,400 persons to the square mile.

The morning sun glinted warmly from the placid muddy waters of the Nile when last I took a trip along the river. The road was a straight and dusty strip, flanked by white-trunked eucalyptus trees and the horny trunks of palms, their fronds like great feather dusters waving in the air. On the right was the river, to the left the green fields of wheat and cotton, and everywhere the fellahin.

A Nile riverboat, flat-bottomed and shallow of draft, its huge mast and cotton sail looming majestically above the trees, pushed slowly down the stream. Ahead was a bridge, far too low for that giant mast. Two men bent to a windlass in the bow, and slowly, with a great groaning sound, the long mast lowered back along the boat, until the sail overflowed the deck and trailed astern. The prow moved beneath the bridge, one man like a pygmy beside the giant tiller in the stern, until, with a shout, the men in the boat bent to their windlass again, the mast stood slowly upright, and the sail filled in the gentle breeze.

Water buffalo, called gamoosa, with their patient staring eyes, plodded in endless circles, turning horizontal water wheels, lifting water from the river into sluicelike channels, running through the fields. Some beasts had cloths across their eyes, as though to blind them to the monotony of their round. On the backs of others tiny children lay, switches in hand, while other children slept or played in the shade of eucalyptus trees.

Here was a family too poor, perhaps, to own a water wheel, and two men, clad in long white drawers, dark backs glistening from their labor in the sun, crouched and turned the crank handle of a long wooden cylinder, within which a screw drew up water to the level of their fields. One could not help but wonder, as he passed, how many landlords had ridden by that field in the past 5,000 years while fellahin worked thus with their tambours, or Archimedean screws, beside the flowing stream.

A woman walked along a river path, water pot balanced on her head, baby slung across one hip, sunlight glancing from the massive bronze anklet or "wedding ring" worn on one bare ankle. Behind her strode another woman, clad in the black milaya, or body-length veil, with a bright cascade of ornaments shining in the sun.

These fellaha women, and thousands like them up and down the river's banks and along the myriad canals, would that day wash their clothes, their cooking pots, and perhaps themselves, some using clay for soap, in the green-brown waters, then scoop up pots of water to carry on their heads back to the drinking water barrels in their village homes. Children would romp or play about them during the day, the boys in white one-piece robes and little more, the girls in bright dresses of cotton, some with ribbons in their hair, the youngest children with shaven heads, stained red with henna dye.

The road turned abruptly to follow a canal, and ahead a raftlike ferry rested against the bank. Onto the ferry crowded a dusty throng of men and women, together with their cattle, until the gunwales dipped into the stream. Finally, with others still clamoring to jump aboard, men and women laid hold of a rope stretching from bank to bank and hauled themselves across, to debark on the other side and send the ferry back.

Everywhere, as I rode, stretched the green of growing things or the rich darkness of a fallow field, in sharp contrast to the tan and naked desert which, though out of sight, closed in just a handful of miles away. In these fields, as long as the sunlight lasts and sometimes into the night, with perhaps 10 days off during the year for the great Moslem feasts, the fellah bends to his work, using tools no more complex than a hoe, a simple wooden plow, his gamoosa or a donkey—and the strength of his own arms.

He lives in a village, and, just as he himself is a man of the soil, so his village home is of the soil, mud daubed over a framework of palm leaves or river weeds. It contains, at the most, three tiny rooms with earthen floors, shared by his animals, his wife and children, sometimes his parents and their parents as well.

It was sobering, as always, to watch men whose vision is narrowed to the mud and soil beneath them, whose villages are crowded into patches of unwanted land. Yet 17,000,-000 men, women, and children, three-fourths of Egypt's people, are fellahin, dwelling in this manner along the Nile and its canals. Seldom during the centuries that have marched so big with portent down that narrow river valley, have these farmers lifted their gaze to events much beyond their village ken. The same is true today. They, the fellahin and their children, will be there, little changed, when Colonel Nasser and his followers are gone.

Distressingly enough, in one sense, the fellahin will be there in even greater numbers as the years roll on, for the population of Egypt is increasing today at the rate of 20 per cent every 10 years. This means that, under present circumstances, another 50 years will see Egypt's population twice its present 23,000,000, just as 50 years ago it was less than half its current figure.

This is the problem; for Egypt's land, unfortunately, cannot increase in like degree. The present cultivable area, at best, could be enlarged by 25 per cent and no more. The rest of Egypt is wasteland. Only close along the Nile, for hundreds of miles south to Upper Egypt and the Sudan, can the fellah raise the crops which have made Egypt (despite the oil income of Arabia and Iraq) the richest of the Arab lands.

Egypt's normal population increase is 1.8 per cent yearly of the total. In 1953 the increase was 2.3 per cent. As sanitation, pure drinking water, and other amenities find their way increasingly into the villages under the prodding of the Egyptian Government, the mortality rate will further decline and the rate of increase will jump.

I visited a small village of fellahin not far from Cairo, which was different from the others in that its homes were built upon the relatively clean sands of the desert, rather than upon the mud of the river plains. For this reason the mortality rate of the village was lower than the average. Consequently, according to its omda, or mayor, the village had a special problem. His village was of concern to district officials because its people were not dying off quickly enough to make room for those who were being born.

These are the grim facts with which Egyptian officials have to deal. This is the problem which underlies all others in Egypt. The government which solves, or comes close to solving, Egypt's population problem will remain in power. The government which cannot cope with it is doomed.

When the Suez Canal settlement was signed with Britain in July, 1954, Egyptian officials were free to admit that one of the last foreign scapegoats had been removed upon which they could fall back should they fail to achieve their economic goals. Little time was spent in vindictive statements against the British, who for so long had been posed as the chief enemy of Egypt. Instead, Lieutenant Colonel Zakaria Mohieddin, Interior Minister, and one of the most important members of the military junta which governs Egypt, said: "Now that this agreement has been signed, the preoccupation of all Egyptians should be to build the new Egypt on a basis of work and work alone." Wing Commander Hassan Ibrahim, at that time Minister for Presidency Affairs, declared: "There is still a lot of work to be done to fulfill the promises we made to the nation a couple of years ago."

The first and most obvious answer to Egypt's problem is birth control. Yet it is the answer from which almost all Egyptian officials shy away. The Koran does not explicitly forbid the practice of birth control for Moslems. But there is a strong body of tradition discouraging such use, centering in Al Azhar University in Cairo, the font of Islamic interpretation today. To fly openly in the face of the conservative religious leaders of the land is more than Egyptian officials care to do. As a start, however, the Egyptian Government has accepted the assignment of an American planned-family expert from the United Nations Technical Assistance Administration.

There is an even more discouraging aspect to birth control. Living in one of the most depressed conditions of any people on earth, the fellahin have almost no diversion save sex. In addition, the average fellah does not see that a large number of sons means the additional fragmentation of whatever small holding the fellah already may have. To the fellah, a large family means an increased labor force on the land and is desirable.

To work a change in the sex habits of these people would require years of patient education, even if there existed (which there does not) a body of social workers trained to impart such knowledge, and even if no opposition were to be met from conservative Moslem elements. Thus birth control, the only real solution, still lies almost untried upon the far horizon, despite the employment of a planned-family expert.

In its place, Egyptian leaders are turning their energies toward palliatives—the reclamation of land and the industrialization of Egypt. Schemes in this direction are huge. Egyptian and American scientists, financed jointly by Point Four and the Egyptian Government, have set up land reclamation projects at Fayoum, southwest of Cairo, and at Behera, in the delta region south of Alexandria. Fayoum is semioasis desert, and needs water. Behera is former river bottom, and has too much water. Hence the selection of these two places, since most of Egypt's wasteland falls into these categories—too much or too little water—and needs different methods of reclamation. When realized, the Fayoum and Behera projects will have cost an estimated $25,-000,000, will have reclaimed 80,000 acres of wasteland, allowing the settlement of 16,000 fellahin families where no one lives today. A similar, and even vaster, irrigation project is taking place throughout Tahrir (Liberation)

Province, a 600,000-acre area in the Western Desert which the military regime is seeking to turn from desert into model farmland at the rate of 30 acres per day.

Keystone of Egypt's economic policy is the Sudd el-Aali, literally the High Dam, scheduled for construction over the next 10 years four miles south of the present Aswan Dam in Upper Egypt. When completed, the High Dam will have consumed 17 times as much material as went into the Great Pyramid of Cheops. In this stupendous effort to increase Egypt's present cultivable area of 7,000,000 acres by 2,000,000 additional acres, Colonel Nasser's government will oversee the greatest engineering project in the history of mankind. In addition to irrigating 2,000,000 acres of presently untilled land, the Sudd el-Aali will allow one or two additional crops to be grown on 700,000 acres of land which now can be watered only during the flood season of the Nile. An important feature of the dam and its associated irrigation works will be the creation of 9,000,-000,000 annual kilowatt hours of electricity to power Egypt's new and existing industry.

Of the two remaining problems to be worked out—financing of the dam and agreement with the Sudan—the first is closer to solution. Total cost of the High Dam will be an estimated $1,300,000,000, of which Egypt has pledged to provide $900,000,000 from her own resources. The remaining $400,000,000 must be sought abroad. Of this amount, the World Bank (on which the United States Government has the largest single voice) has agreed to loan $200,000,000. The United States and British Governments between them have pledged a grant of $70,000,000, with indications that the remaining $130,000,000 will be forthcoming.

Under the Nile Waters Agreement of 1929, which the Sudan now wants revised, Egypt receives about 48,000,-

000,000 cubic meters and the Sudan about 4,000,000,000 cubic meters of the Nile's average annual flow of 84,000,-000,000 cubic meters. The remaining 32,000,000,000 cubic meters passes into the Mediterranean Sea. With the construction of the dam, whose reservoir will hold 130,000,-000,000 cubic meters (nearly four times that of Colorado's Boulder Dam), none of the annual flow need be wasted, except for evaporation loss in the hot climate of Upper Egypt.

The Sudan is pressing to have her share of Nile water increased to a figure between 22,000,000,000 and 35,000,-000,000 cubic meters yearly. Egypt, though willing at least to double the Sudan's present share, has rejected Sudanese figures. The Sudan also demands that Egypt deduct the entire evaporation loss from her share, while Cairo claims this loss should be shared. Finally, the Sudanese town of Wadi Halfa will be inundated by the High Dam's reservoir, and Egypt's compensation for the rebuilding of the town has still to be worked out.

Little work can be done, in other words, before political agreement between Egypt and the Sudan is reached. This is one of the reasons Egypt's military leaders were deeply disappointed when Sudanese opinion swung strongly against union with Egypt after the Sudan gained her independence on January 1, 1956.

At present the Nile flood is unpredictable, flood water ranging from 42,000,000,000 cubic meters in dry years to 150,000,000,000 cubic meters in years of "high Nile." And, as has been seen, a great deal of the flood is lost in the Mediterranean Sea. Creation of the Sudd el-Aali will mean complete and consistent storage, allowing Egypt to plant predetermined amounts of cotton and other crops. This fact, plus the creation of 2,000,000 acres of new farm land

and vast amounts of electrical power, will increase Egypt's annual income, it is estimated, by $650,000,000.

A High Dam Authority, headed by Colonel Samir Helmy and free from the stresses of politics, already has been formed. A contract has been signed with the British firm of Sir Alexander Gibb and Partners, consulting engineers. Colonel Nasser's hope is that the dam will be built by an international engineering consortium including at least British, French, and West German firms.

Though the High Dam project dwarfs all other schemes, Egypt's efforts in the industrial field also are ambitious. Her cotton textile industry, employing 150,000 workers, already boasts one of the most efficient plants in the world in the Spinning and Weaving Company at Mahalla el-Kubra in the Nile delta. Already woolen yarn, silk and rayon, hosiery, and knitwear have begun to be exported.

Steel output, with the help of West German experts, is due for expansion. New food-processing plants are underway. New fertilizer plants, it is hoped, will meet almost the entire needs of the country. Egyptian cement, shoes, and cigarettes are among established products which soon will be joined by jute, paper, and tires. Much of this development is being aided by the technical assistance of the West. Of late, however, the Soviet Union, East Germany, and Poland have promised help to Egypt in the development of her industry.

Under the circumstances, and leaving aside the question of whether East or West provides the aid, these efforts of Egypt are prodigious. Nearly three-fourths of Egypt's population is illiterate and lethargic. Native engineers and technicians are few. Egyptian capital is insufficient to meet the need and must be supplemented by foreign investment money. Risk capital, however, is reluctant to enter a country so frequently marked by strife and unrest, and whose latest revolution is only four years old. These things make an efficient program of expansion even harder.

Yet the expansion must take place. American industrial consultants, called in by the Egyptian Goverment, say that Egypt must double her present industrial plant in 10 years if she is not to lose out to other Middle Eastern lands. Such doubling would cost at least $200,000,000, much of which would have to come from foreign sources.

Then the experts come out with the starkest fact of all. All the reclamation of land which it is possible to achieve, including that promised by the High Dam, plus every scrap of industrial expansion planned—if carried through with the maximum efficiency and dispatch—would only barely keep pace with population increase. Year after year, Egypt must lift herself by her boot straps merely to maintain the *status quo*, so rapidly does her population increase. Thus land reclamation, and industrial and agricultural expansion, must be seen for what they are—palliatives and not solutions.

Egyptian leaders are soberly aware of this. Many of them (who practice birth control themselves) know that limitation of population is Egypt's only answer. Yet they see no easy way of selling it to the people, particularly over the opposition of the qadis, or religious judges. (In some Egyptian social service centers, quiet experimentation is being tried with imparting information on birth control to those fellaha women who voluntarily complain of the burden of large families and whose husbands are willing for such information to be imparted.)

In lieu of birth control, some Egyptian officials talked to the author in the summer of 1954 of settlement of surplus fellahin in the underpopulated Nile valley of the Sudan.

Under this scheme, Cairo officials told me, expropriated Egyptian landlords would be permitted to buy large tracts of land in the Sudan, on which they would settle Egyptian fellahin. This, however, was before the Sudan scotched the plan by voting for independence from Egypt after the liquidation of the Anglo-Egyptian Condominium. Emigration of fellahin to Iraq, and possibly to Syria, also is talked about. Such migration, however, would drain off only a few thousand persons at best.

Thus Egypt's military rulers, who have given every evidence of having the good of their country at heart, find themselves on the horns of a dilemma. Should they fail to press for birth control with all the vigor they possess, the economic situation of Egypt eventually may give their enemies—Wafdists, members of the Moslem Brotherhood, Communists, and others—an opportunity to oust them from power.

If, on the other hand, Egypt's leaders declare that no longer can the country's population be allowed to grow, almost certainly the wrath of conservatives would open upon them, lending fuel to the fires of the dangerous Moslem Brotherhood which seeks a theocratic state and which the regime crushed only with difficulty. Such opposition might be tolerable were the regime assured of popular support. On this issue, however, it is highly doubtful that the country at large would understand what its leaders were about, and the government's popular base would be threatened. Under the circumstances, it would give Colonel Nasser and his fellows small comfort to know that no government which followed them could do much better.

CHAPTER 14

Barbed Wire in the Holy Land

Of all the mighty events that have unfolded through the ages in and around the Jordan River valley, few are likely to prove of more lasting significance to the inhabitants of the area than the founding of a green plantation in 1949 in the salt-encrusted desert a few miles south of Jericho. It is an event which would not have occurred had there been no Palestine War between Arabs and Jews in 1948. The story of this plantation, and of what has happened to it in the years since 1949, sheds light on the vexing problem of Arab-Israeli relations today.

South of Jericho, deep in the lowest river rift on earth, 1,000 feet below sea level, with the Mountains of Moab rising on the east and the wind-scarred hills of Judea to the west, Musa Bey el-Alami, founder of the plantation, is proving that land classified dead and waste throughout history actually is rich enough to bear three crops of fruits and vegetables a year.

On more than 2,000 acres of land reclaimed from desert over the past six years, Musa Bey, an Arab lawyer formerly of Jerusalem, and his Arab refugee workers now grow citrus fruits of all kinds, bananas, grapes, and watermelons, wheat, barley, cotton, beans, eggplants, tomatoes, and a dozen other crops. Shaded by a growing forest of eucalyptus and Australian pine trees—each six inches high when planted in April, 1952—and by date palm saplings beginning to reach above the roof tops, are whitewashed homes for refugees who formerly lived in tents in the camps which stretch along the barren Jordan valley or in hovels in overcrowded villages elsewhere in the Hashemite Kingdom of Jordan. Modern workshops to teach carpentry and mechanical skills stretch along macadam roads on the project, together with poultry houses, a bakery, an electric power plant, pump houses, and, most important of all in Musa Bey's eyes, school rooms and neat little houses with modern plumbing for the refugee orphan boys whom he has taken from the streets of Arab towns and brought to Jericho.

In one sense, Musa Bey's project on the desert is another chapter in the story of men and women the world over who have risen to new heights of devotion when disaster of one kind or another has stripped them of their homes. In another sense, however, Musa Bey's project strikes even deeper than most, for it is located in a land hallowed by religion and history, and is proving that the very plains over which Jesus must have walked on the hot and dusty way to the River Jordan are capable of supporting thousands of persons where none have lived before. In still another way Musa Bey's work is striking, for from the very beginning he met the bitterest kind of opposition, political and technical, from Jordanian and Palestinian officials, and from United Nations and other experts—opposition which did not begin to subside until the project achieved its first success.

The story of the work goes back to 1944 with the establishment in Palestine, then under British mandate, of a nonprofit Arab Development Society, designed to raise the social, economic, and educational standards of Arab villages in Palestine by offering them a sort of native "Point Four" of expert help. At the head of the society stood a distinguished Jerusalem lawyer and former government advocate-general for the British mandate government. This was Musa Bey el-Alami, who scarcely dreamed at that time that soon he would give up the law, which had built him a fortune, for work on the land that would nearly cost him his fortune.

Whatever success the society achieved in the next few years—and it was modest, due to scarcity of funds—was wiped out by the Arab-Israeli war, which in 1948 caused the flight and dispersion of more than 750,000 Arab Palestinians and their establishment as refugees in the surrounding Arab lands. Among these refugees was Musa Bey himself, who saw with greater realism than many of his Arab compatriots that the hundreds of thousands of refugees would not soon be returning to Israel, and that they somehow must be assimilated in the Arab lands if they were to avoid permanent stagnation in refugee camps.

To this end his eyes turned toward the Jordan River valley, in which many thousands of refugees then were camped, and which, though desolate and apparently worthless, at least was a part of Palestine and thus to many refugees preferable to more fertile lands in northern Syria and Iraq. International experts claimed that these empty lands in the Jordan valley were uncultivable because of lack of water and because the soil was too salty to be productive at all. In these estimates of Western experts Musa Bey claims also to have detected an uneasiness lest the establishment of thousands of refugees so close to the Israeli border might provoke tension between them and the new Israeli state.

Curiously enough, at least to those unacquainted with Arab thinking on the Palestine problem, the opposition of Arab leaders to Musa Bey's scheme was more bitter by far than that of Western experts, whose primary concern was the maintenance of at least an uneasy truce in the area. Many Arab leaders were frank to see in the successful settlement of refugees anywhere in Arab lands the destruction of one of their trump cards in Arab-Israeli peace negotiations—the "right" of all refugees to return to their original homes. This view was transmitted by design to the refugees themselves.

Thus it was not until June 29, 1949, that Musa Bey, in the name of his Arab Development Society, gained permission from the Jordanian Government to launch an experimental project on 4,000 acres of land, officially registered as dead and waste, lying west of the Jordan River in the vicinity of Jericho about seven miles north of the Dead Sea. It was a formidable task awaiting Musa Bey and the workers he had recruited from the camps. Armed with hand drills and homemade casings of sheet iron, they stood in a sunbaked area of hard, salt-encrusted clay, interspersed with great patches of seemingly bottomless dust, into which a stick would push as far as the hand would go. East to the wadi of the river itself and west to the naked hills of Judea no vegetation save the hardiest desert plants ever had been known to grow.

Six months after work began, came the miracle. To those who have stood in the greenness now flourishing and looked about at the desert, and up at the Mountains of Moab, stickless and bare, and at the wilderness of Judea with its traditional Mount of Temptation, miracle scarcely seems too strong a word.

Sweet water, so potable it could be swallowed directly from its source, welled up from below for the first time in written remembrance. Within 30 months of that time Musa Bey had sunk 25 wells, and not once did he fail to bring in fresh water. Soon 10 pumps were producing 200,000 gallons of water an hour, and distributing it along nine miles of concrete aqueducts to the fields of the society's plantation. Sixteen thousand forest trees had been planted, 10,000 banana trees, 8,000 vines, 5,000 citrus trees, plus acre on acre of vegetables and grain crops of all kinds. And not once since the first well had been brought in had the water volume dropped.

A complete sewage system had been built for the project; each building had electricity and running water. Five workshops—for carpentry, mechanics, tailoring, shoemaking, and an ice plant—had been started. Two school buildings to accommodate 80 children had been built.

By loaning him engineers and a drilling rig, the Arabian American Oil Company (Aramco) had been the first outside organization to offer Musa Bey encouragement. Aramco, together with its associate, the Trans-Arabian Pipe Line Company, gave him a Star 72 Well-boring machine and a truck to haul it, and it was this machine which replaced the hand tools Musa Bey's men formerly used. Since that time the Ford Foundation, the United Nations, and the United States Point Four program in Jordan have given him aid.

By mid-1953 Musa Bey's first and perhaps greatest task had been accomplished—proving that the Jordan valley could support agriculture. "Land around my project has gone up from nothing to $560 an acre," Musa Bey told me at that time, pointing proudly at private farms which had sprung up in the neighborhood, flourishing on the methods he had introduced. At that time Musa Bey was recognized as a leading example of an Arab refugee who realized that he and his people would not be going back to their old homes, and who was willing, therefore, to better their lot where they were.

For this reason his project met disaster. In December, 1955, when Jordanians erupted in rioting against the Baghdad Pact, rioters sacked Musa Bey's plantation, because it was a visible symbol that the refugees would not be going back to their homes. Trees and crops which had been grown for the refugees' own benefit were destroyed by refugees. His project will go on, but its experience in December, 1955, was one more sign that Arabs in general, and refugees in particular, have not yet accepted the loss of Palestine and the presence of Israel as a permanent fact.

Though the sacking of his project was Musa Bey's sharpest rebuff, he had met this opposition before. Indeed, early in his work he had been forced to abandon the idea of a rapidly growing area of permanent settlement, which would remove refugees from the camps, and had substituted for it the establishment of a training center on his project for refugee orphan children. At this center, as Musa Bey saw it, refugee children would be taught Arabic and English, would learn to be farmers and would study also one more craft of their own choosing, and finally, if they so chose, would be sent out as trained leaders to help other refugees acquire the skills they had learned.

Musa Bey's plantation and its work is a drop in the bucket when compared with the vast pools of hopeless humanity living in camps in Jordan, Egypt, Syria, and Lebanon, and when compared with the truculent refusal of Arab leaders to consider the negotiation of peace with the Jewish neighbor. Musa Bey's experience in December, 1955, is all the more poignant because his optimism and realism are in such stark contrast to the fears, hopelessness, and belligerence which mark the Arab scene today, where Israel is concerned.

The results of this Arab atmosphere allow Western leaders little hope that a workable compromise between Israel and the Arabs currently can be achieved, and Western efforts are largely reduced to maintaining an uneasy balance of power between the two foes. During the continuance of this truce, it is hoped, the prerequisites for compromise gradually can be achieved.

The background which developed this situation goes back long before the British established their mandate over Palestine after World War I. Religious Zionism, or the hope one day of returning to the Promised Land, had marked the Diaspora throughout its history, and late in the nineteenth century the first Zionist Jews came to Palestine to settle Zionist colonies, the first three being Rishon le Zion in Judea, Zichron Jacob in Samaria, and Rosh Pina in Galilee.[1] Other settlements followed, peopled by Jews from eastern Europe, and financed by wealthy Jews in the West, who bought land in Palestine and provided the settlers with tools and capital.

At the turn of the century, under the impulse of Dr. Theodor Herzl, Paris correspondent of the *Neue Freie Presse* of Vienna, Zionism became a political rather than religious movement, dedicated to the establishment of a Jewish homeland in Palestine. In 1897 the first Zionist Con-

[1] For a detailed discussion of Zionist penetration of Palestine, see George Lenczowski, *The Middle East in World Affairs* (Ithaca, N.Y.: Cornell University Press, 1952), pp. 259-99.

gress, held at Basle, Switzerland, formed the World Zionist Organization and elected Herzl as its president.

In 1904, following mass pogroms against Jews in Russia, Britain offered the Zionists Uganda as a place of settlement. This offer was rejected by the Seventh Congress of the World Zionist Organization, which refused to consider any alternative to Palestine. Soon, despite the passing of Herzl in 1904, the Zionist movement had spread throughout the Western Hemisphere, attracting many Jewish adherents in the United States and Britain.

Not all Jews favored Zionism. Reformed synagogues in particular, preaching assimilation in whatever countries they were found, rejected the nationalist implications of Zionism, which declared that all Jews belonged to a separate nationality. The Zionist view found its most effective spokesman during this period in Dr. Chaim Weizmann of Britain, who later became the first President of Israel.

After World War I the Zionists supported Britain's claim to a mandate over Palestine. Indeed, when the Council of the League of Nations confirmed this mandate on July 22, 1922, the text of the mandate incorporated, almost word for word, the language of the Balfour Declaration of November 2, 1917, which had promised official British support in "the establishment in Palestine of a national home for the Jewish people." The way had been cleared for the Zionist penetration of Palestine.

Britain assumed its mandate over Palestine in 1920 at the assignment of the Allied Supreme Council, two years before formal confirmation by the League of Nations. At that time, 1920, there were approximately 55,000 Jews in Palestine. One of the first acts of the mandatory government was to fix yearly quotas for Jewish immigration, despite strong Arab protests. Cooperating with the British in the assimilation and settlement of the Jewish immigrants was the Jewish Agency, official spokesman of world Jewry. President of the Agency was Dr. Weizmann, also president of the World Zionist Organization. A standing executive committee of the Agency in Palestine was headed by David Ben-Gurion, and its foreign department was led by Moshe Shertok (who later changed his last name to Sharett).

From the first the Jewish community in Palestine, aided by outside capital channeled through the Jewish Agency, was better organized than the Arab community in Palestine, which was loosely knit in two major political groups, the first led by Haj Amin el-Husseini, Grand Mufti of Jerusalem, and the second headed by Raghib Bey Nashashibi. The more important of these two groups was the one led by the grand mufti, who also dominated the Arab Higher Committee, an amalgamation of five Arab political parties in Palestine.

Generally speaking, the Arabs, being fundamentally opposed to Zionist immigration, refused to cooperate with the British. To many British mandate officials this was deeply disturbing, since British policy in the Middle East traditionally was pro-Arab. The Arabs even rejected a British offer for the creation of an Arab Agency through which might have been channeled Arab demands, notably for the establishment of a parliamentary government for Palestine, and for the halting of land sales by Arabs to Jews.

In the meantime Jewish immigration continued, more and more Arab land was bought by Jews, and the Jewish community expressed its definition and purpose in the building of modern well-equipped schools, hospitals, and other facilities. The degeneration of Arab-Jewish relations into open fighting was not long in coming, and the mid-1930's were marked by clashes, culminating in 1937 in the so-called Arab Rebellion which lasted through 1939.

In 1937, despairing of agreement between Arabs and Jews, the British produced a proposal for the partition of Palestine, involving a separate Arab state, a Jewish state, and a neutral enclave around Jerusalem and Bethlehem to remain under British administration. This proposal, though rejected by the Arabs, led to a conference in London in 1939, attended by the Zionists on one side, and Arab delegates from Palestine, Transjordan, Iraq, Egypt, Saudi Arabia, and Yemen on the other.

Arab and Jewish demands proved incompatible at the conference. The Arabs demanded independence for themselves and the halting of Jewish immigration. The Jews, on the other hand, demanded unlimited immigration and the establishment of a separate Jewish state. As a result of this conflict, the conference disbanded with no agreement reached.

The next step was the publication by Britain on May 17, 1939, of a White Paper outlining a new policy for Palestine. An independent Palestine state, linked to Britain by treaty, was to be created within 10 years. Jewish immigration was to be limited to 75,000 for the next five years, after which it was to stop altogether. Palestine was to be divided into three zones, in one of which the sale of land by Arabs to Jews was to be allowed. In the second zone such sales were to be restricted, and in the third zone they were to be prohibited.

The White Paper was rejected by the Arabs, who felt it did not go far enough in endorsing Arab aims, and even more forcefully by the Zionists, who saw in the White Paper a reversal of the Balfour Declaration. The League of Nations itself criticized the 1939 document as incompatible with the terms of the mandate requiring Britain to facilitate the establishment of a national Jewish home. The British made no secret of the fact that their marked swing toward the Arabs, as shown in the White Paper, was at least partly to counteract Axis propaganda among the Arabs on the eve of general war.

During World War II a kind of truce existed in Palestine until 1943, when it was broken by a new wave of terrorism, launched this time by the Jews. Despairing of a policy of moderation, the Jewish Agency, led in this respect by David Ben-Gurion, formulated new aims in the so-called Biltmore Program. These aims included the establishment of a Jewish state, taking in all of Palestine; the formation of a Jewish army; and the repudiation of the White Paper of 1939. A final aim was unlimited Jewish immigration, to be controlled by the Jewish Agency instead of by the British.

To achieve these goals, some Zionists employed terror to bend the British to their will. A mounting campaign of murder and pillage, costing a number of British lives, was led by two terrorist groups, Irgun Zvai Leumi and the Stern Gang. A third underground Jewish force, Haganah, formed originally with Jewish Agency backing to protect Jewish settlements from Arab attacks, did not take active part in terrorism.

Simultaneously Zionists in the West drew the attention of Americans and other peoples to the plight of the Jews under Hitler, and to the tragic events resulting from British determination to prevent illegal Jewish immigration into Palestine during the war. The sinking of the *Struma*, an immigrant ship, off the Turkish coast after the British had refused to allow her to dock in Palestine, pointed up the Zionist campaign.

In the United States the Zionists enjoyed marked success in enlisting political support for their aims. Many state legislatures passed resolutions favoring the Zionist cause, and in 1944 a resolution calling for official United States support for Zionist aims was introduced before both Houses of Congress. A vote on the resolution was postponed when General George C. Marshall, then Army chief of staff, declared its passage might harm the Allied war effort in the Middle East. The Zionists did secure, however, a statement of sympathy with Zionist aspirations from President Roosevelt. This political support was to culminate in President Truman's *de facto* recognition of the State of Israel on May 14, 1948, the same day the British relinquished their mandate over Palestine.

On August 31, 1945, President Truman asked Clement R. Attlee, British Prime Minister, for the immediate admission of 100,000 Jewish refugees to Palestine. At British suggestion, an Anglo-American Committee of Inquiry was set up to study the matter. This committee, sympathetic to Zionist aims, recommended in particular that 100,000 immigrants be authorized to enter Palestine, and that limitations on the transfer of Arab land to Jews be rescinded.

Neither the United States nor British Government acted on the committee's recommendations, but appointed a commission of higher officials to study ways of implementing the committee's findings. The higher commission toned down the recommendations of the original committee and proposed instead a revival of the old British plan for the partition of Palestine. The impossibility of reconciling Arab-Jewish views on the matter and President Truman's renewed insistence that 100,000 Jews be allowed to immigrate led Britain, in 1947, to lay the question before the United Nations.

An eleven-nation United Nations Special Committee on Palestine (UNSCOP) drew up majority and minority reports. The majority plan (Canada, Czechoslovakia, Guatemala, the Netherlands, Peru, Sweden, and Uruguay) called for the partitioning of Palestine into a Jewish state, an Arab state, and an internationalized Jerusalem. The minority report (India, Iran, and Yugoslavia) recommended a federated Palestine, with Arab and Jewish communities enjoying local autonomy, and with Jewish immigration permitted for three years up to the absorptive capacity of the Jewish canton. (Australia was the eleventh nation on UNSCOP.)

The Arabs favored the minority plan, since it called for a single independent state with an Arab majority and a limitation on Jewish immigration. The Zionists endorsed the majority report, since it provided for an independent Jewish state. On November 29, 1947, the United Nations voted for the partition of Palestine, with an economic union between the Arab and Jewish states, as recommended by the majority report of UNSCOP. A five-nation UN Palestine Commission was set up to implement the resolution, which called for the establishment of the two separate states within two months after the British withdrawal, scheduled for August 1, 1948.

The Zionists, apparently, had won their struggle. Not only for the Arabs and Jews, but for other peoples as well, the cost had been great. The United States in particular was, and still is, castigated by the Arabs as the one nation which had the most to do with bringing Zionist aims to fruition. Armed groups of Arab volunteers began streaming into Palestine to wage war against the Jews. Violence and casualties mounted. Great Britain, unable to cope with the situation, announced she would terminate her mandate ahead of schedule by May 15, 1948.

On May 14 she did this, and the same day the Zionists in Tel Aviv proclaimed the Jewish state of Israel. Within a

Israel.

few hours President Truman recognized the new nation on behalf of the United States, and the United Nations swiftly followed. Arab states sent their armies to invade Israel and the formal Arab-Israeli war began.

Badly divided, the numerically superior Arab forces were no match for the determined and cohesive Israeli Army, fighting for the first Jewish homeland in 2,000 years. In the opening stages of the war Arab forces were forced to relinquish Tiberias, Safad, the coastal towns of Haifa and Jaffa, and other strong points. While these losses surprised outsiders, they caused shocked dismay among the Arabs themselves. The internal weaknesses within the Arab social and political machine had begun to manifest themselves through the armies which bore the Arab flags.

Only Transjordan's Arab Legion, commanded by Glubb Pasha, made a strong showing, by denying Old Jerusalem and some northern parts of the city to the Jews. Most of New Jerusalem, however, remained in Zionist hands. Next in effectiveness to the Arab Legion was the army of Iraq, which had to move overland several hundred miles to reach the fighting. In the north the forces of Lebanon and Syria made little impression on Jewish defenses. The Egyptian Army was badly mauled in fighting to the south.

On May 20, 1948, in an effort to halt the war, the Security Council appointed Swedish Count Folke Bernadotte UN Mediator for Palestine. The first truce engineered by Bernadotte took effect on June 11. This break in the fighting was used by the Jewish forces to regroup and organize, and to assimilate the war matériel which had begun to flow into Palestine after the British departure.

Proposals by Bernadotte for a federation of Palestine and Jordan, to include an Arab and a Jewish state, were rejected by both sides, and fighting broke out again July 9. This time

Israeli forces were successful on every front. Their advances were ended by a second truce, which began July 18. Still no basis for agreement could be found, and fighting resumed on October 14. Israeli forces captured Beersheba, forced the Egyptians back almost to Gaza, and surrounded a large Egyptian contingent at Falluja. Israeli forces to the north cleared Galilee and advanced into Lebanon. A final burst of fighting between Egyptians and Israelis, during which an Israeli force penetrated Egyptian territory in the Negev and then was forced back, ended the shooting war on January 7, 1949.

In the meantime Count Bernadotte had recommended to the UN General Assembly a change in the UN partition plan which would have given the Negev to the Arabs. This was bitterly opposed by Israelis, who counted on the Negev to support Israel's future population. While his report was in transmission to the UN, Count Bernadotte was assassinated by Jewish terrorists in Jerusalem on September 17, 1948. Subsequently, his proposals were rejected by the government of Israel, which refused to give up the Negev, and which opposed also the union of Arab Palestine with Jordan, and the internationalization of Jerusalem.

From January to July, 1949, armistices were concluded between Israel on the one hand and Egypt, Lebanon, Jordan, and Syria on the other. Iraq still has not signed an armistice with the Jewish state. Negotiations for the armistices were led by Dr. Ralph Bunche, successor to Count Bernadotte, on the island of Rhodes. These armistice agreements confirmed the territorial arrangements existing at the end of the fighting. Israel, in other words, as a result of her victory in the war, today controls about three-fourths of Palestine, more territory than that assigned to her under the UN partition plan. These extra lands Israel refuses to give up on the grounds that she won them in a war in which she was the victim, and not the aggressor.

Originally the Arabs refused to accept the 1947 UN partition plan. Today, however, the Arabs claim they will negotiate final peace with Israel only on the basis of the 1947 resolutions. Principally this would involve the shrinking of Israel territorially, and the internationalization of Jerusalem, now divided into Arab-held and Jewish-held sectors. In addition, the Arabs proclaim the right of the Palestine Arabs who lost their homes to return to Palestine. (By natural increase the number of refugees has swollen to nearly 900,000 today.)

These conditions Israel rejects. Her territory, she claims, belongs to her legitimately. As for the refugees, Israel points out that many of them fled at the urging of their own leaders, who promised them an early return to their homes when the Israelis had been wiped out. Had they not fled, Israel claims, they still would be living in their homes, just as the 190,000 Arabs who now are citizens of Israel.

Stalemate is the result, deteriorating periodically toward renewed open warfare between Arabs and Jews. The United Nations maintains a Truce Supervision Organization along the several Arab-Israeli borders, whose function is to mediate disputes and report its findings back to the UN, whose ward, in a sense, Israel is.

Among the Arabs, political repercussions of the war have been profound. Transjordan unilaterally annexed Arab Palestine and changed her name to Jordan. Humiliation of the Palestine defeat was an important factor leading to the Egyptian revolution of Colonel Nasser and his "Free Officers" group. Through the Arab League the Arab states have launched an economic boycott of Israel. Hundreds of thousands of refugees—100,000 in Lebanon, 85,000 in Syria, more than 200,000 in Egypt's Gaza strip, 475,000 in Jordan —huddle in tent or hut camps, without work, supported by UN rations. These people the Arab host governments refuse permanently to settle, lest this be an acknowledgment that Israel is here to stay.

Along the Jordan-Israeli border villages are cut in half. Others have lost their farmlands to the other side, and hence their livelihood. What this means to the inhabitants of both sides is illustrated by the plight of Beit Safafa, a tiny Arab farming village about 15 miles south of Jerusalem by the narrow rutted road one must use to reach it from Jordan.

Beit Safafa's buildings are of crude cut stone, weathered to the color of the earth around them. Its main street is of dirt, grooved by the endless passage of hoofs and by the coursing of winter rains. Down the center of this street runs a barbed wire fence, cutting the village in two. On one side is Israeli Beit Safafa; on the other side is the Arab town. So it has been since 1949, when the Rhodes armistice agreement gave to Israel the Jaffa-Jerusalem railway, which cuts through the outskirts of Beit Safafa. Once an hour that Jaffa train winds its way through the hills south of Jerusalem, and an Israeli passenger, glancing idly out one window, might see farmers tilling Israeli fields, while through the opposite window Jordanian farmers might be seen in their olive groves or vineyards.

The morning the author was there a little boy on the Israeli side was peering through the barbed wire at a group of Arab boys playing marbles in the dirt. When I trained my camera lens on him, he burst into tears and fled. Within 40 feet of each other two women held babies and sunned themselves in their front yards. Yet one was on the Arab side, the other was on the Israeli. Other women, and men also, walked up and down that main street, barbed wire stretching between them, with never a word across.

The most striking feature of Beit Safafa's division is that the people on both sides of the line are Arab, which, one might suppose, would lead to much smuggling and clandestine interchange between the two. Though this exists to some extent, it is limited by the fact that the Arabs on the Israeli side are there largely by their own choice, for they elected to remain with their lands when the armistice was signed.

Thus in some cases friendship and even blood relationship have cooled to antipathy, a separation aided by the Israeli armed patrols on the one hand and the Jordanian police on the other, who frustrate any attempt at contact, even a "marhaba," or "good morning," and who, if they see a figure slipping across the barbed wire at night, may shoot first and ask questions afterward. Thus Beit Safafa is an unhappy town, its lands bisected, its people divided, uncertain, and fearful lest they be arrested or even shot while going about their daily affairs.

Beit Safafa is not alone in its circumstance. North of Jerusalem lies the border town of Qalqilya. One day, during a jeep trip along the Jordan-Israel border, I kicked off my shoes in the white sanctuary of Qalqilya's mosque, climbed the tight spiral of the minaret, and looked down upon the narrow streets of the market place and on the tiny mud courtyards of the houses of the town. Yellow wheat gleamed on one flat roof, used as a threshing floor. To the west of the town, through the Palestinian coastal plain, ran a line of curious white pillars, marking the boundary between Jordan and Israel. Those coastal fields of dull green olive groves and the brighter green of orange trees, once had belonged to Qalqilya, and now belonged to Israel.

Had the wind been right, Israeli farmers bending over their crops might have heard the muezzin of Qalqilya calling the noonday prayer from the minaret, might even have lifted their heads and seen him. But in that few hundred yards between them—the Israeli farmers on the one hand, and the Arabs of Qalqilya on the other—lay possible death or prison should they have tried to mingle, to speak, or to exchange their goods; not only because their nations still technically were at war, but because between them lay the enmity of farmers who cherished the same fields.

Despite the dangers which attended infiltration, many Arabs—maddened by the constant putt-putting sound of their own water pumps irrigating Israeli crops—slipped across the border at night to steal, or to destroy. So it was up and down the Jordan-Israeli border, and a pattern of petty infiltration had grown up; Arabs creeping across the border to gather oranges from trees they themselves had planted, and occasionally committing sabotage, or even killing, as they went. Almost to the same extent Arab refugees in Egyptian-held Gaza stole across into Israel to maraud and kill. To a lesser extent there were incidents along the Syrian-Israeli border at the Sea of Galilee, where Syrian soldiers fired at Israeli fishing boats approaching the eastern shore of the lake.

All efforts at inducing the Arabs to come to the peace table having failed, and the Arabs' petty infiltrations having increased steadily in intensity, Israel adopted a policy of mass reprisal. The first Israeli reprisal raid took place October 14, 1953, when an Israeli army battalion surrounded the Jordanian border village of Qibya, blew up its buildings, and methodically killed more than 50 men, women, and children. For this raid Israel was condemned by the Security Council; as she was also for a later raid (February, 1955) against Egyptian Army positions in Gaza, in which 38 Egyptians were killed; and as she was also for an Army raid against Syrian gun positions east of the Sea of Galilee on December 11, 1955, when 55 Syrians were killed.

World opinion went sharply against Israel after each of these raids. To the government of Israeli Premier David Ben-Gurion, however, the raids were justified in that Arab infiltration was cut down sharply after each Israeli attack. Yet after each raid Arab tempers rose closer to the exploding point. Colonel Nasser of Egypt declared, in fact, that it was the Israeli attack on Gaza which had determined him to seek massive arms, wherever they might be found.

The raids had another unsettling effect. After the Qibya attack Jordanians in Jerusalem, Ramallah, and Amman let their government know that they were angry over the refusal of the Arab Legion to go to the defense of the embattled town. The Jordan Government was placed squarely on the spot. It knew that its Arab Legion of approximately 20,000 men—though top-notch in discipline and training—could not long hold back numerically superior Israeli forces. Legion intelligence reported that, on the night of the Qibya attack, at least one Israeli regiment was waiting in the hills ready to break across the border should the Legion have come to Qibya's defense. Thus on that night, and on similar earlier occasions, the Arab Legion was held back from border towns lest major fighting develop and additional Jordanian lives and territory be lost.

After Qibya the situation had festered to the point that people on the Arab side were disgusted with the strategy outlined above and let the Jordan Government know about it in demonstrations and riots, which the Legion itself had to quell. Yet the people's anger did not make the Jordanians any more capable of halting an Israeli attack should it come.

Nor did it help the Jordanian authorities to halt petty Arab infiltrations into Israel.

Here was the rub. Israel claimed at the time of Qibya that the program of Arab infiltrations into Israel officially was supported by the Jordan Government. Hence, the Israelis said, they had no alternative but to adopt reprisal raids such as Qibya. In fact, however, as neutral observers saw it, the great majority of Arab infiltrations into Israel were unofficial and unorganized, the work of embittered farmers determined to steal produce from fields which formerly had been theirs, or the work of malcontents out to stir up trouble.

It is probable that another reason than mere reprisal lay behind such events as Qibya. A cardinal point of Israeli policy in the years since the Palestine war has been to seek direct peace talks with the separate Arab governments and thus break the monolithic front which the Arabs so far have preserved in refusing to discuss peace on any terms except the UN's 1947 resolutions.

Israel's view has been that workable peace agreements might be achieved if each Arab government could be brought to discuss the matter in an "isolated" way, apart from the insistent scrutiny of and pressure from other Arab lands. Thus the argument of Israel, when Qibya was discussed in the Security Council, was that such events could be stopped only when the Arabs were willing to sit down and conclude a general peace.

Events have not moved toward this end, however. The Arabs show no disposition to sit down at the peace table; indeed, they appear confident that their own increasing strength, plus their economic boycott of Israel, are working toward the goal they all profess—the elimination of Israel altogether. In the meantime the legacy of bitterness on both sides, growing almost daily, makes the prospects of real peace even slimmer.

For Israelis the situation is acute. Theirs is a small land, 8,048 square miles, about the size of Massachusetts. Israel is shaped like an arrowhead, with its southern tip at the head of the Gulf of Aqaba, and widening back toward the north until it reaches its widest point at Beersheba—about 65 miles from the Mediterranean Sea on the west to the Dead Sea on the east. This southern part of Israel, from Beersheba to Elath on the Gulf of Aqaba, is the desert wilderness of the Negev.

Northward the Negev softens into the Plain of Philistia and the rolling hills of the Shephelah, until Tel Aviv is reached on the Mediterranean coast. North of Tel Aviv stretches Israel's coastal plain, the ancient Plain of Sharon. Here Israel is at her most fertile and also her most narrow. Indeed, standing on the Samarian hills above the village of Qalqilya in Jordan, one can look across the entire width of Israel at this point and see the Mediterranean glinting in the sunlight in the west.

Fifty-five miles north of Tel Aviv the coastal plain terminates with a rush at Mount Carmel, north of which lies Haifa, Israel's major port, and the east-west plain of Esdraelon. Beyond Esdraelon rise the high rolling hills of Galilee, running north to the frontier of Lebanon, one of Israel's four Arab neighbors. Included in Israel is the Galilean Sea (officially Israel's border lies 11 yards east of the lake's eastern shore, though Syria insists the shoreline belongs to her). Also belonging to Israel is part of the western shore of the Dead Sea.

Within Israel's tiny land the chief problems are three. First comes external relations with the Arabs, who surround Israel on every landlocked side. Lebanon, Syria, Jordan, and Egypt are Israel's only contiguous neighbors, and every one of them technically is at war with the Jewish state. In this atmosphere Israel struggles with her second great problem, namely the integration of hundreds of thousands of people of disparate backgrounds into a unified state. Figures alone tell much of the story. Between May 15, 1948, and March 31, 1955, according to the Jewish Agency for Palestine in Jerusalem, Israel absorbed 742,249 new immigrants, including 123,020 from Iraq; 122,792 from Romania; 105,-472 from North Africa; 104,356 from Poland, and 45,887 from Yemen.

In this process Israel's population has been nearly doubled. Almost half these newcomers came from the Middle East and North Africa; in other words, they were Oriental Jews. It is the latter who are the most difficult to settle in a land whose dominant class is Western in outlook. Today almost all the population of Israel's "temporary" transit camps is Oriental, the European Jews having been largely absorbed into the economy. Unemployment is concentrated in the transit camps.

Added to the great problems of Arab relations and immigrant absorption, is the need to develop a viable economy in a land barren at best. Only along the coastal plain and the plain of Esdraelon and a few other spots is Israel naturally fertile. Otherwise the desert must be made habitable, and industry and agriculture made to flourish.

In addition to these natural obstacles, Israel's economy is artificially hampered by her state of war with the Arabs. The latter have imposed an economic boycott on Israel which deprives the Jewish state of a cheap source of foodstuffs and a natural outlet for her manufactured goods. Iraq also has closed down the Iraq Petroleum Company's pipeline to Haifa, thereby reducing the Haifa refinery's output to a trickle and forcing Israel to spend scarce foreign currency for oil. (There is hope that Israel's newly discovered oil fields may reactivate the Haifa refinery and make Israel self-sufficient in oil.) Finally, Israel is forced to maintain an expensive military establishment which consumes more than half the ordinary budget.

The economic task has not been made easier by the existence of a multi-tiered bureaucratic system inherited from pre-state days when a variety of local and international agencies were pressing toward the establishment of Israel. In some cases the overlapping and even conflicting functions of these agencies have been carried over into the state apparatus. Again, the burning urge to pioneer the new state has caused in some instances the creation of desert settlements, and a type of agriculture, whose benefit to the economy as a whole can be questioned.

Without outside financial help during her formative years, Israel scarcely could have survived. This aid included releases from sterling balances ($100,000,000), a loan from the United States Export-Import Bank ($135,000,000), grant-in-aid from the United States Government in excess of $150,000,000, and more than $100,000,000 in gifts from world Jewry. The first two sources, releases from sterling balances and the Bank loan, already have dried up. Grant-in-aid from America is declining, and the natural tendency, barring renewed Arab-Jewish war, is for Jewish charity gradually to subside.

In the Arab-Israeli stalemate the United States, Britain, and France have sought through the Tripartite Declaration of 1950 at least to maintain the *status quo*. This declaration warns both sides that no transgression of present boundaries would be tolerated by the West. In addition the three Western powers have sought a balance of power between the two sides by denying significant quantities of arms both to Arabs and Israelis.

This policy now has been undercut by Egypt's purchase, at the cut-rate price of $80,000,000, of an estimated $200,-000,000 worth of Soviet bloc arms. Syria has followed this up by buying an undisclosed amount of Communist arms. On the ground, except in the category of tanks, Israel still leads the Arabs, qualitatively and numerically, despite the Arab acquisition of Soviet arms. In the air, however, Egypt has acquired a definite lead.

Israel, a nation of 2,000,000 persons, has an estimated 80,000 soldiers under arms, forming the nucleus of an army which can be expanded to at least 200,000 men within 48 hours. In addition, every Israeli village has a secret cache of weapons and a village "reserve" unit, commanded by a professionally trained reserve officer.

Against this immediate potential of 200,000 Israeli soldiers, the Arab nations, with 40,000,000 persons in all, are believed able to field approximately 170,000 men, of which some almost certainly would be kept at home to guard against internal unrest. Egypt's Army, with 80,000 men, is the largest Arab force. Jordan's Arab Legion, British-trained though no longer British-commanded, has about 20,000 men. Iraq's Army numbers approximately 40,000, Syria's 20,000, and Lebanon's 5,000 men. Saudi Arabia might be able to field a force of 5,000 partially trained soldiers. Beyond these standing armies, the Arabs possess virtually no trained reserves.

Israel possesses the additional advantage of a unified army responsible to a single command. Traditionally Arab armies, as has been seen, are loosely coordinated in battle, if at all. To what extent the recent Egyptian-Saudi-Syrian-Yemenite merger would offset this divisive tendency is unknown.

In tank armament the Arabs now have a qualitative advantage. Israel owns about 300 Sherman tanks of World War II vintage, armed with 75-mm. guns. These tanks are inferior to the estimated 30 heavy Stalin tanks and the 50 T-34 Soviet tanks which Egypt has acquired. In addition, Egypt has a number of British Centurion tanks. Israel's over-all superiority in trained manpower, however, is believed to outweigh heavily Egypt's new qualitative superiority in tanks. For the foreseeable future, in fact, Western military observers believe the Israeli Army could master Arab armies combined on the ground.

In the air, the picture is different. Before Egypt concluded her arms deal with Czechoslovakia, Israel was believed to have approximately 50 jet fighters, British Meteors and Vampires. Egypt had perhaps double that number of the same kind of planes. Now Egypt is believed to have acquired 200 Soviet MIG fighters—mainly MIG-15's, but possibly a few faster MIG-17's—and perhaps 40 IL-28 jet bombers, each capable of carrying a four-ton bomb load. These bombers could reach the Israeli cities of Tel Aviv and Jerusalem within a few minutes after leaving Egyptian airfields.

To combat the IL-28 bombers and the MIG fighters, Israel has virtually nothing. Israel's great concern, therefore, is that Egypt might launch a sudden air attack in which Israeli cities would be destroyed before Israel's ground superiority could make itself felt. Egypt, on the other hand, always has feared that Israel might bomb Egypt's Nile dams, thereby destroying the Egyptians' partial control over the Nile flood and reducing the country's economy to ruins. Egypt, in other words, is as vulnerable to Israeli air attack as Israel is to attack from Egypt. This creates a kind of stalemate. Each side has the power to destroy the other; thus, it is hoped, neither will risk war.

In the meantime, Israel has stated her concessions to peace. As quoted by Dana Adams Schmidt in *The New York Times*, they are as follows:

1. Israel would open up the natural lines of communication between Egypt and Lebanon to all forms of Arab traffic. [This would mean opening up the historic road and rail route connecting Egypt with the northern Arab world through Palestine.]
2. Jordan would be offered a free port at Haifa and transit rights across Israel. [This would remove the necessity for Jordan to ship and receive all goods through Beirut and Damascus, or through the inefficient port of Aqaba.]
3. Israel would be prepared to consider transit arrangements to establish lines of communication across the Negev desert between Egypt and Jordan. [Egypt, on the other hand, demands an Arab land corridor instead of transit rights.]
4. Israel would be willing to permit Arab aircraft to fly across Israel in all directions. [Currently all Arab flights must detour around the Jewish state, and vice versa.]
5. Israel would pay compensation to Arab refugees for the property they left behind in territory now part of Israel. [The United States already has offered to help Israel pay compensation. The offer has been rejected by the Arabs unless compensation is accompanied by permission for those refugees who wish to do so to return to their homes in Israel.]
6. Israel would collaborate in the project for unified development of the Jordan and Yarmuk river valleys.
7. Israel would agree to minor frontier adjustments where the border was strategically illogical or economically damaging to adjacent villages.[2] [This would unite villages such as Beit Safafa and Qalqilya with their farmlands.]

These concessions are dismissed by the Arabs as inadequate. They declare they will negotiate only on the basis of the UN's 1947 partition plan, which would involve loss of

---

[2] *The New York Times*, December 20, 1955.

territory to Israel, particularly in the Galilee area and west of Jerusalem and Bethlehem. This condition Israel rejects, on the grounds that her territory was won in a war in which she was the victim.

In fact, the Arabs might not prove so adamant on territorial changes if the prior question of refugees could be settled. The Arabs' minimum demand is that those refugees who wish to do so be permitted to return to Palestine, and that the rest be paid compensation for their loss. So far Israel has refused to approve any sort of UN-supervised plebiscite to determine the wishes of individual refugees.

In this connection Israel sees a factor working in her favor. This is the growing reluctance of the United States (which furnishes 70 per cent of refugee funds) to go on subsidizing the refugees through the UN, while the Arab states in whose lands the refugees live refuse to settle them in any permanent way. Recent reports of the United Nations Relief and Works Agency (UNRWA), assigned to administer refugee relief, have candidly criticized the Arab governments for lack of cooperation on this score.

The tenor of these reports to the UN General Assembly could be construed by Israel as placing constraint on the Arab governments to reach a settlement with Israel before they are forced to assume almost the entire maintenance and support of the 900,000 refugees. The gist of the reports, though cloaked in courteous language, is that the number of refugees drawing UN rations has not decreased in the past eight years, largely because the Arab governments have been extremely slow to accept rehabilitation and settlement of refugees in their own lands even though the UN has granted $200,000,000 to make settlement economically feasible.

The reports have warned that, should UN contributors stop giving to refugee relief, the "host" countries of Lebanon, Syria, Jordan, and Egypt would not be able to bear the burden of their maintenance without severe economic dislocation. The inference is that one day the Arab governments might find themselves with the responsibility of caring for nearly 1,000,000 people and with little external funds to aid them, unless in the meantime they display a more cooperative attitude toward rehabilitation projects which UNRWA has ready and waiting on blueprints, and which are designed to benefit the economies of the host countries as well as provide a livelihood for the unfortunate refugees.

So far the Arabs have not succumbed to this indirect pressure. Basic to their refusal to settle refugees in their own lands is fear that this would mean acknowledgment of Israel as a permanent entity in the Middle East. Though many Arab leaders privately admit that Israel is here to stay, they are afraid to tell their people so. Only if Israel permits all refugees who wish to do so to return to Palestine, Arab leaders say, will Arabs at large accept settlement of the remaining refugees in Arab lands. Thus the merry-go-round continues, with the welfare of the refugees themselves declining steadily.

Jordan and Egypt have been the most cooperative with UNRWA, partly because the burden of the refugees falls most heavily on them. From the beginning Jordan granted her 475,000 refugees citizenship. Yet she cannot settle them in her barren lands. Eventually, it is hoped, the Yarmuk River plan and other irrigation and land reclamation projects will absorb thousands of refugee families.

Egypt, with 200,000 refugees in the arid Gaza strip, has offered from the first to assimilate up to 50,000 refugees in the Sinai Peninsula. But Sinai has no water, and a plan to siphon Nile water under the Suez Canal into Sinai, worked out by UNRWA engineers, so far has not been approved by Egypt. Egyptian leaders, it is believed, first want to settle their problems with the Sudan on the over-all development of Nile water, including the effects of the High Dam.

For religious and economic reasons, Lebanon refuses to accept her 100,000 refugees on a permanent basis. Syria, underpopulated and with spreading plains waiting to be developed, would seem the most logical candidate. Yet Syria, from UNRWA's point of view, has been the most stiff-necked all along. Syrian leaders tell UNRWA that thousands of Syrians live in conditions worse than do the refugees themselves, supported by a daily ration from the UN. What would these citizens do, Syrian officials ask, if they saw UNRWA training refugees for jobs, loaning them money for shops or farms, and settling them on Syrian land? Iraq, whose rich and undeveloped plains need people, returns roughly the same answer to UNRWA pleas. The result is that most of the $200,000,000 which the UN voted for refugee self-help still is uncommitted.

This $200,000,000 is apart from the direct daily relief which UNRWA administers to the refugees in the form of food, blankets, and other doles. For this relief the UN votes yearly in the neighborhood of $30,000,000. The $200,000,-000 figure is to implement the so-called Blandford Plan, a program of rehabilitation and settlement voted by the UN and named for Ambassador John B. Blandford, Jr., the American who headed UNRWA at the time the plan was conceived.

The Blandford Plan aims at making the refugee so valuable, through the acquisition of a new skill, that he would become an economic asset to any country which accepted him. Under the plan refugees are offered vocational training in agriculture and various mechanical trades. When a man's training is finished, UNRWA will loan him enough money to set him up in a small shop or farm—if an Arab government will accept him. It is on this last point that the plan hangs fire.

The Arab governments do have terms which, if met by Israel, probably would bring the Arabs at least to the stage of negotiation. The first is the acceptance by Israel of a token return of refugees, perhaps 100,000. (Arab leaders privately say that no more than this number would wish to live in Israel, if offered the alternative of compensation.) Another Arab requisite is the cession by Israel of some territory, perhaps in the Esdraelon or Galilee sectors.

Other demands, including Jordan's transit rights to Haifa and border rectification, are concessions which Israel claims she is ready to make. Egypt, however, demands a permanent land corridor across the Negev to connect Egypt with Jordan and the northern Arab world. Israel rejects this term since it would cut Israel in two.

Israel would be required by the Arabs to give up her Mount Scopus enclave in the Arab sector of Jerusalem, including the empty buildings of the Hebrew University and Hadassah Hospital. Books and equipment of these two institutions would be returned to Israel, and in compensation Israel would receive the present UN enclave of Government House, and its buildings. Any differential, one way or the other, would be made up by a cash payment.

Arab thinking on the status of Jerusalem still is unclear. Observers believe a possibly acceptable solution would be the maintenance of Jerusalem as a twin city, new Jerusalem under Jewish control and old Jerusalem under Arab aegis, but with free access to and from the sectors, and with the whole city under some sort of UN supervision. Finally, the United Nations would be required to give an ironclad guarantee that the terms of the settlement, territorial and otherwise, would be respected.

The major points of difference between Arabs and Israelis narrow down to the right of some refugees to return to their homes, and the cession of at least a token part of Israeli land. On these issues the two sides are as far apart as ever. A third sticky point is the type of corridor which Egypt would receive across the Negev.

There is another factor which cannot be disregarded in weighing the prospects for Holy Land peace. This is the apprehension of many Arabs that an Israel at peace soon would dominate the Middle East economically. Many Lebanese and Syrian businessmen, for example, would stand to lose heavily should Jordanian transit trade be diverted from Beirut and Damascus to the Israeli port of Haifa. The result of a switch of Jordanian traffic to Haifa, which Jordan seeks, would mean the loss to Beirut of 22 per cent of its entire transit trade, and an even greater percentage loss to the Syrian state railroad. Apart from the question of Jordanian traffic, many Lebanese traders are known to suppose that Israeli merchants, with excellent contacts throughout the business world, might be able to attract a considerable volume of international trade away from Beirut to Haifa, once the latter port's lines of communication became open to the Arab hinterland.

In isolated cases, on the other hand, one is able to find Arabs who secretly give the impression of desiring normal economic relations with Israel. Farmers in south Lebanon, who have been hard hit by the closing of the Israeli frontier to their produce, are believed to feel that the opening of that border would make it easier for them to dispose of their crops.

Even in this instance, farm authorities in Beirut are convinced that Lebanese agriculture in general would suffer if Jewish crops, particularly citrus fruits, were allowed to enter and compete on the Arab market. It is known, for example, that oil companies in Kuwait and Arabia persistently complain that a large percentage of the fresh fruits and vegetables which they now obtain from Lebanon are spoiled through poor handling and packaging. Israeli growers, believed to be better versed in Western packaging techniques, would make a direct bid for this lucrative Arabian market, in the opinion of Beirut observers. (Despite this possible threat, Point Four packaging experts have found it difficult to persuade Lebanese producers to adopt more efficient handling methods, designed to please the customer.)

In the past France was the greatest single buyer of Lebanese oranges. In 1953, however, France switched to buying oranges from Spain, and when Lebanese authorities sought the reason why, they were told that the Spanish fruit could be obtained more cheaply—and in better condition.

Apart from these local instances of apprehension over Israeli competition, a general uneasy feeling appears to pervade the Arab atmosphere that the Israelis possess a superior technology which somehow would allow them to create a demand for Jewish manufactured goods throughout the Arab world. Thus, despite whatever trade barriers the Arab states might throw up, Arab economies eventually would be subject to Israeli domination.

The over-all stalemate on basic terms of agreement between the two sides now has hardened even further, due to renewed Arab confidence in their military strength. This makes for truculence on the Arab side, and increased desperation on the part of Israel, causing even some moderate Israelis to think in terms of preventive war before the Arabs grow strong enough to destroy them.

In this dilemma the United States pins its chief hopes on the ability of Eric Johnston to get both sides to agree to unified development of the Jordan River valley. Four times, as special representative of President Eisenhower, Mr. Johnston has traveled to the Middle East in efforts to persuade both sides that their welfares would be enormously enhanced by joint development of the Jordan River. The plan as finally hammered out by both sides, with Mr. Johnston as mediator, has won the technical approval of Arabs and Israelis. Political agreement, however, has not been forthcoming. Israel is ready to sign approval of the plan; so, it is believed, are Egypt and Jordan. Jordan, with the poorest economy among Arab states and with the heaviest refugee burden, stands to benefit greatly from the Johnston plan. Lebanon and Syria are holding back, and observers see in their reluctance a fear that implementation of the Johnston plan would lead to the opening of Haifa to Jordan, and the consequent loss of Syro-Lebanese transit trade.

For Israel and Jordan the question is critical. Utilization of Jordan River waters for irrigation and hydroelectric power would allow settlement of at least some of Jordan's refugees and would give the Israeli economy its only chance of becoming viable. Every step which the Israelis can take in this direction is being taken. Until the Arabs agree to joint development of the river, Israel is stymied unless, in the face of a threat of war from Syria, she proceeds with unilateral diversion of the Jordan River in the demilitarized zone between Israel and Syria.

Mr. Johnston's first trip to the Middle East, in October, 1953, resulted in the publication of separate Arab and

Israeli plans for utilization of Jordan River waters. On his second and third trips (June, 1954, and January, 1955) Johnston sought, with some success, to narrow down the differences between the two plans. On his return home from his third trip, Mr. Johnston declared that the "ten yard line" had been reached, meaning in particular that both sides now were agreed on the necessity for joint water development and on utilization of the Sea of Galilee, wholly within Israel, as a joint storage reservoir.

When he went to the Middle East for the fourth time in August, 1955, Mr. Johnston took with him a compromise plan which won technical approval from both sides, and also the promise of United States funds to cover two-thirds of the estimated $200,000,000 project. Implementation of the plan, involving a complex series of dams, canals, and storage reservoirs, would give to Lebanon, Syria, and Jordan a total of 60 per cent of Jordan waters now unused, and to Israel 40 per cent.

Specifically the allocations to the Arabs would be: "35 mcm. (million cubic meters) to Lebanon, from the Hasbani River to irrigate 8,700 acres; 132 mcm. to Syria in three different areas along the Yarmuk and Jordan rivers; 480 mcm. to the Hashemite Kingdom (Jordan) to irrigate some 125,-000 acres."[3] Israel would receive a total of 400 million cubic meters. Though Israel objects to the scaling down of her demand for water from 550 million cubic meters to 400 mcm., she is believed ready to agree to the plan for the sake of relaxed tensions which presumably would follow. Objections raised by Syria and Lebanon, however, have thrown the whole plan into jeopardy.

[3] Georgiana G. Stevens, "The Jordan River Valley," *International Conciliation*, No. 506 (January, 1956), p. 273.

Step by step since the Palestine War in 1948, the Western powers have sought to foster a spirit of compromise through such projects as the Blandford Plan, the 1950 Tripartite Declaration, and the Johnston plan. Each project has been undercut, either by Arab-Israeli intransigeance or latterly by Soviet interference. Bitterness, meanwhile, has mounted on both sides, with the Arabs speaking increasingly of a second round of fighting and Israel forced to think in terms of a preventive war, or "active defense," to protect herself before the Arabs grow too strong. As a result the spirit of compromise, and consequently real peace in the Holy Land, appears as far away as ever.

Selected Bibliography

ABDULLAH. *Memoirs of King Abdullah of Transjordan.* London: Jonathan Cape, Ltd., 1951.

ALDINGTON, RICHARD. *Lawrence of Arabia.* Chicago: Henry Regnery Co., 1955.

ALLEN, H. B. *Rural Reconstruction in Action.* Ithaca, N.Y.: Cornell University Press, 1953.

ARMSTRONG, H. C. *Lord of Arabia, Ibn Saud.* Beirut, Lebanon: Khayat's College Book Cooperative, 1954.

ASAD, MUHAMMAD. *The Road to Mecca.* New York: Simon & Schuster, Inc., 1954.

BARATZ, JOSEPH. *A Village by the Jordan.* New York: Roy Publishers, 1955.

BERNADOTTE, FOLKE. *To Jerusalem.* London: Hodder & Stoughton, Ltd., 1951.

BLUNT, WILFRED SCAWEN. *The Seven Golden Odes of Pagan Arabia.* London: Chiswick Press, 1906.

COON, CARLETON S. *Caravan: The Story of the Middle East.* New York: Henry Holt & Co., Inc., 1951.

DICKSON, H. R. P. *The Arab of the Desert.* London: George Allen & Unwin, Ltd., 1949.

DOUGHTY, CHARLES M. *Travels in Arabia Deserta.* New York: Random House, Inc., 1946.

EDDY, WILLIAM A. *F.D.R. Meets Ibn Saud.* New York: American Friends of the Middle East, Inc., 1954.

FATEMI, NASROLLAH SAIFPOUR. *Oil Diplomacy, Powder Keg in Iran.* New York: Whittier Books, Inc., 1954.

FERNAU, F. W. *Moslems on the March*. New York: Alfred A. Knopf, Inc., 1954.

FISHER, SYDNEY NETTLETON. *Social Forces in the Middle East*. Ithaca, N.Y.: Cornell University Press, 1955.

GIBB, H. A. R. *Mohammedanism, An Historical Survey*. London: Oxford University Press, 1949.

GLUBB, JOHN BAGOT. *The Story of the Arab Legion*. London: Hodder & Stoughton, Ltd., 1952.

HAAS, WILLIAM S. *Iran*. New York: Columbia University Press, 1946.

HITTI, PHILIP K. *History of the Arabs*, 5th ed. New York: The Macmillan Co., 1952.

HOGARTH, D. G. *Arabia*. Oxford: Clarendon Press, 1922.

————. *The Penetration of Arabia*. London: Alston Rivers, Ltd., 1905.

HOSKINS, HALFORD L. *The Middle East: Problem Area in World Politics*. New York: The Macmillan Co., 1954.

HOURANI, GEORGE FADLO. *Arab Seafaring in the Indian Ocean in Ancient and Early Medieval Times*. Princeton, N.J.: Princeton University Press, 1951.

IZZEDDIN, NEJLA. *The Arab World: Past, Present, and Future*. Chicago: Henry Regnery Co., 1953.

LAMB, HAROLD. *Suleiman the Magnificent*. Garden City, N.Y.: Doubleday & Co., Inc., 1951.

The Home Letters of T. E. Lawrence and His Brothers. New York: The Macmillan Co., 1954.

LAWRENCE, T. E. *Seven Pillars of Wisdom*. Garden City, N.Y.: Doubleday & Co., Inc., 1947.

LENCZOWSKI, GEORGE. *The Middle East in World Affairs*. Ithaca, N.Y.: Cornell University Press, 1952.

LILIENTHAL, ALFRED M. *What Price Israel*. Chicago: Henry Regnery Co., 1953.

MOULD, ELMER W. K. *Essentials of Bible History*, rev. ed. New York: The Ronald Press Co., 1951.

NAGUIB, MOHAMMED. *Egypt's Destiny*. Garden City, N.Y.: Doubleday & Co., Inc., 1955.

NASSER, GAMAL ABDEL. *Egypt's Liberation: Philosophy of the Revolution*. Washington, D.C.: Public Affairs Press, 1955.

PALGRAVE, WILLIAM GIFFORD. *Through Central and Eastern Arabia*. London: Macmillan & Co., Ltd., 1883.

PATAI, RAPHAEL. *Israel Between East and West*. Philadelphia: The Jewish Publication Society of America, 1953.

PEROWNE, STEWART. *The One Remains*. New York: E. P. Dutton & Co., Inc., 1955.

PHILBY, H. ST. J. B. *Arabian Days*. London: Robert Hale, Ltd., 1948.

———. *Sheba's Daughters*. London: Methuen & Co., Ltd., 1939.

———. *The Empty Quarter*. London: Constable & Co., Ltd., 1933.

———. *Arabian Jubilee*. London: Robert Hale, Ltd., 1952.

———. *A Pilgrim in Arabia*. London: Robert Hale, Ltd., 1946.

RIHANI, AMEEN. *Around the Coasts of Arabia*. London: Constable & Co., Ltd., 1930.

ROOSEVELT, KERMIT. *Arabs, Oil, and History*. New York: Harper & Bros., 1949.

RUTTER, ELDON. *The Holy Cities of Arabia*. London: G. P. Putnam's Sons, Ltd., 1930.

SANGER, RICHARD H. *The Arabian Peninsula*. Ithaca, N.Y.: Cornell University Press, 1954.

SCHECHTMAN, JOSEPH B. *The Arab Refugee Problem*. New York: Philosophical Library, Inc., 1952.

SCHROEDER, ERIC. *Muhammad's People*. Portland, Me.: The Bond Wheelwright Co., 1955.

SHWADRAN, BENJAMIN. *The Middle East, Oil and the Great Powers*. New York: Frederick A. Praeger, Inc., 1955.

SPEISER, E. A. *The United States and the Near East*. Cambridge, Mass.: Harvard University Press, 1950.

STARK, FREYA. *Baghdad Sketches*. London: John Murray, 1946.

———. *A Winter in Arabia*. London: John Murray, 1945.

———. *Seen in the Hadhramaut*. London: John Murray, 1938.

THOMAS, BERTRAM. *Arabix Felix: Across the Empty Quarter of Arabia*. London: Jonathan Cape, Ltd., 1932.

THOMAS, LEWIS V. and FRYE, RICHARD N. *The United States and Turkey and Iran.* Cambridge, Mass.: Harvard University Press, 1951.

TWITCHELL, KARL S. *Saudi Arabia.* Princeton, N.J.: Princeton University Press, 1953.

ROYAL INSTITUTE OF INTERNATIONAL AFFAIRS. *The Middle East: A Political and Economic Survey.* London: Oxford University Press, 1951.

Periodicals:

Among American periodicals and newspapers *The Middle East Journal, International Conciliation, The New York Times*, the New York *Herald Tribune*, and *The Christian Science Monitor* have been particularly helpful. The *Sunday Times*, the London *Economist*, the London *Observer*, and the *Manchester Guardian* have been among British publications used.

Index

305

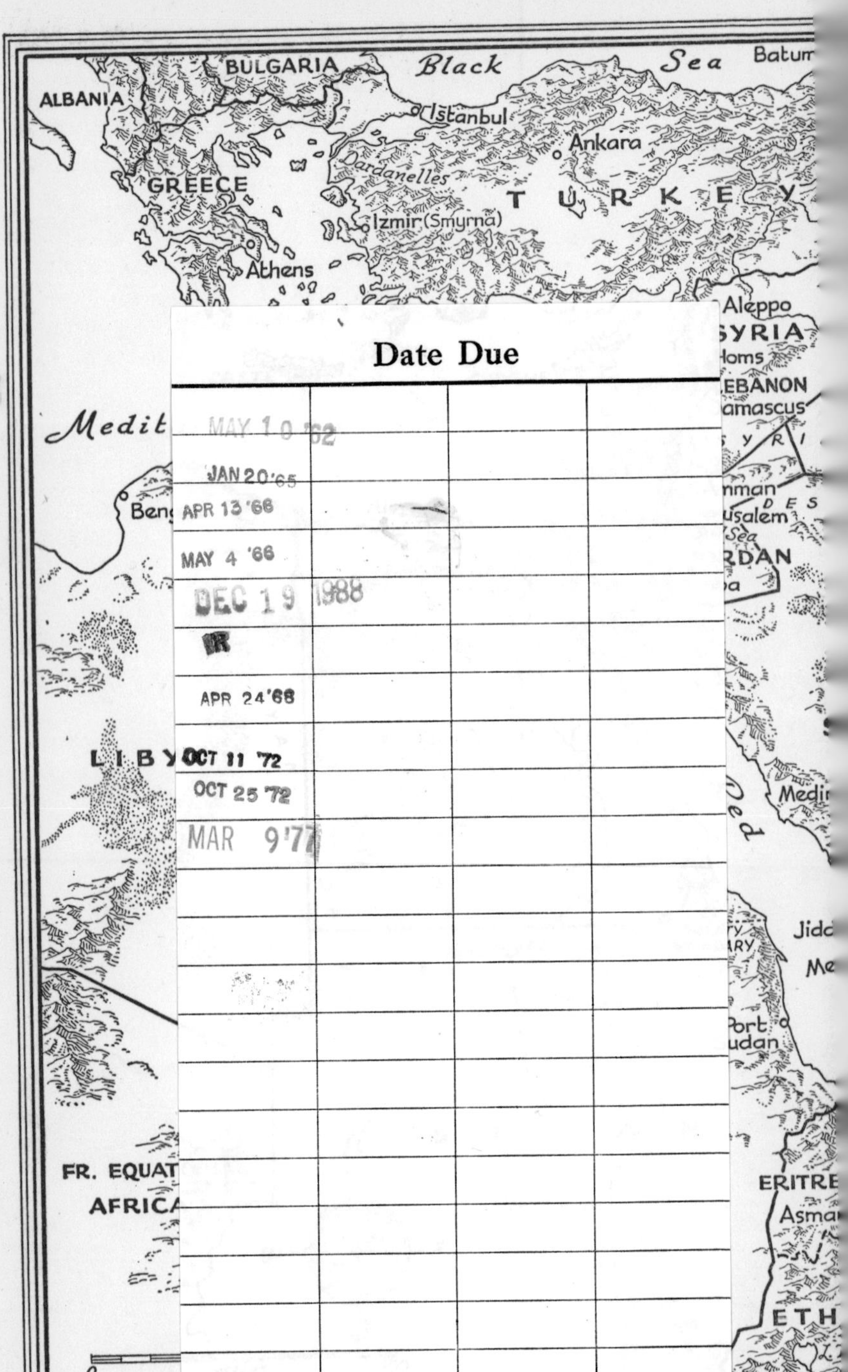
BULGARIA
Black
Sea
ALBANIA
Istanbul
Ankara
GREECE
Dardanelles
T U R K E Y
Izmir (Smyrna)
Athens
Aleppo
SYRIA